Canadian Symbols of Authority

This mace, symbol of the dignity and authority of a free people, has been carried across our mighty Dominion ... it will remain ever an emblem of our common love of order and freedom and loyalty to each other and to our Sovereign.

The Honourable Reginald Spakes
Speaker of Newfoundland Legislature
5 April 1950

Canadian Symbols of Authority

Maces, Chains, and Rods of Office

Corinna A.W. Pike & Christopher McCreery

DUNDURN
TORONTO

Editor: Jennifer McKnight
Design: Courtney Horner
Printer: Friesens

Library and Archives Canada Cataloguing in Publication

Pike, Corinna A. W.
    Canadian symbols of authority : maces, chains, and rods
of office / Corinna A.W. Pike and Christopher McCreery.

Includes index.
Includes bibliographical references.
Issued also in electronic formats.
ISBN 978-1-55488-901-3

    1. Signs and symbols--Canada. I. McCreery, Christopher
II. Title.

CR212.P55 2011   929.90971   C2011-901162-X

1 2 3 4 5   15 14 13 12 11

We acknowledge the support of the **Canada Council for the Arts** and the **Ontario Arts Council** for our publishing program. We also acknowledge the financial support of the **Government of Canada** through the **Canada Book Fund** and **Livres Canada Books**, and the **Government of Ontario** through the **Ontario Book Publishing Tax Credit** and the **Ontario Media Development Corporation**.

Printed and bound in Canada.
www.dundurn.com

Dundurn	Gazelle Book Services Limited	Dundurn
3 Church Street, Suite 500	White Cross Mills	2250 Military Road
Toronto, Ontario, Canada	High Town, Lancaster, England	Tonawanda, NY
M5E 1M2	LA1 4XS	U.S.A. 14150

To the Honourable Charles C. Clarke, 1826–1909

Speaker of the Ontario Legislature, clerk of the Ontario
Legislature, and first student of Canada's maces

Her Majesty Queen Elizabeth II, Queen of Canada, wearing the Sovereign's insignia of the Order of Canada and the Sovereign's insignia of the Order of Military Merit.

TABLE OF CONTENTS

Foreword	His Royal Highness The Duke of York, KG, GCVO, CD	9
Foreword	Terrance J. Christopher, OMM, LVO, CD	11
Acknowledgements		13
Chapter One	Canadian Symbols of Authority and Traditions of Ceremonial Protocol in Canada	17
I	**Rods of Office**	23
Chapter Two	Historical Roots of the Black Rod	25
Chapter Three	The Black Rod of the Senate of Canada	29
Chapter Four	Black Rods in the Provinces	43
	Quebec	46
	New Brunswick	48
	Alberta	51
	Prince Edward Island	54
Chapter Five	Baton of the Speaker of the House of Commons	57
Chapter Six	Baton of the Chief Herald of Canada	65
Chapter Seven	Tipstaffs and Batons of Canadian Police Forces	69
II	**Parliamentary Maces**	79
Chapter Eight	Origins and Development of Parliamentary Maces	81
Chapter Nine	The Mace of the Senate of Canada	101
Chapter Ten	The Mace of the House of Commons	115
Chapter Eleven	Provincial Maces	131
	Ontario	132
	Quebec	138
	Nova Scotia	143
	New Brunswick	148

	Prince Edward Island	154
	British Columbia	159
	Manitoba	169
	Saskatchewan	173
	Alberta	179
	Newfoundland and Labrador	185
Chapter Twelve	Territorial Maces	195
	Northwest Territories	196
	Yukon Territory	206
	Nunavut	210
Chapter Thirteen	Municipal and Academic Maces	219
III	**Badges and Chains of Office**	223
Chapter Fourteen	Insignia of Chains of Office of the Canadian Orders	225
	The Order of Canada, Sovereign's Badge	226
	The Order of Military Merit, Sovereign's Badge	227
	The Order of Merit of the Police Forces, Sovereign's Badge	229
	The Most Venerable Order of St. John of Jerusalem	240
Chapter Fifteen	Uniforms and Badges of Civil Authority	245
Chapter Sixteen	Collar of the Sergeant-at-Arms of the House of Commons	287
Chapter Seventeen	Collars of Office of the Canadian Heraldic Authority	295
IV	**Future Prospects**	305
Conclusion	Additions and Changes	307
Appendix I	Ushers of the Black Rod of the Senate	311
Appendix II	Sergeants-at-Arms of the House of Commons	312
Appendix III	Maces Currently in Use — Reference Chart	313
Notes		315
Glossary		337
Bibliography		340
Photo Credits		345
Index		352

FOREWORD

by His Royal Highness The Duke of York

Aside from the obvious flags and coats of arms, there are many other symbols of authority in use around the world. The massive gilded silver maces present in all of Canada's legislatures, and the chains of office worn by the Governor General, Chief of the Defence Staff and Chief Herald, represent a few of the fascinating and beautiful objects used by officers of the Crown.

The history of Canada can often be illuminated by individual objects. For instance, elements of the mace used in the Senate originated with the mace that was used by the Legislative Council of Lower Canada in the 1790s. This object has survived fire, theft and revolt and continues its stately function in the upper chamber.

Not all of the objects examined herein are ancient, and this also reflects the evolving nature of symbols of authority. The continuing role that these symbols of authority play in the ceremonial life of the great country of Canada is a testament to their enduring quality.

This book by Christopher McCreery and Corinna Pike reveals much about the history of Canada's many symbols of authority, their origin, history, development and the offices associated with them.

As a member of the Royal Family, and as someone who has been educated in Canada and is proud to have close links with Canada, I believe that this book will serve an important purpose by revealing a wealth of information hitherto unavailable in a single volume.

FOREWORD

by Terrance J. Christopher

This unique book examines the elements that comprise Canada's symbols of authority. It provides the reader with an historical perspective of our Canadian institutions, their history, and the meaning of the traditions and symbols that are associated with them. This book not only embodies a history of the actual objects, but also provides insight into the high offices to which they are associated.

With regard to black rods and legislative maces, their presence and use can be traced to Canada's first legislatures and the birth of democracy in a young country.

While this book is significant in that it traces our history over centuries, it demonstrates how ceremonies and protocol have played such a vital central role in the development of Canada's traditions. It is also a reminder that we must preserve and safeguard our traditions and symbols of authority, for they play an important part in defining us as Canadians. These objects also symbolize the continuity of Canada's governing institutions through the union of the Crown and democracy.

Like much of our national history, the story and origins of Canada's symbols of authority are also shared: one, which connects us to members of the Commonwealth, France, and even the United States.

I congratulate Corinna A.W. Pike, FGA, DGA, and Dr. Christopher McCreery, MVO, for their historical expertise, meticulous research, and dedication to bringing Canada's symbols of authority to life. Their work has helped reveal part of Canada's symbolic lexicon, about which little has been written and which has often been ignored.

Lieutenant Commander Terrance J. Christopher, OMM, LVO, CD
Former Usher of the Black Rod of the Senate

ACKNOWLEDGEMENTS

The authors owe considerable thanks to a number of officials and experts who from the beginning of this project took a keen interest in seeing it completed. Their enthusiasm and willingness to assist were crucial to the success of this work.

In particular, the former Usher of the Black Rod, Lieutenant Commander Terrance Christopher, OMM, LVO, CD, provided both authors with a wealth of information and encouragement. The former sergeant-at-arms of the House of Commons, the late Major General Gus Cloutier, CMM, CVO, CD, is remembered with affection.

The Speakers of the Senate and House of Commons, the Honourable Noël Kinsella and the Honourable Peter Milliken, were of great assistance.

We are extremely grateful to the Canadian Association of Former Parliamentarians for their kind donation and continuous support throughout this project. Our special thanks goes to Doug Rowland, CD, former chairman of the Canadian Association of Former Parliamentarians and Francis LeBlanc, President, Education Foundation of the Canadian Association of Former Parliamentarians.

Special acknowledgement is given to Bruce Patterson, Deputy Chief Herald of Canada, for his advice on various heraldic issues and for editing the text. In London, England, our appreciation goes to Clive Cheesman, Richmond Herald at the College of Arms, for giving valuable assistance with the editing. Chief Herald of Canada Dr. Claire Boudreau also provided invaluable advice and assistance on a number of occasions.

At the provincial and territorial levels, considerable gratitude goes to the Speakers and the Clerks of all the legislative assemblies across Canada. For assistance in the processes of gathering material for the book, our appreciation is extended to Beverley Bosiak (Deputy Clerk, Legislative Assembly of Manitoba), Charles MacKay (Clerk, Legislative Assembly of Prince Edward Island), Patrick Michael (former Clerk, Yukon Legislative Assembly), and John Quirke (Clerk, Nunavut Legislative Assembly).

At the Parliament buildings in Ottawa, we would like to acknowledge and thank Kevin MacLeod, CVO, CD, Usher of the Black Rod/Canadian Secretary to the Queen; Jan Potter, Mace Bearer of the Senate; and Kevin Vickers, Sergeant-at-Arms of the House of Commons. The Principal Clerk Procedure of the Senate, Charles Robert, was of assistance in matters related to the symbols of Quebec. From overseas we are grateful to Jill Pay, Serjeant-at-Arms, House of Commons, Westminster, England; and Brent Smith, Serjeant-at-Arms, House of Representatives, New Zealand.

Particular gratitude is extended to the sergeants-at-arms of all the provincial and territorial legislatures who have been very accommodating and hospitable in assisting with the research and who provided opportunities to inspect and handle the maces and rods for detailed assessment. Much appreciation goes to the following sergeants-at-arms: Curtis Adamson (Prince Edward Island), Daniel Bussières (New Brunswick), Rudy Couture (Yukon), Dennis Clark (Ontario), Garry Clark (Manitoba), Elizabeth Gallagher (Newfoundland and Labrador), Ken Greenham, CD (Nova Scotia), Brian Hodgson CD (Alberta), Anthony Humphreys (British Columbia), Simanuk Kilabuk (Nunavut), Pierre Paquet (Quebec), Patrick Shaw (Saskatchewan), and Brian Thagard (Northwest Territories).

Many people from various professional backgrounds have given considerable time and energy and have been a great aid to the research: David Monaghan, Curator of the House of Commons, and his assistant Kerry Barrow; Michael Laffin, Manager of Operations, Nova Scotia House of Assembly; Andrée Godin, Culture and Sport Secretariat, Fredericton; Greg Griffin, Jeffries & Co., Victoria; Robert Edge, Canada Club, London, England; Robert Harrison, Archives Officer, House of Lords, England; Joanne Bird, Curator, Prince of Wales Northern Heritage Centre, Yellowknife, and her staff; Yves Minjollet, Manager of the Musée Nationale de la Légion d'honneur, Paris; Suzanne Whitmore, Library of Parliament, Ottawa; Herb LeRoy, Private Secretary to the Lieutenant Governor of British Columbia; Irene Roughton, Assistant Registrar, Chrysler Museum of Art, Norfolk, Virginia; Jeanie Tummon, Curator of the Ontario Provincial Police Museum, Orillia; Sergeant Jacques Vézina, Sûreté du Québec; Patricia McRae, Archivist, Rideau Hall, Ottawa; Sophie Chevalier-Forget, Royal Canadian Mounted Police Historian; Charles Reid, Clerk of the South Carolina House of Representatives; Lady Jennifer Gretton, Lord Lieutenant of Leicestershire; and Martin Pelletier, Assemblée nationale du Québec.

René Chartrand, former curator of Parks Canada and renowned expert on all things related to uniforms and badges in early Canada, was particularly helpful in matters related to New France. Nigel Arch, LVO, Director of the Kensington Palace State Apartments, was incredibly helpful in relation to the history of court uniforms in the United Kingdom.

Megan Schlase of the Vancouver City Archives was helpful in providing a great quantity of information about the Vancouver City mace and its history. Appreciation is owed to Mayor's Officer and Serjeant-at-Mace David Thornton, the Bassetlaw Museum, and the Charter Trustees of East Retford, England, for providing photos of the highly important Retford Maces.

We are most thankful to the Library of Parliament for always responding to our requests for books and pamphlets in a timely fashion. The staff at Library and Archives Canada was similarly helpful in locating a number of files and documents related to the House of Commons mace and territorial maces. Throughout this project the backbone has been supported by the friendly and helpful staff at the different legislatures across Canada and the staff of the legislature libraries.

Christopher McCreery, MVO
Halifax, Nova Scotia

Corinna A.W. Pike, FGA, DGA
London, United Kingdom

CHAPTER ONE

Canadian Symbols of Authority and Traditions of Ceremonial Protocol in Canada

We often think of Canada as a very young country where both institutions and traditions are recent creations taken from other countries and applied to the Canadian context. Yet Canada's record of uninterrupted democratic government is only surpassed by two other countries: the United Kingdom and the United States.[1] We have one of the longest histories of functioning and evolving democratic institutions in the world. Our federal Parliament and various provincial legislatures embody a democratic tradition that is as rich and diverse as the people of Canada.

Since the era of the Governors of New France and the Sovereign Council, which aided in the governance of the fledgling colony, Canada has been a monarchy. For more than half a millennium Canada's head of state has been a Sovereign, represented by a governor or governor general. Within this framework, which over time evolved to become a constitutional monarchy, the continuity of the Crown came to be fused with representative and responsible democratic bodies to form what is affectionately known in constitutional circles as "Peace, Order and Good Government." Even our rebels, such as the Métis leader Louis Riel, were intent on retaining the Crown as the locus of power.

This is the first book to examine the various symbols of authority used by the Queen, her representatives the governor general and the lieutenant governors, police commissioners, state officials, and the federal, provincial, and territorial legislatures. The parliamentary maces used throughout Canada, like the Crown, embody continuity in an ever-changing political world. They are not symbols of a foreign land imposed upon Canada, but rather they are like old friends that are part of the Canadian symbolic and ceremonial lexicon. They have also adapted to the Canadian context and thus been made symbols of the nation.

Despite this rich symbolic and ceremonial heritage, little is known and even less understood about the various maces, chains of offices, and batons that are used throughout Canada. Aside from a few pamphlets, the objects and offices discussed in this book have only been seen from a distance by Canadians.

His Excellency the Right Honourable David Johnston, CC, CMM, COM, CD, governor general and commander-in-chief of Canada, wearing the chancellor's chain of the Order of Military Merit.

They comprise not only symbols of democracy and authority, but are part of the rich heraldic and artistic heritage of Canada. Given that these symbols have been developed at different times over the past two centuries, each is a token of the age during which it was created. Similar in form, but unique in their symbolism, Canada's chains of office and maces are not only physical representations of specific offices and legislative bodies, but are also an integral part of our ceremonial history. Sovereigns, governors general, and prime ministers come and go over time, but a number of maces, such as that used by the Senate, date back to a time when Canada was little more than a sparsely populated strip of land along the St. Lawrence River.

If little is known about the actual symbols of authority used throughout Canada, then it is true that even less is understood about the different state ceremonies and protocol that accompanies each of these objects of national identity. While much has been inherited from the French and British, in some jurisdictions a similar wealth of Native Canadian traditions has been incorporated, and these traditions have been melded together into a Canadian body of heritage, traditions, and ceremony.

The protocol associated with the use of Canada's various symbols of authority is largely unwritten, and in most respects has been passed down through an oral tradition. In 1934 the secretary to the governor general Sir Allan Lascelles developed the *Green Book*, which until the 1980s served as the basis of knowledge and procedure for events involving the governor general, from levees to investiture ceremonies. The *Green Book*, although useful within the context of viceregal offices, was not a government-wide protocol manual. In 1967 Prime Minister Lester Pearson directed the Privy Council Office to develop *The Manual of Official Procedure of the Government of Canada*. This mammoth two-volume work constitutes the most comprehensive guide to protocol and government traditions in Canada, but it was not maintained or updated and largely fell out of use by the 1980s. With the departure of Canada's great courtiers — such as Esmond Butler, who served successive governors general from 1957 to 1985, and Gordon Robertson, who served almost every prime minister from William Lyon Mackenzie King to Pierre Trudeau, rising to the post of Clerk of the Privy Council — some of this knowledge was forgotten. Who of Canada's state officials would know anything about the Great Seal defacing ceremony that is supposed to transpire after the adoption of a new Great Seal of Canada? Given that the last such event occurred more than fifty years ago, it is, to some degree, understandable that memory of these events has evaporated.

In the provinces manuals of procedure have been developed and are used to varying degrees. It is often at the provincial, territorial, and municipal level that citizens are more exposed to representatives of the Crown and their democratic institutions. Most Canadian municipalities have a long history of mayoral chains of office, and these constitute symbols of municipal authority which have yet to be studied.

In addition to examining the physical and historical nature of each symbol of authority, the authors have attempted to explain the context in which these symbolic elements of the state are used. Where a mace is placed or when a chain of office is worn is as important as what the particular object is made of and who manufactured it. The intent of this work is not to provide a comprehensive history of protocol in Canada, as such a work would be multiple volumes in length and of somewhat limited interest, despite the importance of such a modern compendium.

Those wishing to learn more about the heraldic history of Canada should consult Sir Conrad Swan's *Canadian Symbols of Sovereignty*, Alan Beddoe's *Canadian Heraldry*, and Kevin Greaves's *Canadian Heraldic Primer*. A history of the Canadian honours system can be found in *The Canadian Honours System* written by Christopher McCreery. Sir Peter Thorne's book, *The Royal Mace*, provides a concise history of the development of the mace in England and the United Kingdom. In-depth analysis of the development of maces can be found in Chris Given-Wilson's *The Royal Household and the King's Affinity*, and Walter Paatz's *Die Akademische Szepter und Stäble in Europa*. Although somewhat dated, Charles Clarke's *The Mace and Its Uses*, published in 1881, provides the first serious study of maces in Canada.

Much credit is owed to Clarke for being the first Canadian student of "symbols of authority." Clarke, as Speaker of the Ontario provincial parliament, took an earnest interest in legislative maces little more than a decade after Confederation. He speaks to the level of reverence that many early parliamentarians had for these symbols of the struggle to attain democratic bodies. Both citizens and legislators often forget that the achievement of democracy and independence in Canada was not an event. It was a long struggle that reaches back to the Royal Proclamation of 1763 and the Quebec Act of 1791. These were not just events that pertain to what would become the provinces of Quebec and Ontario, but to all of what would become Canada. Similarly, Newfoundland's use of the mace in 1838 would have a role in the rights and privileges of legislatures throughout Canada and the British Empire, from Australia to Sri Lanka. These are connections that all Canadians should feel, as these stories are a part of our common history.

We would be well advised to examine more closely how Canada developed into one of the most successful democracies in the world. The mace, like the ballot, political parties, partisanship, and the Crown, has played a role in our democratic life as a nation.

Given that this book examines symbols of authority the reader might justifiably ask why the Crown is not examined. The Crown plays a dual role as both a symbol of authority and, more importantly, as the ultimate symbol of the state's sovereignty and power. That it has such a ubiquitous presence in the symbols of authority used throughout Canada is further evidence of this fact. A unifying element in the Canadian state, both symbolically and legally, the Crown symbolized more than authority alone. The St. Edward's Crown, which is most frequently reproduced and used throughout Canada on coats of arms, flags, and badges, is a shared symbol, used in the sixteen Commonwealth countries of which Elizabeth II is Queen. The shared nature of this pre-eminent symbol of authority is the principal reason why it is not examined in its own right herein.

For ease of understanding, this work is divided into three sections. The first examines the various rods and staffs of office, while the second examines the myriad of different legislative maces used throughout Canada. The final section delves into the history and development of chains and badges of office, with an additional chapter devoted to the rise and fall of civil uniforms.

I

Rods of Office

CHAPTER TWO

Historical Roots of the Black Rod

Canada has employed a Gentleman Usher of the Black Rod since 1791, making it one of the oldest offices in the land, surpassed only by the position of the Sovereign, governor general, and Bishop of Quebec. In pre-Confederation Canada, Newfoundland, New Brunswick, Prince Edward Island, Manitoba, and Upper and Lower Canada (later the Province of Canada) all possessed legislative councils that were attended upon by a Gentleman Usher of the Black Rod. A physical black rod was also used in many of these bodies. Following Confederation, only Quebec, New Brunswick, Nova Scotia, and Manitoba retained a legislative council. Black rods continue today to be used in four jurisdictions in Canada: federally in the Senate by the Usher of the Black Rod, and provincially in the legislative assemblies carried by the sergeants-at-arms of New Brunswick, Alberta, and Prince Edward Island.

The office of Gentleman Usher of the Black Rod dates from 1348 and the founding of the Most Noble Order of the Garter by King Edward III.[1] On 13 April, in the thirty-fifth year of King Edward III's reign, he appointed William Whitehorse to the "Officium Hostiarii Capellæ Regis infra Castrum de Windesor,"[2] being paid 12 pence a day for his services.

The Order remains England's premier honour and is one of the oldest orders of chivalry in the world. On St. George's Day, the Usher, who would become the Gentleman Usher of the Black Rod, led the procession of Knights of the Garter towards St. George's Chapel, which is part of Windsor Castle. Once all the knights were assembled in the chapel it was the role of the Usher of the Black Rod to close and guard the doors. With time, the Usher became known by the name of his rod of office, the Black Rod.

The first reference to the Usher can be found in letters patent dating from 1361, appointing Whitehorse "usher of the free chapel of Wyndesor Castle."[3] The word "usher" comes from the Latin word *ussarius*, which means "doorkeeper." Initially the Usher was an official associated solely with the Order of the Garter, as it would be sometime before he gained a parliamentary role.

The functions of Black Rod were further refined during the reign of King Henry VII and augmentations to the statutes of the Order of the Garter. With this, the Black Rod's role expanded to include parliamentary duties. In 1522, the Usher of the Black Rod was given responsibility for "all the doors where any councils are held, as well in Our High Court of Parliament, as in other places."[4] Originally the Black Rod was carried in place of a mace as a symbol of authority, empowering the Usher to arrest those contravening the statutes and ordinances of the Order of the Garter.

King Henry VIII commanded that the Black Rod must be a "Gentleman of Name and Arms," and hence the term "Gentleman Usher of the Black Rod" was coined.[5] The design of at least part of the Black Rod is set out in a 1552 statute that commands that the black rod have at one end a "Lion the Ensign of the English."[6]

One of the reasons that the Usher of the Black Rod carries a black rod and not a mace as his symbol of office relates to the blunt nature of a mace. During the reign of King Edward III it was decided that a mace was too rough an instrument to be used to maintain order amongst Knights of the Garter, and later in the House of Lords. The general idea behind this was that the bearer of a black rod would be less likely to seriously injure a member in any attempt to maintain order.

Royal France's premier national order, *l'Ordre du Saint-Esprit*, possessed an office similar to the Gentleman Usher of the Black Rod. The "huissier de l'ordre du Saint-Esprit" was a ceremonial officer who carried the mace of the ordre du Saint-Esprit. Although somewhat more elaborate than the black rod, the purpose was the same. The French adopted this officer in the sixteenth century.[7] As France did not possess an elected assembly, this officer was limited to serving members of the ordre du Saint-Esprit and did not perform other functions, such as the parliamentary duties of his British counterpart.

It was during the seventeenth century that we find the first references to the Black Rod's most public duty, summoning the House of Commons to attend the Sovereign in the House of Lords; or in Canada, to attend the Queen or governor general in the Senate. A 1614 *Journals of the House of Commons* entry for the House of Commons noted that the Black Rod came to inform the members of Parliament that the King called for them to come to the House of Lords.

The office has become more closely associated with the House of Lords and the Senate in Canada than with its original assignment to guard assemblages of Knights of the Order of the Garter. In the United Kingdom, the Gentleman Usher of the Black Rod continues to participate in ceremonies related to the Order of the Garter.[8]

Until 1883 it was the responsibility of each Gentleman Usher of the Black Rod to procure his own black rod. The oldest of these known to exist dates from 1683 and continues to he held by the family of Sir Thomas Duppa (Black Rod from 1683–1694). The designs of the black rods used in the House of Lords, in the Legislative Council of New Brunswick, and in the Senate of Canada are all similar. This general design has been maintained since the seventeenth century.

The Earl of Elgin, Canada's governor general from 1847 to 1854, commented, "the office of Black Rod is not a sinecure, in England it is a very honourable and responsible office, but it is not so understood in Canada."[9]

In a number of countries throughout the Commonwealth it has become the custom for the upper chamber to employ a Gentleman Usher of the Black Rod, who carried an instrument known as the black rod. This was true in the case of Ireland, prior to its union with Great Britain in 1801; as well as South Africa, Australia, New Zealand, Jamaica, Trinidad and Tobago, and all of Australia's states except Queensland. The Senate of Northern Ireland also used a Black Rod.

CHAPTER THREE

The Black Rod of the Senate of Canada

Prior to Confederation, many of the various colonies that joined to form Canada had upper houses, known as legislative councils. This was true in the case of Upper and Lower Canada, Nova Scotia, New Brunswick, British Columbia, Newfoundland, and Prince Edward Island. In Lower Canada, the legislative council predated the granting of representative government, being founded in 1774. The first Gentleman Usher of the Black Rod served the Legislative Council of Lower Canada, being paid £50 per annum.[1]

After Confederation, the office of Gentleman Usher of the Black Rod was created for the Senate of Canada. René Kimber, the Gentleman Usher

The Usher of the Black Rod of the Senate of Canada, Kevin MacLoed, CVO, CD, leading the viceregal procession prior to a Royal assent ceremony.

of the Black Rod who had served the Legislative Council of the Province of the United Canadas, was appointed the first Black Rod for the newly created Senate. Since that time, the Usher has been appointed by letters patent issued under the Great Seal of Canada.[2] In November 1867, one of the first debates to transpire in the Senate chamber concerned the office of the Gentleman Usher of the Black Rod and his duties. The first report of the select committee on contingent accounts of the Senate (internal economy) decided that the duties of the sergeant-at-arms to the Senate should be discharged by the Gentleman Usher of the Black Rod.

There was some dissent, and Senator Ulric-Joseph Tessier, who happened to be the last Speaker of the Legislative Council of Canada, noted that "there was a high dignity and importance attached to the office in England, and the incumbent was regarded as a person of eminent rank."[3] The honourable Senator thought it was unreasonable to ask the Gentleman Usher to carry the Senate mace, as this had not been done in the old legislative council or in the House of Lords. Initially it was decided "that the duties of the Sergeant-at-Arms to the Senate, as well as those of the Gentleman Usher of the Black Rod, may, and should be discharged by the same individual."[4] In colonial times a sergeant-of-the-mace had been employed by the Legislative Council of Lower Canada, and in 1841 when the Legislative Council of the Province of Canada was convoked, a sergeant-at-arms was appointed to assist the Gentleman Usher of the Black Rod in the upper chamber. Thus a precedent had been set long ago.

The situation was not immediately resolved, and in May 1869, Captain Juchereau de St. Denis LeMoyne, son of the first clerk of the Senate, was appointed acting sergeant-at-arms.[5] In 1873 Le Moine was appointed sergeant-at-arms to the Senate and clerk of the Senate's French journals section.[6] In 1884 Le Moine was appointed sergeant-at-arms of the Senate by letters patent under the Great Seal of Canada. It is interesting to note that the term changed from sergeant-at-arms *of* the senate to sergeant-at-arms *to* the Senate at this time. Following Le Moine's retirement in 1923 no new sergeant-at-arms was appointed.[7] In 1927 the *Journals of the Senate* reveal that Charles Larose was employed as "mace bearer." This is the first time that this designation appears. Larose was subsequently re-designated "Assistant Gentleman Usher of the Black Rod" in 1931, serving in that post until 1946, and would be succeeded by his son C. Bonner Larose, who served as Assistant Gentleman Usher from 1947 to 1962.[8]

The position of Assistant Gentleman Usher appears to have been used when a person was appointed to the post, while the term "mace bearer" was used when the Senate merely required someone to carry the mace for ceremonial purposes, and not necessarily to assist the Gentleman Usher of the Black Rod. From 1964 to 1984 the Senate continued to employ an Assistant Gentleman Usher of the Black Rod. The first person to hold this post was Lieutenant Colonel Alfred Fortier, who served from 1964 to 1976. He was succeeded by Lieutenant Colonel Charles Askwith, who served in this capacity from 1977 to 1983 and then as Acting Gentleman Usher of the Black Rod in 1984, prior to the appointment of Major René Jalbert. For a period between 1983 and 1988 there is no mention of an Assistant Usher and it appears that the mace was carried by a person informally titled "mace bearer." In 1989 R.E. Gladstone was appointed Deputy Gentleman Usher of the Black Rod, but this position did not last. From 1992 to 1999 the mace was carried by a Senate messenger who subsequently joined the Senate Protective Services. From 1999 to the present the mace has been carried by a person formally styled "mace bearer"; the position was held by Richard Logan from 1999–2003, and by Jan Potter from 2004 to the present day. Potter is also the first female to hold the post, although Patricia Lapointe, a Senate page, became the first female to carry the Senate mace on 20 November 2001. The first woman appointed to carry a legislative mace was Phyllis LeBlanc, who was appointed sergeant-at-arms of the Legislative Assembly of New Brunswick in February 1995.[9]

Curiously, the Senate of Canada is the only legislative body in the Commonwealth to have its mace carried by a "mace bearer."[10] In other jurisdictions it is carried by the Usher of the Black Rod or another similarly styled but more junior official — such as an Assistant Usher of the Black Rod — who is entrusted with the symbol of Royal authority in the upper chamber.

In the United Kingdom the Gentleman Usher has discharged the administrative duties of the sergeant-at-arms to the House of Lords since 1971,[11] and thus his title is "Gentleman Usher of the Black Rod, Secretary to the Lord Great Chamberlain, and Sergeant-at-Arms of the House of Lords."[12]

At the Senate in 1997 Mary MacLaren was appointed to the office and the title changed from Gentleman Usher of the Black Rod to simply Usher of the Black Rod. This change did not transpire without some debate. There has long been discussion about the title, and some have suggested that when a female holds the office it should be known as "Lady Usher of the Black Rod," and when it is a man "Gentleman Usher of the Black Rod."

The Black Rod

During the parliamentary fire of February 1916, Lieutenant Colonel Ernest Chambers led the rescue operations in the Senate precincts. Although the Senate was not sitting that evening, Chambers was present because he had a private apartment behind the Senate chamber. Chambers was responsible for rescuing the Senate mace, although the black rod was lost in the fire along with the Gentleman Usher of the Black Rod's uniform.[13] It is believed the black rod that was destroyed in the fire was purchased at the same time that Sir Allan Napier MacNab procured a mace for the Legislative Assembly of the United Canadas in 1845,

It is possible that it was manufactured by E. Chanteloupe of Montreal. It was approximately 100 centimetres in length and made of black ebony with silver-gilt fittings. The head was topped with a crowned lion seated upon a pedestal, the collar of which was engraved with maple leaves. One quarter of the way down the rod was a decorative knop also depicting natural maple leaves. The middle of the rod was more elaborately decorated with maple leaves, as was the foot knop. The design for this black rod, although different from the current Senate black rod and that used in New Brunswick, conforms with the general design included in Elias Ashmole's *The Institution, Laws and Ceremonies of the Most Noble Order of the Garter*, published in 1672. Indeed Ashmole depicts two designs, one of a rod topped by a lion on all fours, similar to the original Senate black rod, and another with a lion

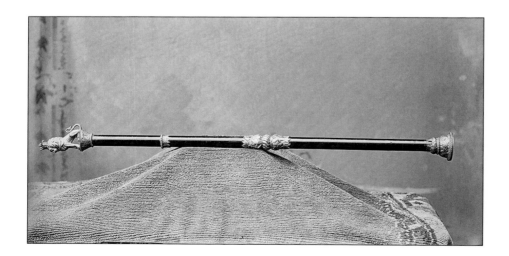

The black rod of the Senate of Canada, 1867–1916.

holding a shield and the Royal cypher, similar to the current black rod used by the Senate.

Shortly after the parliamentary fire the Senate's Committee of Internal Economy met and decided to commission a new black rod. On 10 March 1916, Garrard & Co. Ltd., the Crown Jewellers, were contracted to produce a new black rod for the Senate of Canada. They were instructed to model it upon the black rod of the House of Lords. The British branch of the Empire Parliamentary Association, the forerunner of the Commonwealth Parliamentary Association, acted as an advisor to both the Senate and Garrards. In March 1918 the association asked the Senate if they would be permitted the honour of presenting the new black rod to the Senate, "which would mark their friendly feelings towards their parliamentary colleagues in the Dominion of Canada."[14] Rather than simply have one or two members of British Parliament donate money towards the new black rod, it was decided to limit donations to 10 shillings each. British members of the House of Lords

Senator identification pin displaying the upper end of the black rod.

and members of the House of Commons covered the cost of the new black rod through these subscriptions. A total of ninety-one members of the House of Lords — including Lord Mount Stephen and former Governor General Lord Lansdowne — made a donation towards the new black rod. In the Commons, one hundred and forty members donated to the project.[15]

The new black rod was presented to Prime Minister Sir Robert Borden on 21 June 1918, at Westminster by Lord Finlay, the Lord Chancellor, and J.W. Lowther, Speaker of the House of Commons.

> Our members on learning of the destruction of the Black Rod in use in the Senate, requested leave to present the new Black Rod to the Senate of Canada.
>
> We know that our action cannot restore the traditions historically associated with the previous Black Rod which had been in use ever since the days of the Legislative Council of old Lower Canada and before the great Dominion of Canada was constituted by the union of the Provinces.[16]

Sir Robert Borden being presented with the black rod of the Senate of Canada by the Empire Parliamentary Association, 1918.

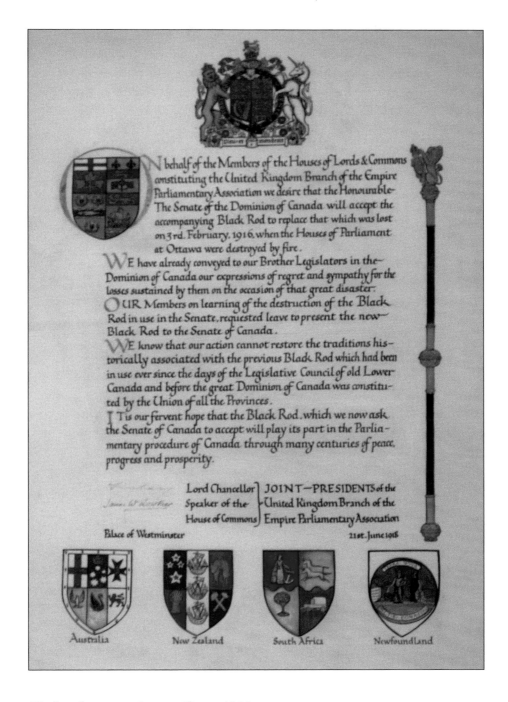

Black rod presentation certificate, 1918.

The black rod was delivered to Canada on 30 August 1918, and a small press conference was held in the prime minister's office where Sir Robert

Borden presented the black rod to the Speaker of the Senate and the Gentleman Usher of the Black Rod. As the Senate was not then sitting, it would not be until 1919 that the new black rod could be put into action. On 28 February 1919, Sir James Lougheed, the government leader in the Senate, moved a vote of thanks to the Empire Parliamentary Association for the new black rod.

The Senate's black rod carries the Royal cypher of King George V and includes maple leaf decorations on the orb-shaped knops. A 1904 British gold sovereign is set into the base, displaying the allegory of St. George slaying the dragon. It is interesting to note that the black rod used in the House of Lords, which dates from 1883, was modified during the reign of King Edward VII and also includes a 1904 gold sovereign. Amongst other things, the gold sovereign denotes the "date of appointment of the present holder of the office of the Gentleman Usher of the Black Rod in Canada [Ernest John Chambers]."[17]

Ceremonial

The Usher of the Black Rod carries out many of the same functions in the Senate as the sergeant-at-arms of the House of Commons does, but he has the added role of attending upon the Queen or governor general when either of them is present. He is responsible for many of the ceremonies that transpire in the chamber. This usually only occurs during Royal assent, the speech from the throne, the installation of a new governor general, or during a Royal visit. The Usher of the Black Rod leads the ceremonial procession of the Queen or governor general into the Senate chamber.

When the Queen or governor general is present, the Speaker of the Senate commands the black rod to "proceed to the House of Commons and acquaint that House that it is His Excellency's [or Her Majesty's] pleasure they will attend him immediately in this House."[18] The Usher of the Black Rod retires from the Senate chamber and proceeds to the House of Commons. There he knocks three times with his black rod on the outer doors of the House of Commons. Once he gains entry into the lobby a messenger knocks three times on the inner doors of the House of Commons with a wooden mallet. Canada has not followed the British tradition of having the doors of the House of Commons slammed in the face of the Usher of the Black Rod. The Usher of the Black Rod is admitted to the Commons by the sergeant-at-arms. The slamming of the door in Black Rod's face is believed to have originated after an incident that occurred in the British

Ernest John Chambers, VD, wearing court dress, holding the replacement (post-1918) black rod.

House of Commons in the seventeenth century. The Commons *Journals* from 10 May 1641, record that "exception was taken to Mr. Maxwell coming to the House with a message, without his black rod, and coming in before he was called in."[19]

Lieutenant Commander Terrance Christopher, OMM, LVO, CD, Usher of the Black Rod, 2002–2008.

After Black Rod is admitted he advances to the bar and bows to the Speaker and proceeds up the middle of the House to the table, bowing a second time when he is halfway between the bar and the table. He bows a third time on reaching the table. He then delivers his message, bowing to each side of the House after he has uttered the words: "this honourable House." After delivering his message from the Senate, he bows to the Speaker and then bows two more times: once when he reaches the end of the table and again when he reaches the bar. The Usher of the Black Rod then leads the procession of the Speaker of the House of Commons, the sergeant-at-arms, and members of the House of Commons through the corridors of Parliament to the Senate chamber. Upon entering the Senate chamber, only the Usher of the Black Rod is allowed to proceed past the brass bar at the far end of the chamber. Members of the House of Commons are required to stand behind the bar. Of course the prime minister and members of the federal cabinet, although members of the lower house, are already present as they are members of the Queen's Privy Council for Canada.

During ordinary sittings of the Senate, undertaken without the presence of the Sovereign or governor general, the Usher of the Black Rod leads the Speaker's parade prior to the daily opening and sits at a desk in the centre aisle of the Senate near the brass bar so that he can control entry to the Senate floor.

The Usher of the Black Rod carrying the Black Rod of the Senate during a Royal Assent ceremony.

Black Rod of the Usher of the Black Rod of the Senate of Canada (1918–present)

Material: Black rosewood with 18-carat gold and sterling silver-gilt mounts.

Length: 99 centimetres.

Upper End: The rod has at the top the heraldic lion serjant erect (sitting on its haunches) holding in its paws a crowned shield displaying the Royal cypher of King George V surrounded with a garter with the motto *Honi soit qui mal y pense*, all upon a round knop decorated with maple leaves. This uppermost mount is made of 18-carat gold with blue enamel in the garter and red enamel in the crown.

Left: Black rod of the Senate, upper end.
Right: Black rod of the Senate, middle section.

Black rod of the Senate, lower end.

Shaft and Knop: Black rosewood in two sections with a silver-gilt knop halfway down alongside which is an engraved inscription. The knop is decorated with maple leaves.

Foot Knop: Silver-gilt knop decorated with maple leaves; the base of the knop is inset with a 1904 British gold sovereign with the reverse facing out displaying St. George slaying the dragon.

Engraving: Located alongside the central knop.

PRESENTED TO THE SENATE OF CANADA BY
MEMBERS OF THE UNITED KINGDOM BRANCH
OF THE EMPIRE PARLIAMENTARY ASSOCIATION
TO REPLACE THE BLACK ROD LOST IN THE FIRE
OF 3RD FEB. 1916.

FINLAY
   LORD CHANCELLOR
J. W. LOWTHER   JOINT-PRESIDENTS
   SPEAKER OF THE HOUSE
     OF COMMONS
PALACE OF WESTMINISTER
21ST JUNE 1918

Manufacturer and Distinguishing Marks: London hallmarks for 1917–1918 with maker's mark "SG" for Sebastian Garrard of Garrard & Co. Ltd.

CHAPTER FOUR

Black Rods in the Provinces

Presently four provincial black rods are known to exist. Only those provinces which continue to possess an actual black rod are examined in detail herein.

Lower Canada possessed the oldest legislative council in Canada, dating back to 1774. Prior to Confederation, the Province of Canada (Canada East and Canada West), Manitoba, New Brunswick, Newfoundland, Nova Scotia, and Prince Edward Island all had upper chambers known as legislative councils. These were bodies in which the members were appointed by the Crown for life.[1] These councils composed part of the bicameral structure of colonial legislatures that existed in most of British North America. Following Confederation, Ontario, British Columbia, Saskatchewan, Alberta, and Newfoundland did not adopt legislative councils. In many ways the legislative councils were akin to provincial Senates. In 1968, the last of the provincial legislative councils, that of Quebec, was abolished.

Each legislative council had an individual who acted as Gentleman Usher of the Black Rod. Although it is not entirely clear if these colonial and provincial Ushers of the Black Rod actually possessed a physical black rod for ceremonial use, we do know that a court sword was often carried by all colonial Gentleman Ushers of the Black Rod. Because the legislative councils met with less frequency than the legislative assemblies, the post of Gentleman Usher of the Black Rod was usually filled by a messenger or other employee of the legislative council.

Today in Canada, three legislatures use a black rod: the Legislative Assembly of New Brunswick, the Legislative Assembly of Alberta, and the Legislative Assembly of Prince Edward Island.

While Prince Edward Island can lay some claim to having previously employed a Gentleman Usher of the Black Rod, Alberta has never possessed such an official.

In these provinces today, the black rod is carried by the sergeant-at-arms on certain ceremonial occasions. The physical rods are of recent manufacture, Alberta first using one in 1998 and Prince Edward Island adopting theirs in 2000.

New Brunswick, which possesses the oldest existing black rod in Canada, has a long tradition of incorporating the instrument into legislative ceremonies involving the lieutenant governors. The presence and use of black rods in Alberta and Prince Edward Island may seem unusual, given that Alberta never had an upper house and Prince Edward Island's upper chamber has long been extinct. This is a uniquely Canadian innovation, one developed to offer the sergeant-at-arms in Alberta and Prince Edward Island a special *accoutrement*, other than the mace, to carry when in attendance upon the Queen, governor general, or lieutenant governor. This Canadian tradition is one developed to honour the Crown and to display the central place that provincial legislatures play in the governance of the country.

Dormant Black Rods

Only two dormant black rods are known to exist in Canada. However, it is valuable to examine the presence of the office of Gentleman Usher of the Black Rod in colonial British North America.

The Legislative Council of Nova Scotia was established in 1837 and continued to function following Confederation, only being abolished in 1928. At the first session of the legislative council on 25 January 1838, the members were required to take their oath of loyalty to the Queen. The Gentleman Usher of the Black Rod was then dispatched to the House of Assembly to let them know "It is His Excellency's pleasure they attend him immediately in this House [the Legislative Council]."[2] J.J. Sawyer served as the Council's Gentleman Usher of the Black Rod from 1838 to 1874. He was replaced by Robert Romans in 1874.[3] The position continued to exist as it is mentioned in the lead-up to subsequent speeches from the throne, until the legislative council was abolished in 1928. Although a physical black rod was not used in Nova Scotia, it was the only province to have a Gentleman Usher whose sole responsibility was to act in that role. From 1874 until 1888 Robert Roman was Nova Scotia's Gentleman Usher of the Black Rod. After 1888 references to a separate office cease.

Given that Nova Scotia did not possess a legislative mace until 1930, it is not surprising that the legislative council never had a physical black rod. The Gentleman Usher of the Black Rod simply carried a court sword.

The first reference to a Gentleman Usher of the Black Rod being present in Upper Canada appears in July 1800. There is a reference to the post being filled by a George Law who was accorded an annual salary of £30, rather significantly less than the £50 paid to his Lower-Canadian counterpart. It is not known if a physical black rod existed for the Legislative Council of Upper Canada; however we do know that the Gentleman Usher of the Black Rod and sergeant-at-arms of the legislative council were given £6.5.0 to cover the cost of a court sword.[4]

Given that the mace from the Legislative Council of Lower Canada was used following the 1841 union of the two provinces into the Province of Canada, and that there is no record that the legislative council or assembly possessed a mace following the 1813 ransacking of York by the Americans, it seems unlikely that there was ever a physical black rod for the Legislative Council of Upper Canada. When Upper Canada was united with Lower Canada and combined to become the Province of Canada, the new legislature was endowed with a Gentleman Usher of the Black Rod from its inception in 1841; this officer was inherited from the Legislative Council of Lower Canada.[5]

Upon becoming a province in 1870 the Manitoba Legislature was structured as a legislative council and legislative assembly. The first meeting of the legislative council was convened on 15 March 1871, and the lieutenant governor was attended upon by "Captain Villiers, acting as the Gentleman Usher of the Black Rod."[6] Villiers held this post until 1874 when it was filled by Victor Beaupré, who would remain until the last meeting of the council on 4 February 1876. These men were styled acting as Gentleman Usher, and nothing more substantive. It is likely that they had multiple duties with the council or they were present only for speeches from the throne.[7] Given that the Legislative Council of Manitoba was very small, consisting of only seven members including a Speaker, it would have been an onerous expense to have a full-time Black Rod. As with other provinces there is no mention of whether or not a physical black rod existed.

Newfoundland's legislative council, known as the Board of Council, was created in 1832 upon the adoption of a new colonial constitution. It met for the first time in January 1833, and an official styled Gentleman Usher of the Black Rod was present. The council was suspended between April 1841 and January 1843 when the constitution was suspended and both the legislative council and legislative assembly were combined into an amalgamated assembly until 1854 when the council and assembly were again separated. It is not certain what role, if any, the Gentleman Usher of the Black Rod played during this period. The council employed a Gentleman Usher of the Black Rod until the council ceased to exist when the Commission of

Legislative Council of the Dominion of Newfoundland, 1934. The Gentleman Usher of the Black Rod, holding a long wooden rod staff, can be seen in the back row.

Government was established in 1934 and Newfoundland reverted to being a British Crown colony. The last holder of this post was Charles F. Garland, who served from 1929–1934.[8] In the photo depicting the last sitting of the legislative council, Garland can clearly be seen at the back of the council chamber holding a plain wooden staff approximately 2 metres in length. The whereabouts of this black rod is unknown.

The Act of Union with Canada stipulated that no legislative council was to be established when the colony became a Canadian province in 1949.

QUEBEC

Quebec possessed the oldest legislative council in Canada, a body that would expand as a result of Canada's growth. The upper chamber transformed from the Legislative Council of Lower Canada, to the Legislative Council of the Province of Canada, to the Legislative Council of Quebec, and ultimately into the Senate of Canada. Following the establishment of British rule in Quebec, it was decided that it was "at present inexpedient to call an Assembly,"[9] however a legislative council was established by the Quebec Act of 1774.[10] This was known as the Legislative Council of Quebec. In 1791, under the Constitution Act of 1791, Quebec was partitioned into Upper and Lower Canada. Lower Canada was given a legislative assembly and a legislative council. The first meeting of the new legislative council transpired in 1792. Prior to the first meeting of the legislative council, William Boutillier was appointed Gentleman Usher of the Black Rod, and this was confirmed by a Commission issued by the lieutenant governor on 31 October 1792.[11] The *Journals* records that "shortly after, a Message was delivered by Mr. Wm. Bouthillier, Gentleman Usher of the Black Rod,"[12] and with this message the age-old ceremony discharged by the Black Rod in Britain was brought to Canada. The original black rod used by the Legislative Council of Lower Canada is believed to date from the early nineteenth century, roughly the same period that the legislative council mace (now used by the Senate) has been dated to. The original legislative council black rod was used by the Legislative Council of the Province of Canada and was transferred to the Dominion Parliament following Confederation and was lost in the fire of 1916.

In total, ten men held the post of Gentleman Usher of the Black Rod in Lower Canada, the Province of Canada, and Quebec. The first Gentleman Usher of the Black Rod to the Legislative Council of the Province of Canada, René Kimber, was the first person to hold this post in the Senate of Canada following Confederation.[13]

Following Confederation, the provincial government commissioned Ottawa artisan Charles Zollikoffer to produce a black rod for the Legislative Council of Quebec. Zollikoffer also made the mace for the Legislative Assembly and Legislative Council of Quebec, along with the mace for the Ontario Legislative Assembly. Sadly this black rod was lost in the 1883 fire that destroyed the original Quebec Parliament buildings. A new black rod was commissioned from Cyrille Duquet of Quebec City, who was a local jeweller and optician. It is believed that like the new mace made for the legislative council and the black rod were designed by E.E. Taché, deputy minister of Crown lands, who also designed the Parliament buildings. The black rod was used in the Quebec legislative council until the council was abolished in 1968. The black rod is now on display at the National Assembly in Quebec City.

Black Rod of the Legislative Council of the Province of Quebec (1884–1968)

Material: Gilded base metal.

Length: 73.5 centimetres.

Upper End: The rod has at the top end a lion sejant (sitting on its haunches) with a small crown on its head; the lion is positioned above a flared pedestal fitting, which is decorated in maple leaves.

Shaft: The black wood shaft is in two main parts. Midway down the upper section there is a beaded gilded collar encircled with maple leaves. The central fitting is baluster-shaped and has a gadrooned middle knop with maple leaves above and below.

Lower End: The flared gilded knop at the base has encircling maple leaves.

NEW BRUNSWICK

New Brunswick was partitioned from Nova Scotia in 1784 and shortly thereafter a colonial legislative council and legislative assembly were established. There is no mention of a Gentleman Usher of the Black Rod in the *Journals* of the legislative council until 28 December 1837.[14] Earlier entries simply note that two members of the council were sent to the legislative assembly to inform them that the lieutenant governor required their attendance in the council chamber.[15]

As New Brunswick did not adopt a formal legislative mace until 1937, the black rod served as the principal symbol of authority for the New Brunswick legislature (that is both the legislative council and the legislative assembly) until the council was abolished. A ceremonial staff was used by the sergeant-at-arms of the legislative assembly when he attended the lieutenant governor at openings of the provincial legislature, Royal assent ceremonies, and viceregal installation ceremonies. This ceremonial staff is examined in part II of this book.

Following Confederation, the Legislative Council of New Brunswick continued to function until 7 April 1892, when it was abolished. The last Gentleman Usher of the Black Rod was John E. Perks. The black rod carried by the Usher dates from 1834–1837 and bears the Royal cypher of King William

Final session of the New Brunswick Legislative Council, 7 April 1892.

IV. There is no record of a previously extant New Brunswick black rod, and so this black rod is likely to be the only one ever used in the province, being one of those elements, like the mace of the Senate, that graduated from colonial to federal or provincial usage following Confederation. Thus it is the oldest black rod in Canada. Since 1892 it has been used in processions of the lieutenant-governors into the legislative assembly.

Black Rod of the Legislative Council of New Brunswick (1834–1892)

Material: Black ebony with gilded sterling silver mounts.

Length: 101 centimetres.

Upper End: The rod has at the top end a heraldic lion serjant erect (sitting on its haunches) holding in its paws a crowned shield displaying the Royal cypher of King William IV surrounded by the garter with the motto *Honi soit qui mal y pense*, all upon a round knop decorated in the traditional manner with oak leaves. This uppermost mount is silver-gilt with blue enamel in the garter and red enamel in the crown.

Shaft and Knop: Black ebony wood in two sections tapering towards the top. Positioned halfway down is a silver-gilt knop decorated in the traditional manner with oak leaf foliate forms.

Foot Knop: Missing, although was present at the final meeting of the legislative council in 1892.

Manufacturer and Distinguishing Marks: London hallmarks for 1834–1837 with maker's mark "J.J.E.," likely that of John James Edington. This is one of the oldest surviving black rods in the Commonwealth.

ALBERTA

The Alberta black rod being carried in the Alberta legislature by Sergeant-at-Arms Brian Hodgson, CD, during the 2005 Alberta centennial celebrations in the presence of Her Majesty the Queen.

Although Alberta never had a legislative council it accepted the gift of a black rod from the Royal Canadian Legion. The Alberta black rod is carried by the legislature's sergeant-at-arms on special occasions. Like its Senate counterpart, the Alberta black rod has a strong Commonwealth connection.

On 28 January 1998, a special ceremony was held in the rotunda of the Alberta Legislature. The Alberta-Northwest Territories Command of the Royal Canadian Legion presented the Speaker of the legislative assembly with a black rod to be used by the sergeant-at-arms.

In 1994 the Commonwealth Parliamentary Association held its annual conference in Banff, Alberta. Stanley Schumacher, then the Speaker of the Alberta Legislature, was presented with a British gold sovereign, a coin, by the Parliament of the United Kingdom. Schumacher was subsequently presented with an ebony rafter by the Parliament of Sri Lanka in 1995. The sergeant-at-arms, Brian Hodgson, developed the idea of combining these two elements into a black rod for the legislature. The Chief Herald of Canada, Robert Watt, designed the black rod, which was crafted by Charles Lewton-Brain.[16] The new black rod was introduced to the legislature by the lieutenant governor, Bud Olson, during his speech from the throne. It was first used in the presence of the Queen during her 2005 centennial visit to the province.

The 1905 British gold sovereign was set into the base of the Alberta black rod as has been the tradition with both the black rods used in the Senate of Canada and in the British House of Lords. A 1905 gold sovereign was chosen, as this was the year that Alberta entered Confederation as a province.

The Alberta black rod is carried within the legislative building by the sergeant-at-arms when he is escorting the Queen, members of the Royal family, governor general, or lieutenant governor. The black rod is also carried when the sergeant-at-arms attends the lieutenant governor for speeches from the throne, Royal assent, and during formal functions held in the legislature hosted by the Speaker at which the lieutenant governor is present.

Black Rod of the Legislative Assembly of the Province of Alberta (1996–present)

Above: The Alberta black rod, view of the end piece with 1905 gold sovereign.
Left: The Alberta black rod, upper end.

Material: Ebony wood with gilded-silver mounts.
Length: 114 centimetres.
Upper End: A heraldic lion is modelled in the round at the upper end; the demi-lion rampant is placed within a coronet of Canadian maple leaves alternating with Alberta wild roses, four of each. Beneath the coronet there is an engraving of the Royal cypher "E II R." This is mounted to the top end of the wooden shaft.
Shaft: Black ebony from Sri Lanka. Midway down the shaft there is a plain silver-gilt band with a planished textured surface.

Lower End: A cone-shaped, silver-gilt fitting, engraved on the side with the badge of the Royal Canadian Legion. The bottom of this fitting is inset with a 1905 British gold sovereign, displaying the reverse with St. George slaying the dragon.

Manufacturer and Distinguishing Marks: No maker's marks. Designed by Robert Watt, Chief Herald of Canada, and crafted by Charles Lewton-Brain, a Calgary goldsmith.

PRINCE EDWARD ISLAND

From its inception in 1770, Prince Edward Island's legislative council was fused with the executive council (cabinet).[17] It was not until 1838 that the legislative council was made separate from the executive council. The body was maintained after Confederation and it functioned until 1893 when the legislative council was merged with the legislative assembly. Then that portion of the legislative council that was merged with the legislative assembly was abolished on account of the expense of maintaining it and a variety of local issues.

In 1838 the legislative council was established as a body independent of

The sergeant-at-arms knocking three times with the Prince Edward Island black rod.

Sergeant-at-Arms Curtis Adamson leading the procession while carrying the Prince Edward Island black rod.

the executive council, and at this time the colony's first Gentleman Usher of the Black Rod was appointed. While there is no evidence to suggest that either the colonial or provincial legislative councils possessed a physical black rod, there are references to various persons holding the post of "Gentleman Usher of the Black Rod and Serjeant-at-Arms."[18] It would appear that the black rod served both the legislative assembly and the legislative council. The legislative council did possess what can best be described as a ceremonial staff, although it is entirely likely that the staff was carried either in place of a mace or black rod. The staff is 237 centimetres long and is made of wood and painted black and gold.

Although the province has not had a legislative council since 1893, Alberta's adoption of a black rod in 1998 helped influence the decision to adopt a Prince Edward Island black rod. The black rod is carried by the sergeant-at-arms when he is in attendance upon the Queen or lieutenant governor. The black rod was presented to the legislative assembly on 23 November 2000.

Black Rod of the Legislative Assembly of Prince Edward Island (2000–present)

Material: Painted oak wood.

Length: 90 centimetres.

Upper End: The top end is painted in gold and the rest has been decorated and turned with a variety of rings, painted to symbolize the heritage of the province.

Gold: (top end)	The Crown (Lieutenant Governor)
Silver:	Speaker of the Legislative Assembly
Red:	The Clerk of the Legislature
White:	The Clerk Assistant
Blue:	The Sergeant-at-Arms
White:	Four rings to represent the four pages of the legislature
Green:	The Province of Prince Edward Island
Light Green:	Three rings to represent the three counties that the province is divided into: Prince, Queen, and King.

Shaft: Two Prince Edward Island pennies from 1871, examples of the only coins ever minted for the province. One displays the reverse (depicting part of what became the armorial bearings of the province, taken from the original great seal of the colony), and the obverse of the other is shown (Queen Victoria). Below the coins are twenty-seven incised grooves representing the electoral districts of Prince Edward Island. The rod terminates at the base with a metal fitting.

Manufacturer and Distinguishing Marks: No maker's marks. The P.E.I. black rod was manufactured by Lloyd Kerry. The two Prince Edward Island coins were donated by Doug Morton.

CHAPTER FIVE

Baton of the Speaker of the House of Commons

The baton carried by the Speaker of the House of Commons is one of the most recent additions to the Canadian symbolic lexicon. It is also of a uniquely Canadian character, as no other Speaker in the Commonwealth or around the world carries a baton of office. In France, the president (Speaker) of the French Senate wears a breast star and sash of office. The presidents of many South and Central American countries wear sashes of office composed of the various national colours. However, batons have traditionally been reserved for senior civil officials in Britain and military officers holding the rank of field marshal.

The use of batons as a mark of honour and position can be traced back to Roman times, although, unlike the mace, the baton was never intended as a weapon but rather a symbol of status. In the United Kingdom, a number of senior state officials carry batons: most notably the Earl Marshal, field marshals, and the Lord High Constable of Scotland.

In the courts of Byzantium, it was the marshal's responsibility to organize mounted troops. The term "marshal" was brought to England in 1066, and William the Conqueror appointed the first marshal, who eventually became responsible for organizing all state ceremonies. King Richard III (1452–1485) was the first to present England's Earl Marshal with a gold baton. The Earl Marshal is one of the senior officers of state in England and is responsible for the organization of coronations, state funerals, and other state events. The baton carried by the Earl Marshal is gold with black enamelled ends, the top displaying the Royal arms of the United Kingdom while the lower end displays the Earl Marshal's arms.

The use of batons by military officers started with the French under King Louis XIV. The design originally consisted of a "baton which is blue strewn with gold lilies."[1] A standardized pattern for the Baton of France was developed around 1758. One recipient of a baton was François Gaston de Lévis, who succeeded the Marquis de Montcalm as commander-in-chief of the French forces in North America. Lévis was made a marshal of France, also known as a Maréchal de France, after his return to Europe.[2] Prior to 1789 the baton carried by French marshals had gold ends, the shaft being covered with light blue velvet, decorated with gold fleurs-de-lys. France also possessed sergeants-of-the-rod that were present at certain state ceremonies. One account of a ceremonial parade in Paris, dating from 24 September 1684, noted that one could see "the Sergeants of the Rod of Chatlet, two by two, all wearing black coats, swords at their sides holding their blue batons or rods sprinkled with gold lilies."[3]

There is record of a baton being carried by officials in New France as a symbol of authority. The "*Prevost qui a des fonctions dans les villes et toujour, va, on est envoyé avec les armes du Roy, portent le Bâton de commandement, dans les côtes et habitations de la colonie.*"[4] This translates as: "The Provost who has duties in the cities and always goes where he is sent with the arms of the King, bearing his baton of office, into the territories and settlements of the colony." Unfortunately a description of this baton does not survive.

The first British field marshal's baton was presented to the Duke of Wellington following his victory over the French at the Battle of Vittoria on 21 June 1813, where

France, pre-French Revolution marshal's baton and leather presentation case.

Wellington captured the baton of Marshal Jourdan. So delighted with the victory, the Prince Regent (the future King George IV) wrote to the Duke "You have sent me, among the trophies of your unrivalled fame, the staff of a French Marshal,

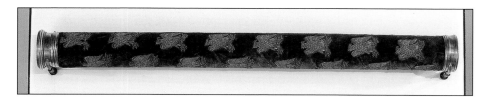

Napoleonic French marshal's baton.

Right: British field marshal's baton top. Below Right: British field marshal's baton, upper end displaying St. George slaying the dragon. Below Left: British field marshal's baton, formerly carried by King Edward VIII.

and I send you in return that of England."[5] In the United Kingdom the last field marshal's baton was presented in 1994 to field Marshal the Lord Inge. The baton has remained largely unchanged since the time of Wellington: a red velvet baton topped with a golden allegory of St. George slaying the dragon, with shaft of the baton decorated with crowned lions. Although no Canadian has ever reached the rank of field marshal, two of Canada's governors general, the Duke of Connaught and Viscount Alexander of Tunis, both held the distinction. At state events, Lord Alexander regularly carried his field marshal's baton while in uniform.

Speaker's Baton

In 1988 the Canadian Heraldic Authority (C.H.A.) was created by Her Majesty

The armorial bearings of The Honourable John Fraser, PC, OC, CD, Speaker of the House of Commons, 1986–1993.

Badge of the Honourable John Fraser, including the Speaker's batons.

the Queen, and immediately following the establishment of the C.H.A., the new institution was flooded with petitions, or requests for arms. In 1991, the then Speaker of the House of Commons, John Fraser, petitioned for a heraldic grant. On 15 December 1992, Speaker Fraser was granted arms which included a pair of green batons that were crossed behind his shield of arms. The concept was developed by Robert Watt, then Chief Herald of Canada.

To mark the 125th anniversary of Confederation, John Fraser commissioned the manufacturing of the Speaker's baton. The baton was designed in 1991–1992 on the basis of Fraser's heraldic grant, although it was not until 1993 that Fraser presented the baton to the House of Commons. When he presented the baton, John Fraser commented that it is "a fully Canadian creation, this new symbol of office is part of a centuries old tradition in Parliamentary governments."[6]

The baton is described in heraldic terms as "a rod Vert at either end tipped and dovetailed inwards Argent ensigned with a lion sejant Argent its dexter forepaw resting on a coronet érablé Argent the rim set with twelve jewels Gules."[7]

61

The baton is green, the colour of the House of Commons. The lion symbolizes "the majesty of parliament," and the ends of the baton are intended to refer to the tabs worn at the neck of the Speaker's formal uniform, and to battlements, and thus the idea of standing on guard for the Parliament of Canada.[8] The twelve jewels in red, set in silver, represent both the twelve provinces and territories that Canada consisted of in 1992, and also represent the national colours, red and white.

The baton is carried by the Speaker when he proceeds to the Senate to participate in a speech from the throne, Royal assent ceremony, or the installation of a new governor general.

It is logical to assume that with time the Speaker of the Senate will adopt a baton of office similar to that of his House of Commons counterpart. A crimson-coloured baton topped with a crown or a replica of the Speaker's chair would be an appropriate symbol of the high office held by the Speaker of the Senate. Like the baton of the Speaker of the House of Commons, the Senate Speaker's baton could be carried during state events, at levees, and at other significant ceremonies. Like the viceregal and commissioners recognition badges, the baton will likely become a more recognized symbol of the Speaker's office.

Badge of the Honourable Peter Milliken, Speaker of the House of Commons, 2001–2011.

Baton being carried by Speaker of the House of Commons, the Honourable Peter Milliken.

Baton of the Speaker of the House of Commons

Material: Lacquered wood with silver mounts set with red garnets.

Length: 51 centimetres.

Upper End: The silver mount at the top of the baton is of a lion sejant with a paw resting on a maple leaf coronet, the band of which is set with twelve red garnets representing the provinces and territories of Canada at the time the baton was made. The lion sits on a circular base above dovetailed battlements.

Shaft: The robust shaft is wood with green lacquer, representing the green of the House of Commons.

Base: The dovetail detail is again repeated on the silver mount at the bottom. On the underside of the base is the engraved arms of the Honourable John Allen Fraser, the Speaker of the House of Commons of Canada who commissioned the making of the baton.

Engraving: The arms of the Honourable John Allen

Above: Baton of the Speaker of the House of Commons, lower end.
Right: Baton of the Speaker of the House of Commons, upper end.

Fraser with the legend PRO REGINA ET PATRIA.

Manufacturer and Distinguishing Marks: No hallmarks. The baton was made by Mr. Erik Roth of St. Jacobs, Ontario.

CHAPTER SIX

Baton of the Chief Herald of Canada

The carrying of batons or staves by heralds has a long history in the United Kingdom, one that has been recently transplanted in Canada. When the Canadian Heraldic Authority was established in 1988, one of the first heraldic devices developed by the C.H.A. was a baton which was used in the grants of arms of three officials: the Herald Chancellor of Canada, the Deputy Herald Chancellor of Canada, and the Chief Herald of Canada. Each of these three batons are slightly different, and it was only in 2006 that the Chief Herald's baton was brought to life. The concept was created by Robert Watt in 1989.

During the opening ceremonies of the XXVI International Congress of Genealogical and Heraldic Sciences, held in St Andrews, Scotland, on 21 August 2006, Chief Herald Robert Watt carried the Chief Herald's baton for the first time at a public event.

Left: Shield of the Herald Chancellor of Canada.
Right: Shield of the Deputy Herald Chancellor of Canada.

Robert D. Watt, LVO, Chief Herald of Canada, 1988–2007, carrying the Chief Herald's baton of office and wearing the Chief Herald's collar of office.

Material: Painted arbutus wood.
Length: 45 centimetres.
Baton: The stylized baton flares out in the same manner at the top and bottom. The red painted ends and the predominant white background on the shaft represent the main national colours of Canada. Down the length of the baton a

Left: Baton of the Chief Herald of Canada.
Above: Shield of the Chief Herald displaying the Chief Herald's baton.

blue stripe spirals and is charged with white maple leaves. The blue is symbolic of Canada's rivers and waterways from which the names of Canadian Heralds are derived. The shields close to the two ends are the arms of the Chief Herald. The two circular flat ends are plain and also painted red.

Manufacturer and Distinguishing Marks: No maker's marks. The baton was carved by Dr. Alden Sherwood from Cortes Island, British Columbia, and painted by Cathy Bursey Sabourin, Fraser Herald.

CHAPTER SEVEN

Tipstaffs and Batons of Canadian Police Forces

In England and Wales the office of the tipstaff is believed to have been created in the fourteenth century. Both the office and the symbol of the office are known as a tipstaff. The office of the tipstaff has both a law enforcement and ceremonial component, and this continues in England, Wales, Australia, and Northern Ireland.[1] Before the advent of the first modern police force — the London Metropolitan Police, which was established in 1829 by Sir Robert Peel — the enforcement of the law was left to various other officials, such as sheriffs, constables, and bailiffs. The tipstaff was an office empowered to enlist any constable, sheriff, bailiff, or member of the public to assist in carrying out the tipstaff's duties. Tipstaffs were also the only people permitted to make arrests within the precincts of the Royal Courts of Justice in London. With the advent of plainclothes detectives in 1842, tisptaffs gained a new importance as a method for officers to identify themselves in the era before police badges were worn.

The original tipstaffs were made of metal or wood and surmounted by a crown. The crown was threaded and could be unscrewed from the top of the tipstaff, which revealed a compartment where warrants of arrest were contained. They gained the dual function of transporting arrest warrants and serving as a truncheon. Indeed this is where the modern-day police truncheon, sometimes referred to as a nightstick or "billy club," originates. In the broadest sense, the tipstaff that was carried by early police officers came to serve as their badge of office in an era long before police uniforms.

Victorian-era tipstaff.

Solid wooden Victorian tipstaff painted with a crown and the Royal cypher of Queen Victoria.

In some parts of Canada, notably Upper Canada, tipstaffs were carried by policemen and officers of the court. The constable's baton, carried by constables in Upper Canada, was in the shape of a traditional tipstaff, bearing a crown on the head with a cylindrical body. In court tipstaffs were also carried by constables charged with guarding prisoners held in the dock. There is a record of twelve tipstaffs being procured for the court in London, Upper Canada. These were 213 centimetres in length, 2 centimetres in diameter, with a rectangular head and "the name of each township on each staff in plain legible letters."[2]

Canadian policemen carried truncheons into the 1940s, and these largely replaced the tipstaff. With the advent of standardized police uniforms, such a distinctive identification symbol was no longer required, and the uniform would replace the tipstaff and truncheon as a symbol of the Crown's authority as enforced by law officers. Crossed tipstaffs are often used on the rank insignia of senior police officers in Canada and throughout the Commonwealth, thus in this miniaturized form they continue to be present.

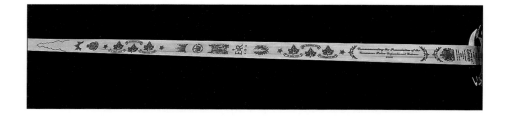

Blade of the chief constable's sword.

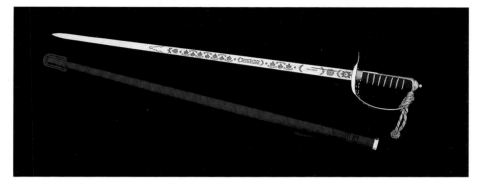

*Above: Chief constable's sword,
Vancouver Police Department.
Right: Deputy Chief Constable
Bob Rolls holding the chief
constable's sword.*

Presently three Canadian police forces possess tipstaffs: the Ontario Provincial Police (OPP), the Royal Canadian Mounted Police (RCMP), and the Sûreté du Québec. The OPP was the first force in Canada to have a ceremonial tipstaff presented to it, when in 1969 the lieutenant governor of the province bestowed a tipstaff on the commissioner of the OPP. Next was the RCMP, which was presented with a commissioner's tipstaff by the Canadian Association of Chiefs of Police in 1970, and most recently the Sûreté du Québec, which was presented with a bâton de commandement in 1983. In place of a tipstaff the Vancouver Police Department has a departmental sword that is carried on ceremonial occasions and used during the change of commander ceremonies, at which a new chief constable is commissioned.

Ontario Provincial Police Tipstaff

The OPP was the first police force in the country to be presented with a ceremonial tipstaff. This occurred on 13 November 1969, when Lieutenant Governor W. Ross Macdonald presented Commissioner Erik Silk with a commissioner's tipstaff in Toronto. The OPP tipstaff has been used at every commissioner's change of command ceremony since 1969. The head of the tipstaff unscrews and a copy of the Ontario Order-in-Council appointing the commissioner is kept inside.

Material: Gilt silver and leather.
Length: 56 centimetres.
Tipstaff Head: A gilt St. Edward's-styled crown with open arches.

Commissioner Julian Fantino, COM, OOnt, reviewing members of the Ontario Provincial Police.

Royal Canadian Mounted Police Tipstaff

Throughout its history, the RCMP has possessed two commissioner's tipstaffs. The first was presented by the Canadian Association of Chiefs of Police on 3 September 1970. Arthur G. Cookson, president of the CACP, Regina's chief of police, and a former member of the RCMP, presented the commissioner's tipstaff to RCMP Commissioner William L. Higgitt. It was presented as a mark of gratitude to the RCMP for their near century of service to the Crown and also as a symbol of unity of all the police forces throughout Canada. In presenting the tipstaff, Cookson commented: "It is our hope today that on behalf of the Force, you will accept from the Association, this tipstaff

Commissioner William L. Higgitt holding the original RCMP commissioner's tipstaff.

which we have caused to be created in England by craftsman skilled in their ancient art and which has been embellished with insignia of the Force by Canadian craftsmen who have likewise excelled themselves."[3]

The crown and shaft were produced by Firmin & Sons of London, while Stokes Cap & Regalia Ltd. of Toronto covered the shaft with red-brown coloured smooth-grained leather. Bond-Boyd Co. Ltd. of Don Mills, Ontario, was responsible for production and attachment of the commissioner's rank to the top band, the RCMP coat of arms to the middle band, and the four versions of the RCMP badges used since 1873: the North West Mounted Police, Royal

North West Mounted Police, Royal Canadian Mounted Police with Tudor crown, and Royal Canadian Mounted Police with St. Edward's Crown. The original tipstaff was used from September 1970 until September 2001.

A second commissioner's tipstaff was produced, largely out of parts of the original tipstaff by Staff Sergeant Robin Gomes, former senior armourer from the armourer's shop at the RCMP depot in Regina, Saskatchewan. The original tipstaff had become worn over the years, the leather was cracked and the stitching had become loose, while the large St. Edward's-style crown had been damaged on several occasions. There was also the fact that the commissioner's rank insignia had changed from a crossed sword, baton, and crown to a crossed sword, baton, pip, and crown. The three collars of the old tipstaff, originally made by Firmin & Sons, which included various versions

Tipstaff of the commissioner of the Royal Canadian Mounted Police.

of the RCMP cap badges produced by Bond-Boyd Co. Ltd., were reused. A new nonagonal (nine-sided) head and base were manufactured from brass and gold-plated.

The commissioner's tipstaff represents the solemn responsibility and authority of law enforcement borne by the commissioner of the RCMP, who is the head of Canada's national police force. It is traditionally presented by an outgoing commissioner to the incumbent of the office at the commissioner's change of command ceremony, which is held in Ottawa. During the commissionership of Guiliano Zaccardelli tipstaffs were provided to deputy commissioners and commanding officers "as outwards symbols of their authority in the field."[4]

Original RCMP commissioner's tipstaff, top end.

Present-Day RCMP Tipstaff

Material: Gilt silver, gilt brass, and wood.

Length: 75 centimetres.

Shaft: Cocobolo wood.

Tipstaff Cap: A nonagogal, gilt-brass shape bearing a St. Edward's-style crown on the flat part of the head, with the rank of commissioner — a crown, one pip, and a crossed sword and baton device — on the face of the head. This incorporates part of the original gilded sterling silver collar made by Firmin & Sons.

Tipstaff Middle: Gilt-silver collar bearing the current coat of arms of the Royal Canadian Mounted Police. The collar was made by Firmin & Sons and the badge was produced by Bond-Boyd Co. Ltd.

Tipstaff Base: Gilt-silver bearing the four coats of arms (cap badges) used by the RCMP: the current RCMP coat of arms with St. Edward's Crown, the RCMP coat of arms with a Tudor-style crown, the North West Mounted Police Badge, and the Royal North West Mounted Police Badge. The foot of the base is a nonagonal gilt brass fitting, engraved with the seventeen ensigns of the force and the RCMP logo depicting an RCMP constable riding a horse.

Shaft: Brass, covered in red-brown smooth-grained leather.

Manufacturer and Distinguishing Marks: None.

Sûreté du Québec Bâton de Commandement

The Sûreté du Québec's bâton de commandement is the French equivalent of a tipstaff, although the symbolism is drawn from the batons carried by officials of the Roman Empire, tracing its origins to the second century.[5] The bâton de

Base of the Sûreté du Québec bâton de commandement.

Normand Proulx, COM, director général of the Sûreté du Québec, 2002–2008, holding the bâton de commandement.

commandement is carried by the director general of the Sûreté, and it is the principal symbol of the director general's authority as head of the force. Created in 1982, the bâton de commandement was presented to Director General Jacques Beaudoin by the provincial Minister of Justice Marc-André Bédard on 27 October 1983. The top of the baton unscrews, and contained within the cylinder is a certified reproduction of the act that founded the Sûreté in 1870. The baton was designed by Gilles Beaugrand of Gilles Beaugrand Inc, Montreal.[6] Six artists worked on the project: Jean-Guy Tourangeau, Roger Sénécal, Gérard Auclair, Jean-Claude Proulx, Gabriel Robitaille, and André Robitaille.

Material: Silver gilt and enamel.

Tipstaff Head: Octagonal in shape, flat, bearing a fleur-de-lys on the top.

Tipstaff Base: Octagonal in shape, flat, bearing a fleur-de-lys on the bottom.

Shaft: White enamel decorated with the date "1870" at the top and appliqués of gold oak leaves interspersed with gold fleurs-de-lys.

Manufacturer and Distinguishing Marks: None.

II

PARLIAMENTARY MACES

CHAPTER EIGHT

Origins and Development of Parliamentary Maces

Parliamentary maces in Canada are closely modelled on their British counterparts used by the Parliament at Westminster. However, it should be noted that maces are not only British in origin; their roots can be traced to many countries, including France, Afghanistan, and India, and dates back to ancient times. Maces continue to be used in legislatures the world over. In parts of Canada, maces have been used since the birth of representative government, "the Houses [Legislative Assembly and Legislative Council of the Province of Canada] followed punctiliously the usage of the British Parliament. In each chamber the entry of the sergeant-at-arms and deposition of the mace marked the beginning of the session."[1] Other provinces, such as Nova Scotia (despite being the cradle of Canadian democracy), did not adopt a mace until early in the twentieth century.

History of the Mace

It is worthwhile to examine the origins and development of ceremonial maces and how this weapon of war has come to be transformed into a "symbol of authority."[2] There is no doubt that in the minds of citizens, as well as Parliamentarians, that "an almost mystical significance has come to be attached to the mace."[3] The mace symbolizes that a particular legislature has the "Royal Favour" and has been given the authority to govern with the consent of the Sovereign: "loyally they [the mace] govern and rule on behalf of their Sovereign."[4] Today the Speaker's authority, as well as the independence of the legislature, is symbolized by the mace. The evolution of the mace provides a fascinating history of democratic development whereby the legislature gradually ceased to be subjugated by the monarch. Today the mace is an essential part of parliamentary tradition and function, symbolizing "the authority of the Crown exercised by the Legislature,"[5] whether it be the Senate, House of Commons, or provincial/territorial legislative assembly.

Ancient Times

The origin of the mace as a symbol of authority is somewhat of a mystery, primarily because of its ancient roots and the multiplicity of uses for which maces have been employed throughout history. Maces have been used as ceremonial emblems in two distinct periods: first in ancient times in the Near East until the rise of the Greek Empire, and secondly from the Middle Ages to the present. "In both periods an object that had originally started as a weapon developed into a symbol of authority and was retained long after that role had ceased to have any combat effectives."[6]

Ceremonial maces and sceptres were the earliest symbols of power, dating back to 3000 B.C. and the Sumerians. Maces, staves, rods, and sceptres have a closely related history, all originating as weapons and evolving through reform and revolution into symbols of sovereignty and authority. In the second century B.C., Persian sculptors carved statues of their various monarchs carrying staffs; these staves were often studded with golden nails. While such staves were intended as weapons, the inclusion of somewhat functional gold nails would have also served as a symbol of great wealth. Only the very rich would have been in a position to use a precious metal, normally reserved for jewellery, as part of a weapon. Around this same time the Sabine King bore a long staff to denote his dignity and position, and this staff was known in Greek as a "skeptron."[7]

Hebrew poetry contains a number of references to a "shevet," which translates as a rod, staff, or sceptre. These references usually refer to those in authority holding a "shevet" or strong rod. Both the New and Old Testaments of the Bible are full of similar mentions of rods and staves being held and used by those in authority, from the staff of Jacob to the rod of Moses.[8] The mace was largely abandoned as a weapon following the development of helmets and armour.[9]

Middle Ages

In the Middle Ages a new type of mace (taken from *massue* or *masse*, a club) became a popular weapon amongst horsemen. Medieval maces had a flanged head, usually with six points. This sort of weapon was much more effective at penetrating chain mail and armour than a sword.[10] Contemporary accounts have noted that the mace is "reputed to be a terrible weapon at close quarters."[11]

A wooden mace and knotted club are depicted in the Bayeux Tapestry being carried by William, Duke of Normandy, and by his half-brother Odo, Bishop of Bayeux.[12] The Scandinavian kingdoms used similar instruments, both in battle and mythology. The Norse god Odin, ruler of the universe, granted his most

Bishop Odo carrying a mace as depicted on the Bayeux Tapestry.

valiant son a mace as a sign of special favour. During the Crusades the leader of the Saracens and Turks also carried a ceremonial mace. It is quite likely that the use of maces became associated with a certain level of prestige and importance over less ornamental weapons.[13]

In battle a mace was carried in addition to a sword and shield. This is in part why today the Usher of the Black Rod and sergeant-at-arms both carry swords, although these have been transformed into ceremonial court swords rather than battle swords.

In Chaucer's *The Canterbury Tales*, the "Knights Tale" recounts "Some wol ben armed on his legges well And have an axe, and some a mace of stele." Chaucer's translation of Ramon Lull's *Libre de l'Ordre de Cavalleria* (*The Book of the Order of Chivalry*) well illustrates the symbolism associated with the mace:

> The mace is given to the Knight to signify strength of courage. For like as a mace or pole-axe is strong against all arms, and smiteth on all parts, right so force or strength of courage defendeth a Knight from all vices, and enforceth virtue and good customs.[14]

The prestige acquired by the mace during the Crusades helped to enhance its symbolic potency and resurgence. By the sixteenth century the mace began to fall out of favour as a battle weapon, and from here its nascent ceremonial usage grew into a full instrument of authority, rather than a blunt instrument for the infliction of physical harm.

Sir Peter Thorne, a former sergeant-at-arms of the House of Commons at Westminster, notes that there were three reasons why the mace experienced a resurgence during the Middle Ages. The first was that the mace had gained a great deal of prestige during the Crusades; its adoption by Royal bodyguards in France, Burgundy, and England also enhanced its perceived importance; and finally, like the baton, the mace had become a symbol of authority that could be traced back to ancient times.[15] From the fourteenth century through to the sixteenth century it "remained in fashion for many of the leading figures to be painted or sculpted with flange headed maces,"[16] thus depicting them as both symbolically and physically powerful.

Sceptres, emblems, and ceremonial maces as emblems of authority developed from a variety of sources: "a) short scepter or rod representing power to govern or punish; b) long scepter derived from the shepherd's staff, which represents the rulers support and comforting role; c) specialized emblems like the pastoral crook and the flail of the Egyptian Kings, which symbolize the basis of their wealth."[17]

The earliest ceremonial maces were used to protect the King's person. These were used by the bodyguards of King Richard I of England and King Phillip II of France. These sergeants-at-arms carried a "pheon," which was akin in many ways to a non-ceremonial mace. It was around this time that Parliament started to look upon the powers of the mace with some envy. Parliament presented King Richard II with a petition requesting that no sergeants of any town could carry their town's mace outside their own bailiwick — this was to prevent the exercise of a town's authority outside its limits.[18] In municipalities maces had long been symbols of authority with which the general public was acquainted. Few people would have ever been to London, let alone been given the opportunity to observe the House of Commons in session.

It is recorded that there were once two slabs in the Church of Culturé, Sainte Catherine, Paris, which displayed two sergeants-at-arms in armour and two in civil dress, each carrying a silver mace richly ornamented and enamelled with fleurs-de-lys. This church was founded by Louis IX (St. Louis) at the request of certain sergeants-at-arms, in commemoration of their defence of a bridge at the Battle of Bovines in 1214. Sergeants-at-arms attended the King of France during the Crusades and are believed to have carried maces. In both England and France, Royal sergeants-at-arms were used to increase Royal authority and presence, and the mace became an element of the public display of power. From an ordinance passed by Thomas Duke of Lancaster in 1414 at the Siege of Caen we have a description of a silver mace that indicated the "high position held at that period by the Royal body-guard."[19] Sergeants-at-arms in England formed part of the garrison for Windsor Castle and the Tower of London well before 1272. The use of *sergents d'arms* in the French Royal Household was common, both as Royal bodyguards and functionaries of the household. The French and Burgundian influence on the development of sergeants-at-arms into Royal bodyguards and bearers of maces was quite strong. Nevertheless, in 1376 French sergeants-at-arms were stripped of their role as Royal bodyguards when they were dismissed by King Charles V.[20]

There is little recorded about the earliest ceremonial uses of the mace in the English Parliament. Some believe that its use was introduced around the time Parliament was divided into the House of Lords and the House of Commons during the reign of King Edward III (1327–1377). The origin of the mace being carried by a sergeant-at-arms in attendance upon the Speaker is an extension of the carrying of maces by the King's bodyguards whenever the King processed into a meeting of his subjects.[21]

In 1377 Sir Thomas Hungerford was elected Speaker of the House of Commons. This was the first time that a person had taken this title, although the role is certain to have existed before this point.[22] There is no mention of a mace being used at this juncture, although by 1388 there is evidence that sergeants-at-arms were attending both the House of Lords and the House of Commons. In 1414 the House of Commons sent a petition to King Henry V to appoint Nicholas Maudit as sergeant-at-arms and to "be intendent at all parliaments during his life as serjeant at arms for the Commons."[23] Maudit would be the first permanent sergeant-at-arms appointed to the Commons.

In practice, a sergeant-at-arms was loaned to the House of Commons and the mace was intended to symbolize an element of the Sovereign's authority that the House would not have otherwise possessed.

It is difficult to ascertain exactly when Parliament in England started using the mace. We are aware that Parliament attempted to restrict the use of civic maces in 1344, as their use was seen as an infringement on parliamentary prerogative. The number of sergeants-at-arms was limited to thirty and their duties were limited to attend and protect the King, arrest offenders, and to serve the Lord High Steward when sitting in judgment upon a peer.

During the reign of Queen Elizabeth I, Sir Thomas Gargrave was elected Speaker and there is a record of his acceptance of the office. Gargrave "departed with the other members of the House of Commons to their own House, the Sergeant of the same carrying the mace all the way before the said speaker, which was in the like sort before him until his return from the Upper House, being presented to the Queen and allowed of."

By 1640 the tradition of having a mace present during debate and transactions in the House of Commons had become entrenched. Mr. Pym, a member of the House of Commons, remarked that "it is a new doctrine, that we can do nothing without a Speaker or a mace."[24]

Maces were not only presented to and used by municipal bodies, but they have at various times been given to guilds and universities to symbolize a degree of Royal favour and a heightened degree of autonomy. A silver mace with a crystal globe was given to the Lord High Treasurer of Scotland in 1690 to serve as a symbol of his office. Civic maces as symbols of autonomy predated the use of legislative maces, although it is in Parliament that they have gained the most significance. The evolution of the mace from purely a weapon of battle to a symbol of authority was partially due to French influence. In France, various universities and institutions outside the Royal household possessed maces as an indication of the autonomy granted to these institutions.[25] From this we can discern the idea that maces are also signs of Royal favour and grant certain powers and rights to not only the individual who is responsible for maintaining the instrument, but the institution to which the mace is attached.

Perhaps the most infamous incident involving the mace occurred at the conclusion of the Long Parliament during the English Civil War. On 10 April 1653, Oliver Cromwell, the Lord Protector, entered the House of Commons and ordered "take away that bauble [the mace]. Ye are no longer a Parliament. The Lord has done with you. He has chosen other instruments for carrying on his work." It is believed that this was the mace made by Thomas Maundy in 1649 that had been paid for by the House of Commons at public expense, not a gift from the Sovereign as maces traditionally were.[26] The mace was subsequently removed and replaced with a mace devoid of Royal symbols.[27] The smaller silver-gilt mace used by the Corporation of Retford measures 71 centimetres in length, and is a fine example from the early seventeenth century. Originally thought to have been made during the Commonwealth period (1649 to 1660) and altered afterwards, another theory suggests earlier, the Royal symbols then relating to King Charles I. It is understood to have been donated circa 1640 by Gervase Clifton Bart. A much later description observes: "The head is a curious

Top: The lesser Retford mace.
Bottom: The large Retford mace.

Commonwealth coronate, formed of a looped cable enclosing cartouches with the arms of England and Ireland."[28] Following the Restoration in 1660, the Corporation of Retford acquired a second much larger and very ornate silver-gilt mace circa 1679, measuring 122 centimetres long. Both these maces today are part of the Borough of East Retford civic plate. The maces used prior to this time in the House of Commons were supplied by the sergeant-at-arms of the day and not paid for by the Sovereign or Parliament.

Following the Restoration in 1660 the mace was returned to the House of Commons. The new mace is believed to contain some parts of the original 1649 "bauble" mace, although much of it is believed to have been melted for its bullion.[29] A mace has been used continuously in the British House of Commons and the House of Lords since that time.

One of the less well known uses of maces is as instruments enabling sergeants-at-arms to arrest people and to aid in the administration of justice.[30] Originating in a time when most people could not read, the mace, emblazoned with the Royal arms, was an outward sign of authority, and a person carrying a mace was an official of the Crown. The Lower House [Commons] has at its command a "Royal Serjeant at Arms who could arrest and commit without a warrant and whose emblem of office was a mace stamped with the royal arms."[31] The mace bestows upon its rightful bearer the power to arrest a person without a warrant,[32] although this power has seldom been used. On at least two occasions in Canadian history the mace has been used by sergeants-at-arms in the apprehension and arrest of people charged under a Speaker's warrant. This occurred in 1838 when the Speaker of the Newfoundland legislative assembly ordered the arrest of three residents of St. John's.

Top: The British House of Commons mace.
Bottom: Showing the arms plate beneath the arches of the British House of Commons mace.

Positioning of the Mace in the Chamber(s)

In the British House of Commons, long before the establishment of legislative assemblies in Canada, the mace was simply held by the sergeant-at-arms for the duration of a sitting. The table that now sits before the Speaker's chair was, until the end of the sixteenth century, a small table used by the clerk with no physical room for a mace to be placed.[33] The mace eventually came to be placed on an enlarged table, to allow the sergeant-at-arms to undertake other duties in the House without the suspension of a sitting which would have occurred if the sergeant-at-arms were to leave the House with the mace. These traditions have evolved to their present state in Britain, Canada, and many other countries in the Commonwealth.

The Senate

In the Senate, the mace is carried by the mace bearer, who follows the Usher of the Black Rod. In earlier times the Usher of the Black Rod was assisted by a Senate sergeant-at-arms. This position ceased to exist following the death

The British House of Commons mace under the table (left), and the mace on the table (right).

of the last office-holder and was replaced by a Yeoman Usher of the Black Rod and later an Assistant Usher of the Black Rod, although this position has been designated mace bearer in recent years. The Senate mace is laid lengthwise down the table that sits in front of the Speaker's chair. The head of the mace is placed on a red cushion. The placement of a mace lengthwise with the head pointing towards the Speaker, although not common, has been the practice in a number of legislatures, notably Quebec's national assembly and the old Irish House of Commons.[34]

The Senate mace is paraded into the chamber prior to each sitting by the Speaker's parade, which is comprised of the Usher of the Black Rod, mace bearer, Speaker, two clerks, and two Senate pages. In the case of the appointment of a new Senate Speaker, as soon as members of the Senate have gathered in the chamber, the mace is paraded in by the Usher of the Black Rod, mace bearer, and clerk of the Senate. The mace is then deposited under the table on a red cushion. The clerk of the Parliaments then reads the Commission appointing the Speaker, and the Speaker is escorted to his chair by two prominent members of the Senate, usually the Leader of the Government and Leader of the Opposition in the Senate. The mace is then brought from beneath the table and placed on top of the table, with the head of the Crown facing the Speaker.

The House of Commons

In the House of Commons, the mace is placed on a cushion on the floor under the table during the election of a new Speaker. When the Speaker ascends and takes the chair, the mace is placed across the table with the crown of the mace pointing to the government side of the chamber.[35] At every sitting of the House of Commons, prior to the reading of the prayers, the sergeant-at-arms places the mace on the table at the end furthest away from the Speaker.[36]

When the Speaker vacates his chair and the House goes into a Committee of the Whole, the sergeant-at-arms places the mace on a rack below the table. In England, Sir Simonds D'Ewes's *Journal of the Senate* notes that by 1640 it had become custom for the mace to be removed from the table when the House was in a Committee of the Whole. When the mace is not on or under the table or being carried by the sergeant-at-arms no member except the Speaker is allowed to speak. If no mace is present in the House of Commons (or the Senate) then no business can be transacted until it is returned.

The mace is carried in the right arm by the sergeant-at-arms before the Speaker when members of the House of Commons are called to attend the Queen or governor general in the Senate chamber. The sergeant-at-arms does not bring the mace into the Senate chamber, as there is already a symbol of authority present, the Senate mace.[37] The House of Commons mace is left in the Senate lobby with a House of Commons messenger.

In both the Senate and the House of Commons, when a stranger is brought to the bar the sergeant-at-arms or mace bearer stands beside the stranger with the mace on his shoulder. The reason for this is to impress upon the stranger the authority of the chamber and to prevent the stranger from launching an attack upon any honourable member.

Provincial and territorial legislatures generally follow the same mace usage as the House of Commons. These traditions are observed in many Commonwealth countries. One exception to this is Quebec's national assembly, where the mace is placed lengthwise along the table as opposed to across the table. This follows the Senate tradition of placing the mace and the same practice used at the first meeting of the Legislative Assembly of Lower Canada in 1793.

Maces in North America and the Caribbean

Canadian legislatures are not unique in their use of parliamentary maces. Indeed throughout the Commonwealth, most legislative assemblies possess and use a mace of some description. This is true for both those countries that retain the Queen as head of state and those that are republics. All of the thirteen colonies that made up what would become the United States of America enjoyed some form of representative government prior to the American Revolution. Like colonial Canada, the thirteen colonies had governors and lieutenant governors, and in some cases a mace.

That parts of Canada were quick to adopt maces is not surprising, as it was primarily the Loyalists — American refugees from the Revolution who remained loyal to the Crown — who played the most significant role in the development of democratic institutions in what developed into British North America. There is a long and proud connection between the two countries, one that should not be forgotten.

Prior to the American Revolution, both the Dominion of Virginia and the Colony of South Carolina utilized a mace. Their design was not unlike the mace used in the Canadian Senate today. South Carolina is the only state that continues to use its mace, and it is a proud tradition deeply imbedded in the political culture of their House of Representatives.

Benjamin Smith, Speaker of the Commons House of Assembly of the Province of South Carolina, ordered that a mace be purchased along with robes and a Speaker's chair in 1755. The mace was completed by Magdalen Feline of

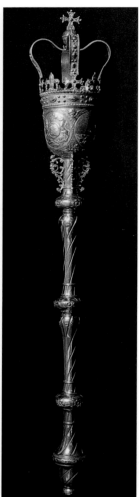

Left: A close-up view of the South Carolina mace head.
Right: The South Carolina mace.

London, England, in 1756. It is of a traditional English design. The head of the mace is divided into quarters, displaying respectively the Royal arms of King George II, the Great Seal of South Carolina, an allegory of agriculture represented by a farmer with his plough, and an allegory of commerce represented by a woman sitting on a wharf holding a ship and a coin purse. The mace was commissioned on 8 March 1756, for £90. During the American Revolution the mace was hidden by Loyalists. At one point they attempted to sell the mace to the

House of Assembly of the Bahamas in order to raise money for the Loyalist cause. The transaction was never completed, and thus the mace remained in South Carolina. It reappeared in 1819 when it was discovered in the vault of a local bank. Since 1880 the mace has been used daily at the opening of each meeting of the South Carolina House of Representatives, where it is placed in front of the Speaker. When the Senate and House meet jointly the mace is borne at the head of the procession. On 30 May 2006, the South Carolina House of Representatives passed a motion stating "that it is with great Southern pride and respect for this striking and lasting symbol of democracy that members of the South Carolina House of Representatives pause in honour of the Two Hundred and Fiftieth Anniversary of the Mace."[38] It is a testament to the versatility of maces that even in the United States they are viewed as historic symbols of democracy.

The tradition of important towns possessing maces is British in origin, but not unique to the United Kingdom. In Canada a number of cities, most notably Vancouver, British Columbia, possess a municipal mace.

In pre-revolutionary America we know of one instance where a mace was presented to a town. On 1 April 1754, Lieutenant Governor Robert Dinwiddie presented a mace to the corporation of the city of Norfolk, Virginia.[39] Prior to the Revolution the mace would precede the mayor of Norfolk during the opening of the city council. During the American

The Norfolk Virginia colonial mace.

Revolution many of the residents remained loyal to the Crown, and it is not surprising that the mace was well hidden from destruction. The mace survived the January 1776 burning of Norfolk and the American Civil War, during which Norfolk was occupied by Union forces. The Norfolk mace is used primarily during special parades. Two replicas of the original have been manufactured.[40] Following the Revolution, with the destruction and removal of many Royal symbols, the mace was sold at auction, "the disposition of the proceeds of the same [to be deposited] in the state treasury."[41]

The House of Representatives in the United States has used a mace since 1789. One of the first resolutions passed by the newly constituted House was to establish the office of sergeant-at-arms and to provide a mace for him to carry.[42] In the United States the mace of the House of Representatives is the only visible symbol of the federal government's authority other than the flag of the Republic.[43] This American mace has an interesting Canadian connection. The current House of Representatives mace has been used since 1 December 1842, and was crafted by William Adams at the cost of $400,[44] the original mace having been lost when the then recently completed Capitol Building was burned by British and Canadian troops on 24 August 1814, during the War of 1812. A temporary painted wooden mace was used until the adoption of the current mace in 1842.

The U.S. mace is generally employed in the same way as Canadian and Commonwealth maces. It is carried in front of the Speaker by the sergeant-at-arms prior to the opening of the daily session. When the House is in session the mace stands on a green marble pedestal located to the right of the Speaker's chair. When the House is in committee the mace is moved to a pedestal next to the sergeant-at-arms' desk. When the House moves into a Committee of the Whole House or during a State of the Union Address, the U.S. equivalent of a speech from the throne, the mace is moved into a lower position, nearly out of sight. In place of a mace the United States Senate has a ceremonial gavel as its symbol of authority.

The mace of the House of Representatives of the United States is 117 centimetres tall and composed of a bundle of thirteen ebony rods, representing the original thirteen states. The rods are bound together by a band of silver, which draws reference from the fasces carried by the Lictors in ancient Rome. The top of the mace is decorated with a silver globe which is surmounted by an eagle with outspread wings.

Maces are used throughout the Commonwealth, both in monarchies and republics. Canada has had a long association with those Caribbean members, such as the Bahamas, Barbados, Jamaica, and Antigua and Barbuda. Even

The United States of America House of Representatives mace outside the Capitol Building.

Trinidad and Tobago, which is a republic, continues to use a pair of maces, one for their House of Representatives and one for their Senate. Jamaica also possesses a mace, employed almost continuously since 1753, used by their legislative council, House of Representatives, governor-in-council, and by the island's Privy Council.

The Canadian House of Commons wooden mace, which was used briefly following the 1916 parliamentary fire, was lent to the House of Assembly of the Bahamas in 1965 after their leader of the opposition threw the Bahamas mace out of a window during a particularly acrimonious debate. The Bahamas mace was broken in half and was no longer serviceable. While attending the Commonwealth Speaker's Conference in London, Speaker Symonette told Canadian Speaker Alan Macnaughton of the damage sustained by the Bahamas mace, and that the island's legislature was currently unable to sit due to the absence of a mace. Speaker Macnaughton immediately had the House of Commons temporary mace dispatched by air to Nassau for use until such time as their mace was repaired.[45] So delighted with the loan of the Canadian mace were the Bahamians that it was returned to Canada freshly gilded.

Australia and New Zealand share much with Canada in terms of parliamentary functions and traditions, and this extends to maces. The mace of New Zealand's House of Representatives obtained its first mace in 1866, more than twelve years after the first sitting of the colonial legislature. This mace perished in the 1907 fire which destroyed New Zealand's Parliament buildings.[46] For two years a temporary mace was used, and it was made of polished puriri wood with gilt decorations. Finally in 1909 a new silver-gilt mace was obtained. Like the 1916 Canadian House of Commons Great Mace, the New Zealand House of Representatives mace is closely influenced by the one used in the British House of Commons. The story of the New Zealand mace mirrors that of its Canadian cousin to a great degree.

Many of the maces used in Canada, especially in colonial times, were inexpensive and improvised affairs. Most are gilded sterling silver or gilded brass, which is in part on account of cost and also because the two materials are more durable. In the case of Upper Canada, Newfoundland, Manitoba, and Alberta, the original maces were fashioned out of wood and local materials. Each of Canada's maces reflects the jurisdiction in which they are used, but also the period in which they were adopted. The maces first used by the Senate and House of Commons were used in previously existing legislatures. The original House of Commons mace was used by the Legislative Assembly of the Province of Canada from 1845 until the establishment of the Dominion of Canada, when that mace was transferred to the newly established House of Commons. Parts of the mace of the Senate originated as the mace used by the Legislative Council of Lower Canada dating from 1793 and was later transferred to the Legislative

Council of the Province of Canada in 1841. Both of these maces were transferred to the new Dominion Parliament in 1867, along with other items, including the chairs used in the original Senate chamber.[47] The cost overruns of building the new Parliament buildings in Ottawa were so extreme that it was decided to reuse much of the furniture, and this also extended to the maces. There was no thought of commissioning new instruments of authority for the infant Parliament.

Another Commonwealth country that has a fairly modern mace is Papua New Guinea. In 1964, more than ten years prior to Papua New Guinea gaining independence from Australia, the Australian Parliament presented the Papua New Guinea legislature with a mace that is a fine example of both local and traditional elements being incorporated into a symbol of authority. The Papua New Guinea mace is 130 centimetres in length and contains 160 ounces of silver. The shaft is made of timbers from Papua New Guinea and Australia, and contains a polished stone ball at the head which is meant to be symbolic of a stone war club — the traditional weapon of many of the peoples of Papua New Guinea. The shaft is three-sided and has three knops. The first represents the highlands, lowlands, and smaller islands, the second represents industry, transport, and communications, and the third represents medicine, education, and Christianity.[48]

Ghana has employed a mace in its parliament since colonial times. Upon attaining independence a new mace was designed, "inspired by the traditional

A 1792 painting of Legislative Assembly of Lower Canada.

linguist's staff."[49] Other ceremonial elements were also created, including a "Seat of State" and "Chair of State," both of which incorporate a variety of local symbols. The British Parliament presented no less than eleven maces to various Commonwealth legislatures in West Africa as they each gained independence in the 1960s and early 1970s.[50]

Symbolism of the Mace

The symbolism of the maces both demonstrates that Parliament is favoured by the Sovereign and is acting with the Sovereign's authority — after all, Parliament is convened and dissolved by the Queen through the governor general (and lieutenant governors in the provinces). In this regard, the mace symbolizes the legitimate right of the legislature to sit under authority of the Crown.[51] All members of Parliament and Senators swear an oath of allegiance — not unlike that given by new citizens — to the Queen of Canada. Although maces were originally symbols of Royal authority and control over the legislature, they have come to be transformed into a symbol of the legislature itself, and occasionally the office of the Speaker.[52] Paradoxically, the mace also symbolizes a certain aspect of the struggle of the elected house to assert its power against the Sovereign and the upper house composed of the titled nobility. In Upper and Lower Canada the mace came to symbolize the attainment of representative and then responsible government, part of Canada's long road to independence.

Much the same as the Crown has become a symbol of a broader institution and system of government — as opposed to a single person — the mace now represents those who serve in the legislature and their service, not only to the Crown, but to the electorate as a whole. This transformation is not surprising given that democratic institutions in Canada have largely been fashioned out of monarchical ones, through evolution and legislative reform becoming representative, responsible bodies of all citizens. "The symbol of the House's authority is the mace."[53]

Structure of this Section

The Senate and House of Commons maces are listed first as these are the senior legislatures in the country. Provinces and territories are listed by the date in which they entered Confederation, not by which date they obtained their mace. Four provinces — Ontario, Quebec, Newfoundland, and British Columbia — had maces prior to entering Confederation, however, it has proven more convenient to list maces by the jurisdiction in which they are used as opposed to the year of manufacture or adoption. A number of maces have been lost on account of fire or misplacement over the past two centuries. An attempt has been made to include relevant details about these instruments as well, despite the absence of photographs. The glossary provides a detailed description of the various parts of a mace, which may be unfamiliar to the reader.

CHAPTER NINE

The Mace of the Senate of Canada

The Senate mace is the oldest parliamentary mace in Canada. Parts of it have survived four fires, two riots, and a rebellion. While the origins of this mace are somewhat of a mystery, we can be certain that the mace was originally used in Lower Canada, most likely by the Legislative Council of Lower Canada.

The Senate of Canada is roughly modelled on the legislative councils that existed in British North America prior to Confederation. These were appointed bodies, although for a brief period between 1856 and 1862 the Legislative Council of the Province of Canada was elected. The fathers of Confederation established the Senate to serve as a chamber of "sober second thought,"[1] where regional interests could be represented.

While the strongest analogy to the Senate may well be the House of Lords,[2] there are a number of key differences. During the debate over the adoption of the British North America Act, which took place in the House of Lords, Lord Carnarvon, the Colonial Secretary who played an important role in Confederation, commented that the Senate "was not a House of Lords, but a second chamber that must be strong, but not so strong as to ignore public opinion."[3] Carnarvon's assessment was fairly accurate, and since Confederation the Senate has largely fulfilled this role. While no money bills can emanate from the Senate, the body does review and improve legislation sent to it by the more junior House of Commons. In the past quarter century the role of the Senate has continued to evolve with the release of many influential reports that examine controversial issues largely ignored by the House of Commons.

Arthur Meighen, the former prime minister, spent a full ten years in the Senate after leaving the House of Commons. Meighen commented that, unlike the Commons, the Senate is "a workshop and not a theatre."[4]

The first legislature of Lower Canada met on 17 December 1792, although there is no mention of a mace being present. On 24 December of the same year, the legislative council ordered that "the sergeant-at-arms attend on this House

The centre block of Parliament, circa 1880 (top) and circa 1916 (bottom).

be provided with a mace for the like uses thereof by him to be made of the mace by the sergeant of the mace in the Lords House in the Parliament of Great Britain, and it is referred to the Committee already charged to report on the mode of providing for the officers of this House, to direct the form of the mace and the expense thereof."[5] In 1793 the sum of £40 was voted by the Council to cover the cost of the mace.[6]

The first reference to a mace being present in the legislative council chamber came on 7 February 1793, when a new member of the council took his oath, "Henry Coldwell Esquire be introduced by the same members preceded by the Black Rod and mace and take his seat."[7] There is no record of when the mace was first used in the Legislative Council of Lower Canada.

A mace for the Legislative Council of Lower Canada was constructed in late 1793 following the first meeting of the Legislative Assembly of Lower Canada. The legislative council's mace was crafted by François Baillaragé of Montreal. Baillaragé described the mace in his diary, and beside Baillaragé's entry was a drawing of a mace that is very similar to that used by the Legislative Council of Lower Canada.[8] It is very likely that this is the mace that is currently used by the Senate of Canada, although it is certain that some augmentations would have taken place in the early 1800s. The diagram contained in Baillaragé's workbook lacks brackets and the knops are of a different shape — however it should be noted that the diagram is quite rough. Baillaragé's description of the mace used by the legislative assembly (the mace on

The Senate of Canada mace.

103

1792 236 Suitte et Montant de l'autre Côté — £ 58. 8. 9
Novembre.
24 finit de vernir les deux Carrioles de Son Altesse
travaillé la valeur d'une Journée. et pour les faire garnire une #
26 livrer dans la remise de Son Altesse les deux Carrioles.
27 livrer un timon et les trois paloniers (bleu) pour Son A.te
a Chetter il y a quelque jours une tinette de beure de trente livres
emprunter pour la payer, de Mr Chenier — 12. 6.
finit le trophée au dessus du Curé, fait porter les deux a l'église
travaillé 6 Jours au dernier.
Commencer les frises de notre paroisse de Quebec.

Decembre
12 livrer a Mr James hady la frise pour la place de l'Orateur dans
la Chambre d'assemblée, Cest 7 guirlandes et 10 rosettes de feuilles
de lorier le tout vaut £ 1. 18.
14 a chetter chez Mr M'Cord pour le théatre dont depeint les
Cernes et Coulises   2 milliers de broquettes — 4. 0
15   ½ livre de pierre bleu — 2. 6
1 livre ocre Jone — 6.
½ livre d°. rouge — 3.
1 livre Colle forte — 1. 6
6 livre witening — 1. 0
17   1 livre azure en poudre — 2. 6.
½ livre rode Pinck — 3. 9
2 brose — 1. 8.
2 pot de terre — 1. 0
donné a Mr J. hady mon Compte, pour être payé il doit m'envoyer l'argent
19 pour le théatre — 2 livres azur en poudre — 5. 0
1 livre Ocre Jone — 6
1 livre Ocre rouge — 6.
10 livre witening — 1. 8.
½ livre noir d'yvoire — 1. 6
J'ai été hier avec Mr M'Kay chez le grand Juge Smith pour prendre
le modelle pour la Masse de la Chambre d'Assemblée de cette
province du bas Canada. C'est une Couronne royale de grandeur
naturelle porte ou surmontant un vase (sur lequel sont peinte
les armes de la Couronne) avec un Manche d'environ trois pieds
de longt. a peu pres Comme en la figure Cy a Coté
24 Mr bouteillée vient de me Commander de la part de Monsieur le grand
Juge, de faire pour lui une verge noire et un lion rampant au dessus,
et la Masse de Mr brassard pour le Conseil législatif.
livré au théatre deux Scenes de Chambre £1. 10 de façon
a chetter pour le théatre 1 livre Rode pinck — 7. 6.
½ livre ocre rouge — 3.
27 toutes les Couleurs fournies Jusqu'à ce Jour font £1. 15. 1
28 Reçu de Mr James hady le payement des frises et rosettes de la Chambre
d'assemblée
a chetter une perre bas de soy fin — 15. 0
une perre escarpin — 6. 6
Dépenses Domestique — 11. 11.
porte en l'autre page — £ 62. 9. 9

donnée a Mr. J. hady
19 pour le théatre ⸺

j'ai été hier avec Mr.
le modelle pour la
province du bas Cana
naturelle porte o
les armes de la Cou
de longst a peup re
24 Mr. bouteillée vient de
juges de faire pour
et la masse de M
livré au théatre a
a chetter pour le théatre

27 toutes les Couleurs fou

28 Reçue de Mr. Jau
a chetter une pierre
une pierre escarpin
Dépenses D'mist

Close-up of Baillaragé's design.

which he modelled that of the legislative council) indicates that the legislative assembly's mace was painted with a coat of arms, which would indicate that the mace was made of wood and not metal.

A long-time deputy clerk of the Senate, Fennings Taylor maintained that the Senate mace had belonged to the Legislative Council of the Province of Canada,[9] having originated in the Legislative Council of Lower Canada prior to the Union. The mace was saved from the flames that consumed the Montreal Parliament on 25 April 1849, during the Rebellion Losses Bill riots. The mace moved to Toronto from 1849 to 1851 and was moved to Quebec City from 1852 to 1856. Again the mace was saved from destruction in 1854 when the Parliament buildings in Quebec City were ravaged by fire. The Parliament then took up temporary quarters at the Convent of St. John in Quebec City, which burned shortly after their arrival. Again the mace was saved. With Confederation and the establishment of the Dominion Parliament in Ottawa, the mace was transferred to the newly constituted Senate.

The Senate mace was used at the opening of the Dominion Parliament on 6 November 1867, when all of the newly appointed Senators swore their oath and signed the Declaration of Qualification allowing them to sit as members of the upper chamber. It would seem that the Senate mace and the House of Commons sergeant-at-arms's chain of office are the only two

BURNING OF THE HOUSES OF ASSEMBLY, AT MONTREAL.—(SEE PAGE 320.)

Burning of the Legislative Assembly of the Province of Canada, April 1848.

constant original physical elements that have survived since Confederation and continue in use to this day.

On the evening of 3 February 1916, fire struck the Parliament buildings. The enterprising Gentleman Usher of the Black Rod, Colonel Ernest J. Chambers, immediately grabbed the mace upon hearing the alarm, although he failed to retrieve his black rod. The Senate was not sitting when the fire broke out, and thus it is miraculous that the mace was prevented from suffering the same fate as its House of Commons counterpart that perished in the flames that consumed the building.

The Senate mace bears the Royal arms of King George III, who reigned from 1760 to 1820, although these Royal arms incorporate the Electoral Bonnet of Hanover, over the central shield, and thus the arms can be dated to 1801–1816.[10] The head of the mace includes an embossed representation of the Great Seal of Lower Canada, depicting a scene of Quebec City. However, the seal "does not show a sufficient number of buildings to allow us to determine what period is involved, although the presence of two church steeples, probably the Anglican and Catholic cathedrals, would indicate a date later than 1804, since the building of the Anglican Cathedral was

Depiction of the Senate mace carved into the Parliament buildings.

completed in that year."[11] It is recorded that on 2 October 1793, Lord Dorchester delivered the new Great Seal of Lower Canada to the colony.[12] Identical to that represented on the head of the mace, we can be certain that this portion of the mace head, and perhaps the entire head, was augmented after this time. Thus it is possible to date this part of the mace to the period of 1804–1816.[13]

The Great Seal of Lower Canada bears the inscription AB IPSO DUCIT OPES ANIMUMQUE FERRO, which translates as "it derives power and courage from the steel itself."[14] This is a quote taken from the *Odes of Horace* [IV 4, 59–60]. This refers to the resilience of Lower Canadians thriving as part of British North America following the Conquest.

The Great Seal of Lower Canada.

In 1969 the Senate mace was taken to the Royal Ontario Museum to be analyzed. It was found that the mace is made of brass, electroplated with gold. As electroplating did not become common until the 1840s, this means that the current plating dates from after that period, but this does not mean that the mace was manufactured then. The hollow parts are made of sheet brass and affixed with soft solder. Officials at the Royal Ontario Museum came to no firm conclusions about the date of the mace.[15] The absence of any trace of mercury gilding could indicate that the mace dates from after 1840, although there are no records of the Legislative Council of Lower Canada adopting a new mace at that time, and even experts have agreed that the absence of mercury gilding does not mean that the mace was never gilded in that fashion.

Given that some maces in England have been updated and adapted, it is entirely likely that the Senate mace is a composition of elements of the original 1793 legislative council mace along with later elements. This would help to explain the presence of the Royal arms of King George III dating from the 1801–1816 period, the Great Seal of Lower Canada dating from post-1794, and several different types of materials and electroplating, despite the fact that some parts of the mace date from before the advent of this technology.[16] The addition of King George III's arms to the 1794 mace is not surprising, since it was customary to add the new Royal cypher to maces in use in England up until the reign of King George II.[17] One can speculate that the entire mace underwent some kind of restoration following one of the parliamentary fires, which would explain the later method of gold-plating.

The Senate mace is carried by a mace bearer. At the opening of the First Parliament of Canada in 1867 and until 1869 this function was carried out by the Gentleman Usher of the Black Rod. In 1869, a Senate sergeant-at-arms was appointed.[18] A similar post of sergeant of the mace had existed in the Legislative Council of Lower Canada from 1792–1837.[19] The Legislative Council of the Province of Canada also employed a sergeant-at-arms between 1841 and 1866. The position of sergeant-at-arms of the Senate was changed to Yeoman Usher of the Black Rod following the death of the only Senate sergeant-at-arms. The title was subsequently changed to Assistant Usher of the Black Rod and most recently the Senate mace bearer.

The Senate mace has, on occasion, been used outside of the Senate chamber. During the centennial of Confederation in 1967 when the Queen visited Parliament Hill, the Deputy Gentleman Usher of the Black Rod of the Senate and the sergeant-at-arms of the House of Commons stood facing each other with their respective maces shouldered on the official platform. The Usher of

Senate mace being carried by Mace Bearer Jan Potter.

Top: Mace Bearer Jan Potter with the Senate mace.
Bottom: Senate Mace.

the Black Rod led the Queen and Prince Philip in procession as they passed between the two maces. This is one of the only occasions where it is know that both maces were used in conjunction and in an outdoor setting.[20]

Great Mace of the Senate of Canada (1867–present)

The arms plate below the crown depicting the Royal arms of King George III.

Material: Gilded brass.

Length: 164.5 centimetres.

Crowned Head: The shape is in the style of St Edward's Crown, where four arches curve upwards and outwards, and then downwards at the intersection.

They are joined to a coronet of alternating crosses paty and fleurs-de-lys, with a circlet decorated with simulated "jewels." The arches are decorated with beaded edges simulating pearls. At the top, also beaded, is the orb and cross paty with bead finials.

Cap: Beneath the crossed arches is the arms plate with the Royal arms of King George III (of the 1801–1816 period).

Head: The cup of the head is divided into four parts, each separated by a short-haired, armless male terminal figure, which are linked to each other at head level by a laurel band. In three of the compartments there are crowned Royal emblems: the rose and thistle together, the harp, and the fleur-de-lys. In the fourth area is a circular representation of the Great Seal of Lower Canada; a scene taken from the

Representation of the Great Seal of Lower Canada on the Senate mace.

obverse, depicting an oak tree by a river with ships at anchor in front of a townscape with two church spires in the distance.

Brackets: There are four simple scroll brackets at the top of the shaft supporting the head of the mace.

Shaft and Knops: Three round, bulbous knops are positioned along the shaft, graduating in size: the largest immediately beneath the brackets, a second at a midway point, and a smaller one nearer the foot knop. Each has a rib around the centre and palm leaf decoration on either side. The main shaft is delicately patterned with spiralling stylized motifs that incorporate roses, thistles, and shamrocks.

Foot Knop: The lower part of the mace flares out in trumpet form with an inverted bell shape below, terminating in a ball and button end piece. Elongated palm leaves decorate the upper area, with similar leaf types over the rest.

Manufacturer and Distinguishing Marks: None. Parts of the mace likely date from 1794, while others were added between 1804 and 1816, with re-plating of the instrument occurring sometime after 1840. Originally used by the Legislative Council of Lower Canada and then the Legislative Council of the Province of Canada.

Senate mace, upper end.

CHAPTER TEN

The Mace of the House of Commons

The House of Commons mace — more commonly referred to as the Parliamentary Mace or Great Mace — is amongst the most important symbols of authority of the Canadian state, perhaps only surpassed by the signature of the Sovereign and the Great Seal of Canada in symbolic importance. The very governance of the country is impossible without its presence.

The current mace is relatively recent, having been adopted in 1917. However, its story provides an interesting window into the heraldic history of Canada. The original House of Commons mace was destroyed in the parliamentary fire of 3 February 1916. The Senate mace survived the fire and continues to be in use.

The original House of Commons mace used since the first session of the Dominion Parliament in November 1867, predated Confederation and the new Parliament. Following the union of Upper and Lower Canada in 1841 into the United Province of Canada (Canada East and Canada West), the then Speaker of the legislative assembly, Sir Allan Napier MacNab, purchased a mace. "This was to a large extent a facsimile of the one used in the British House [of Commons]. It was made of silver, richly gilded and elaborately chased."[1] This new mace was completed in 1845 and has a rather extraordinary history. Like the parliamentary portrait of Queen Victoria which has survived multiple fires and crises, it is difficult to believe that providence did not shine upon the original House of Commons mace in a similar fashion. Adopted in 1845, the original House of Commons mace was first used by the Parliament of the United Canadas located in Montreal. During the 25 April 1849 Rebellion Losses Bill riots, the Montreal Parliament was burned and the mace was seized by one of the rioters but miraculously survived, being left on the porch of Sir Allan Napier MacNab. Sergeant-at-Arms G.K. Chisholm was knocked down by a rioter named Alfred Perry who was wielding an axe handle, and although Chisholm had drawn his sword to defend himself and the mace, Perry

Portrait of Sir Allan Napier MacNab, Bt, Speaker of the Legislative Assembly of the Province of Canada.

the mace in an attempt to smash it. He was prevented from this by two young men, who succeeded "in pulling the mace away from Perry."[2] The mace was then taken to Sir Allan's room at the Donegan Hotel. During this ordeal a small gold acorn was lost off of the mace, and this was subsequently replaced.

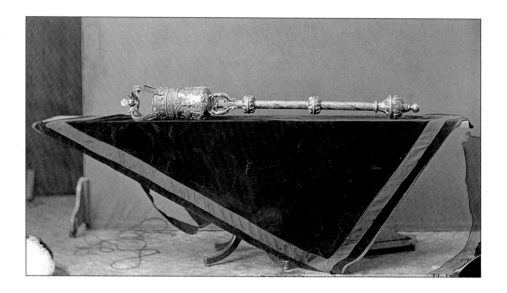

Original mace of the House of Commons.

Sergeant-at-Arms Henry R. Smith, CMG, ISO, VD, with the original House of Commons mace.

Parliament was then moved to Toronto from 1849 to 1851 and moved again to Quebec City from 1852 to 1856. The mace was again saved on two occasions from fire: in 1854 when the Parliament buildings in Quebec City were destroyed and again when the mace was deposited in the Convent of St. John's, which was being used by members of the legislature for meetings.[3] With Confederation in 1867 and the establishment of the Dominion government in Ottawa, the mace was transferred to the new Parliament buildings there.

A number of written descriptions survive of the original House of Commons mace. The Honourable Charles Clarke, Speaker of the Ontario Legislature, wrote in 1881:

> After the Union of the Canadas, and when Sir Allan MacNab was Speaker, the Parliament ordered the purchase of a new mace, and one was procured, in 1845 at the cost of £500 sterling,[4] which is described as a facsimile of that in the English House of Commons.[5] It is composed of silver, richly gilded and elaborately chased, with an entire length of five feet. The top, in the shape of a crown, is of open work, in four pieces, and is surmounted by an orb and cross. The encircling fillet below the crown bears lozenges and pearls. The cup below this band is formed of four segments, each supported from below by the demi-figure of a nude armless woman. Each segment bears a royal Crown, with the letters V.R., and below them one has a rose, another thistle, the third a harp, and the fourth a Prince of Wales plume. An ornamented ring, repeated about the centre of the shaft, then follows. The shaft is about thirty-two inches in length, the head eighteen and the foot nine inches, and has raised fillet running around it diagonally from the base to the head, while the space between the spiral band is elaborately chased with roses, thistles and leaves — probably of the shamrock. The lower portion of the mace is divided into four segments bearing the harp, the rose, the thistle and the plume, while the extreme base is smooth and polished. Just above it are other segments, bearing the floral emblems.[6]

The mace was always rested on a green cushion which sat on the clerk's table located in front of the Speaker's chair.[7]

Tragically, the original House of Commons mace, despite having survived other catastrophes, perished in the 1916 fire. The sergeant-at-arms was out

Chamber of the House of Commons circa 1905. The original House of Commons mace can be seen on the clerk's table.

Parliament the morning after the fire, 4 February 1916.

of the House of Commons chamber when the alarm was sounded, and no one thought to transport the mace out of the chamber as there had been other recent fires of no consequence. Indeed the twenty members present in the chamber at the time of the alarm may have felt unable to handle this paramount symbol of Parliament's authority without enduring the wrath of the sergeant-at-arms.

Immediately following the parliamentary fire, the legislature was moved to the Victoria Memorial Building — what is today the Museum of Nature. Because of the tradition that Parliament cannot sit without the presence of a mace, the Senate mace, which had survived the fire, was briefly employed for use in the House of Commons.[8] It was found too difficult and inconvenient to stage meetings of the Senate and House of Commons, despite the fact that the Senate sat for only short periods of time. Understandably, members of the Senate were quite possessive of their mace and were not overly enthusiastic with their symbol of authority being used in "the other place."[9] The Ontario Provincial Parliament loaned the House of Commons the provincial mace,[10] but this solution was short-lived as the Ontario Legislature was due to resume sitting on the last day of February, thus an alternative had to be devised.[11]

A gilt wooden mace was produced in short order by the House of Commons' own carpenters, and this wooden mace was used until the arrival of the new House of Commons mace. The House of Commons temporary or wooden mace, as it is often called, is perhaps the most highly detailed wooden mace ever used in Canada. Despite the slightly oxidized appearance of the gilt paint, from a distance it looks remarkably similar in proportion to the high-quality metal mace that was destroyed. The temporary mace was also the first in Canada to bear the Royal cypher of King George V. This mace was placed into service on 23 February 1916, when the Ontario mace was returned to Toronto.[12] Members of Parliament seemed unaware that "this mace is only a mockery of gilded wood…. Turned out by a wood carver and coated to look like gold."[13] The temporary mace remained in service until the new House of Commons mace was unveiled to members of Parliament on 16 May 1917.

Scarcely a week after the fire, the Lord Mayor of London, the Right Honourable Sir Charles Wakefield, wrote to Sir George Pearly, the Canadian High Commissioner to London, commenting, "Hearing that the Dominion Parliament lost its mace in the recent fire, the sheriffs of the City of London and myself would feel honoured if Canada would allow us to replace it."[14] Sir Robert Borden and Sir Wilfrid Laurier subsequently conferred and agreed that the mace should be donated by London.

Similar in design to most other Commonwealth maces, the House of Commons mace is largely based upon the House of Commons mace used by the Parliament at Westminster, but with a Tudor-style crown as adopted in the early twentieth century, and quite a number of Canadian symbols. The British House of Commons mace was designed by Thomas Maundy in 1649.

The mace was manufactured and designed by the Goldsmiths & Silversmiths Company Limited of London in 1916. The mace itself is fashioned of sterling silver and bears the British sterling hallmarks for London 1916. It contains over 260 ounces of sterling silver and measures 148.55 centimetres long.

There was some debate as to what Royal cypher the mace should bear. Some suggested V.R. as that is what was placed on the original mace, while others preferred C.R. as this was the cypher that was on the 1660 British House of Commons mace — which the new Canadian mace was being modelled on. Ultimately it was decided to use G.R. as the new mace was being manufactured during the reign of King George V, and even though the general style of the mace was to be similar to the British mace there was no desire to use a version that was an exact replica. It was preferable to have a version that was similar, but that included a variety of Canadian symbols.

The small silver container (7 centimetres high) holding the remnant thought to be from the original House of Commons mace.

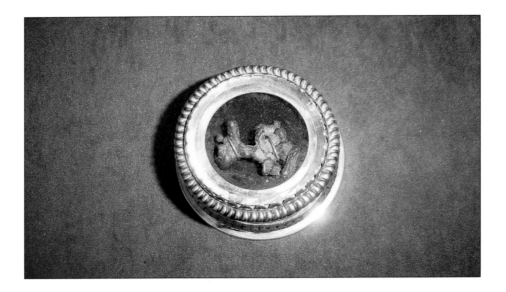

Remnant at one time believed to be part of the original House of Commons mace, presented to Sophia, Countess of Albemarle, and later bequeathed to the Canada Club, London, England.

For some years parliamentary lore held that the current House of Commons mace included some remnants of the original House of Commons mace. A large chunk of metal was retrieved from the ruins of the House of Commons, but when tested it was found that "the remains are all brass with the exception of one or two pieces of lead,"[15] thus, it was decided not to include any non-silver metals in the new mace.[16] Before the results of the tests were known, a small piece of the debris was sent to the Dowager Countess of Albemarle, second daughter of Sir Allan Napier MacNab, "in memory of the association of her family with the history and life of the Dominion."[17] Interestingly, this relic was subsequently mounted in a small, round silver casket and bequeathed to the Canada Club in London where it remains to this day. Whilst there is no certainty about the origin of this fragment, the engraving should, however, be noted:

> The enclosed is a portion of the Mace which was destroyed in the burning of the Canadian Houses of Parliament at Ottawa in 1915 and was presented to Sophia Countess of Albemarle by the present Prime Minister Sir Robert Borden Bart. The interest lies in the fact that when the mob broke into the House

of Commons in 1849 they carried the Mace in Procession to
the residence of Sir Allan Napier Macnab [*sic*] her father, then
Prime Minister, and placed it in his bed for safety.

The new mace was presented to Sir Robert Borden on 28 March 1917, at
the Guildhall in London. The new House of Commons mace was presented
by the Lord Mayor of London, Sir Charles Cheers Wakefield, on behalf of the
Corporation of the City of London.

It was the first time in the long history of the Guildhall that a mace had been
presented. In attendance were Sir Robert Borden, Sir George Perley, Canadian
High Commissioner to London W.F. Massey, and the prime minister of New
Zealand, along with the Australian and South African High Commissioners.

During the ceremony a letter from the recently retired Governor General the
Duke of Connaught was read: "I think it is a most splendid patriotic act of yours,
and is I know most heartily appreciated throughout Canada."[18] Appropriately, Sir
Robert Borden spoke and thanked the Lord Mayor for the gift: "it is my first
duty on the present occasion to express the profound appreciation and thanks
of the Government and people of Canada to the donors of this mace for their
generous gift. It will indeed be an emblem of the tie which binds together the
Mother Country and the Overseas Dominions." Much of the remainder of his
speech focused on the services being rendered by Canadians, Australians, New
Zealanders, South Africans, and peoples from throughout the British Empire in
the First World War. The mace was more than just a gift to Canada; it was seen as
an important symbol of thanks from Britain to Canada and the other Dominions
for the sacrifice they were making in the Great War. The senior Dominion
was being honoured, and thus its sister Dominions were honoured as well.
Other notables present were the Marquess of Crewe, chairman of the London
County Council; Lord Sandhurst, the Lord Chamberlain; two Canadian peers,
Lord Beaverbrook and Lord Shaughnessy; the general officer commanding the
Canadian Expeditionary Force in Britain, Major General Sir Richard Turner; and
the sole female present was Lady Perley, wife of the Canadian High Commissioner.

On 16 May 1917, the House of Commons passed a unanimous vote of
thanks to the Lord Mayor of London for the generous gift of the new mace
as the newly crafted instrument of state was laid on the council table in the
temporary House of Commons housed in the Victoria Memorial building.
Sir Robert Borden extolled the fact that "in its design and execution the mace
forms an emblem of authority well worthy of the great country for which it is
intended."[19] The leader of the opposition, Sir Wilfrid Laurier, responded:

House of Commons mace.

> This emblem and its presentation are evidences of our connection and growing relations with the Motherland. For my part, though I am a democrat to the hilt, I certainly appreciate all these evidences of our parliamentary history as it has come down to us through the ages…. Parliamentary government has come from England to Canada, and this gift to us is an emblem of those parliamentary institutions which are so highly prized especially now that we are under fire in the present world war.[20]

Leading up to the coronation of Queen Elizabeth II in 1953, some discussion arose as to whether or not the Royal cypher on the mace should be changed to reflect the new Sovereign. The suggestion came from the enterprising manager of the Henry Birks & Sons store in Ottawa. Birks came up with the idea because the Quebec legislature had recently requested that similar changes be made to their provincial mace shortly after the death of King George VI.[21]

Since the time of King George II until the early twentieth century, alterations (or augmentations) had not usually been made to a mace after it was completed. This was certainly the practice in the United Kingdom and had been the tradition in most Canadian jurisdictions.[22] Despite this fact, it was decided that the G.R. cypher of King George V should be changed to E.R., of H.M. Queen Elizabeth II. Strangely enough, no other changes were made to the mace. The changes were completed at the Birks silversmith shop in Montreal, and the mace was returned to Parliament on 26 June 1953.

This change is somewhat incongruous as the *E* and *R* of the Queen's cypher were placed on each side of the shield containing the arms of the four founding provinces of Canada. This shield dates from Confederation and was used in a variety of forms until the granting of the Canadian Coat of Arms in 1921. If one

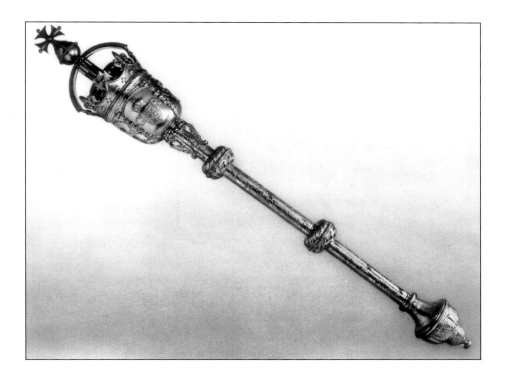

House of Commons mace with Royal cypher of King George V.

did not know that the mace was manufactured in 1916, one would assume that it is the cypher of King Edward VII and not Queen Elizabeth II; however the lettering style is distinctly different.

Temporary House of Commons Mace (1916)

Material: Gilded wood.

Crowned Head: The arches of the crown with beading simulating pearls along the lengths are painted metallic strips that ensue from the main wood block of the mace head. Above where the arches intersect, four small beavers crouch next to the orb and cross finial. The circlet is composed of alternating crosses paty and fleurs-de-lys, with simulated "jewels" along the band.

The crowned head of the temporary House of Commons mace.

Cap: The cap is plain with carved undulations representing fabric folds.

Head: The mace head is decorated with emblems, including roses and oak leaves, together with the Royal cypher of King George V.

Brackets: Beneath the mace head at the top end of the shaft there are four scroll brackets, each with a single leaf form.

Shaft and Knop: There are two bulbous knops spaced along the shaft, which has a spiralling ribbon decoration down its length.

Foot Knop: At the base there is a large foot knop in the shape of an inverted bell, which is simply decorated with roses and stylized leaf forms. The mace terminates with a ball end piece.

Manufacturer and Distinguishing Marks: None.

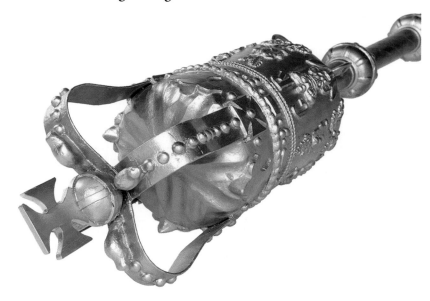

The top end of the temporary House of Commons mace.

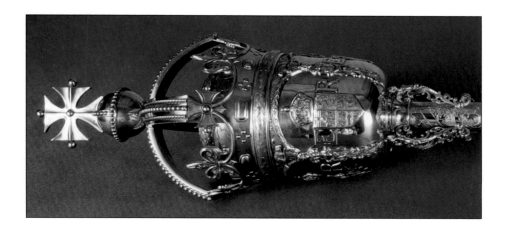

The crowned head of the House of Commons mace.

The Great Mace of the House of Commons (1916–present)

Material: Gilded sterling silver.
Length: 148.55 centimetres.

The arms plate beneath the arches of the House of Commons mace depicting the Royal arms of King George V.

Crowned Head: The crown has a coronet of alternating fleurs-de-lys and crosses paty, four of each, above a band with simulated jewels. The two semicircular arches, which cross over forming four half arches, have beaded ribs simulating pearls. These are surmounted at the intersection by an orb also beaded and a cross paty with bead finials.

Cap: The arms plate beneath the arches carries the Royal arms of King George V, within a circular wreathed border surrounded by foliate decoration.

Head: The head is separated by caryatid figures into four compartments framed under laurel arches; within each spandrel is a beaver. Three of these sections are taken up by a crowned Royal cypher, originally that of King George V when the mace was first commissioned, each combining the rose, thistle, and harp in the style of that period. The initials only were subsequently modernized, with E.R. following the accession of Her Majesty Queen Elizabeth II in 1952. On the fourth side is a crowned shield for the Arms of the Dominion of Canada, composed of the quartered arms of the four founding provinces: Ontario, Quebec, Nova Scotia, and New Brunswick.

Brackets: There are four brackets connecting the upper shaft to the head of the mace, each a female figure combined with delicate openwork scrolls.

Shaft and Knops: Two knops, each with raised spiral gadroons and pronounced central rib, separate two main shaft sections that are chased with a spiralling ribbon interspersed with floral emblems: Canadian maple leaves, roses, thistles, and shamrocks.

Foot Knop: The mace terminates with a rounded button beneath an inverted vase and bell-shaped knop, which has floral decoration that includes fleurs-de-lys, roses, and thistles.

House of Commons mace, showing the brackets.

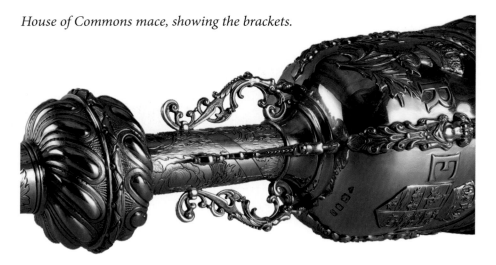

Shaft detail of the House of Commons mace.

Engraving: Inscription on the foot knop:

THIS MACE

REPLACING THE ORIGINAL MACE

OF THE

HOUSE OF COMMONS OF THE DOMINION OF CANADA

DESTROYED BY FIRE ON FEBRUARY 3rd 1916

WAS PRESENTED BY

COLONEL THE RIGHT HONOURABLE SIR CHARLES CHEERS WAKEFIELD

LORD MAYOR OF LONDON

AND THE SHERIFFS OF LONDON

GEORGE ALEXANDER TOUCHE ESQ MP AND SAMUEL GEORGE SHEAD ESQ

JUNE 1916

Manufacturer and Distinguishing Marks: The mace carries the hallmarks "G & S Co Ld" for the Goldsmiths & Silversmiths Company Ltd., London, England, 1916.

Other: On delivery there was an error in the inscription which dated the fire as "February 17th 1916." This was subsequently corrected.

CHAPTER ELEVEN

Provincial Maces

As with the two houses of Canada's federal Parliament, all of Canada's provincial legislative assemblies possess their own mace. The sporadic adoption of maces by provincial legislatures has more been the result of local circumstances than part of any pattern. Like Canadian federalism, developments have not always come from the federal government. Indeed Nova Scotia, which was the first jurisdiction in North America to attain representative government (1758) and then responsible government (1848), did not adopt a mace until 1930. Ontario and Quebec were the first to adopt maces, although this is not surprising because prior to Confederation the Province of Canada — unlike New Brunswick, Nova Scotia, and Prince Edward Island — utilized a mace for both the legislative assembly and legislative council. Both British Columbia and Newfoundland entered Confederation having had a long history of legislative assemblies and the presence of a mace in their respective chambers.

Since 1930 and the presentation of a mace to the Nova Scotia Legislative Assembly, a tradition of gifting provincial and territorial maces has developed. Every provincial mace adopted since this time, aside from British Columbia's, has been presented as a gift, whether it be from an individual philanthropist, an association, or, in one instance, another provincial government. Every province has a sergeant-at-arms.

As Canada is a constitutional monarchy, made up of thirteen different jurisdictions, the symbolism of the mace in the provinces is the same as their federal counterparts. The symbolism incorporated into the various provincial maces is representative of not only the province, but also the period during which the mace was crafted. The symbolism of provincial and territorial maces have the same significance as their federal counterparts. Thus, a wide variety of provincial coats of arms, flowers, and animals are incorporated alongside the various incarnations of the Royal arms of Canada, the Royal arms of the United Kingdom, and the Royal cyphers of Canada's various Sovereigns.[1]

The retired or historical maces of Canada's provinces tend to be less symbolically rich than those currently in use, however, they serve as a window into periods when maces were sometimes constructed in great haste, and had to endure fire, theft, misuse, and general wear. Notwithstanding the simplicity of the earlier ones, they were still regarded as legal accoutrements.

ONTARIO

Upper Canada was founded by Loyalists fleeing the American Revolution. With them they brought a strong desire to remain loyal to the Crown and to foster the creation of institutions modelled on those of Great Britain. Thus, it is not surprising that their first Parliament was opened with a mace. Although crude in construction it was a potent symbol of the continuity of tradition and loyalty that served as the cornerstone for the foundation of what would become Canada. Upon their arrival, Loyalists petitioned King George III for an assembly in the Province of Canada. Loyalist refugees "naturally wanted to live under representative institutions,"[2] and this gave rise to the Constitutional Act of 1791. The Act was essentially an amendment to the Quebec Act of 1763, and it was designed to "apply the British Constitution, as nearly as possible to colonial conditions."[3]

The first Parliament of Upper Canada was convened at Niagara by Governor John Graves Simcoe on 17 September 1792. Although the setting was primitive, Simcoe, who himself had been a member of the British Parliament, "was determined to open Parliament with all the ceremonies and traditions that distinguished the opening of the English Parliament, as far as could be adapted to the condition of the colony." Simcoe was "determined to have all the fixings of Westminster for his new domain,"[4] thus, the first Upper Canada mace was created. It was made from wood and quite simple in appearance.

During the War of 1812, the United States occupied York (present-day Toronto). On 27 April 1813, the Americans captured the city and looted public and private buildings, removing not only items of monetary value, but trophies of war. Included among the pillaged items was the wooden mace of Upper Canada. Canadian and British troops retaliated by burning the White House and Capitol in Washington, D.C., which resulted in the destruction of the mace of the U.S. House of Representatives.

The Upper Canada mace was eventually presented to the United States Naval Academy Museum at Annapolis, Maryland, where it remained until 1934. As a gesture of friendship and goodwill, President Franklin Delano Roosevelt sent a message to the U.S. Congress requesting authority to return the mace to Canada.[5] For many years Charles Clarke, Speaker of the Ontario Legislature, had pressured American authorities for the return of the mace. As part of Toronto's centennial celebrations, a memorial plaque was unveiled by the United States Daughters of 1812 to commemorate the lives of members of the United States Army and Navy who were killed in action during the War of 1812. In conjunction with the plaque unveiling, the Imperial Order of Daughters of the Empire unveiled a plaque commemorating the defenders of York who lost their lives in the war.

The president noted "the suggestion has been made that it would be a gracious act of the United States to return this historic mace to Canada at the time of the unveiling of the tablet… It [the mace] symbolizes the orderly rule of such government in Canada, continuing from that day to this."[6] On 4 July 1934, the warship U.S.S. *Wilmington* entered Toronto Harbour under the command of Captain A.F. Nicklett.[7] Rear Admiral William D. Leahy presented the mace to Lieutenant Governor Herbert Bruce on behalf of President Roosevelt and the American people.[8] Following a massive parade, Lieutenant Governor Bruce noted "the friendly association of our neighbouring democracies during the past 12 decades has been, we believe, a shining example to the world and a magnificent vindication of the principles by which our citizens are inspired."[9] A keen student of history, Bruce would later reflect upon the symbolism of the mace and its importance. "In the British Empire the Mace has been for many centuries the emblem of sovereignty and authority borne by the Sergeant-at-Arms as his warrant for demanding obedience to the commands of the peoples representatives assembled in Parliament. It is likewise a symbol of those democratic ideals of free constitutional government by which the splendid history, also, of your own nation has been illuminated and ennobled in the sight of all men."[10]

After more than a century, the mace was reintroduced at the closing of the twentieth session of the legislature in 1938 when it was carried by Ontario's sergeant-at-arms, C.S. Rutherford, VC.[11]

After the looting of the Upper Canada mace in 1813 there is no evidence that the colony adopted a new mace. The painting of Governor General Sir Charles Metcalfe opening the second Parliament of the Union in 1844 does not display a mace, only a large ledger book on the clerk's table, which was located at the governor's stoop. Following the 1837 rebellions in Upper and Lower Canada, Governor General Lord Durham recommended that the two colonies be united into one province. Thus the Province of Canada was established in 1841, made up of Canada East and Canada West. There is no mention of a mace being used at the opening of the first legislative assembly, which took place in Kingston at the local general hospital. It is probable that if a mace was used it came from Lower Canada, possibly the mace currently used by the Senate of Canada, but we can only speculate as to what instrument of authority was employed.

Dissatisfied with the situation, the Speaker of the legislative assembly, Sir Allan Napier MacNab, ordered that a new mace be produced.[12] The full story of this mace can be found in the section dealing with the House of Commons mace.

With Confederation, Canada West was transformed into the Province of Ontario. The mace used by the Legislative Assembly of the Province of Canada was transported to Ottawa for use by the new Dominion Parliament. The province's newly elected premier, John Sandfield Macdonald, ordered that a mace be produced in time for the inauguration of the Ontario Legislative Assembly. The task was left to Robert Dalton, clerk of the executive council. Dalton arranged for Alfred Todd to oversee the manufacture of the mace and arrange for payment.[13] The project was completed by December 1867, and Charles E. Zollikoffer of Ottawa was paid $200 for his work.[14] Zollikoffer was a Swiss-born Huguenot artist who had a long association with Parliament. He was the man responsible for making a plaster model of the original Parliament buildings that was used for public display prior to construction of

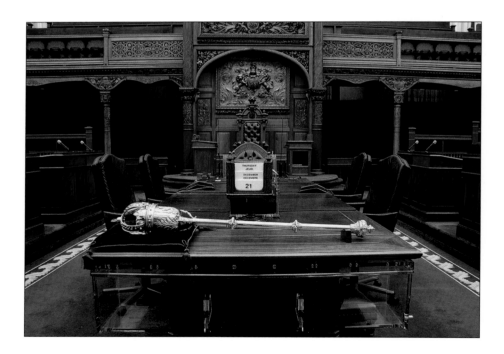

Ontario mace in the chamber of the provincial parliament.

the building.[15] The mace was first used on 27 December 1867, at the opening of the first session of the provincial legislature.

The original mace bore the Crown of Queen Victoria, however, upon the accession of King Edward VII in 1901, it was decided to have the mace altered. Such changes were generally not made to maces in the United Kingdom or other parts of the Commonwealth. Once a mace was constructed it was not altered regardless of who occupied the throne. The cup and crown of the Ontario mace were altered in 1902 by the Dorrien Plating & Manufacturing Company of Toronto.[16] The crown was adjusted to be a Tudor-style crown as adopted in the early twentieth century, while the cup was changed to include the Royal cypher of King Edward VII. The original cup was retained by the company until 1906 when it was turned over to the provincial secretary for safekeeping.[17]

In December 2008 the Ontario mace was altered for the first time in more than a century with the addition of two diamonds. The diamonds, one polished and the other rough, came from the De Beers Canada Victor Mine, located in the James Bay Lowlands on the traditional lands of the Attawapiskat First Nation. De Beers was anxious to commemorate the opening of Ontario's first diamond mine and donated three stones: two for the mace and one for display

Sergeant-at-Arms Dennis Clark carrying the Ontario mace leading the speaker's parade into the Ontario legislature.

at the Ontario Legislature. The setting for the diamonds was designed by Reena Ahluwalia, while the stones were cut on site at the legislative assembly. The setting contains three ounces of platinum that was mined in Canada and provided by Vale Inco. The setting was installed by Corona Jewellers. The augmented mace was unveiled at the Ontario Legislature on 24 March 2009.

Mace of Upper Canada (1792–1813)

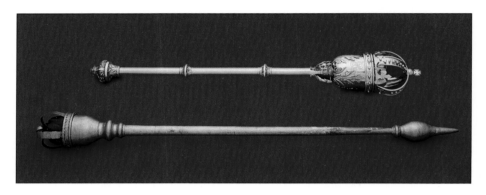

Material: Gilt wood with metal fittings on the head of the mace.
Length: 141.5 centimetres.
Crowned Head: Comprised of a simple circlet with four arches of plain bended metal, with a small orb at the intersection.
Cap: A domed cap beneath the arches is painted red.
Head: Shaped very simply as a plain urn, with no decoration.
Shaft: This is plain and tapers towards the foot.
Foot Knop: A plain, bulbous, spindle-shaped knop terminates with a small metal end piece.
Manufacturer and Distinguishing Marks: None.

Mace of the Province of Ontario (1867–present)

Material: Gilded copper.
Length: 115.5 centimetres.
Crowned Head: The overall shape of the crown is quite rounded, with a coronet of alternating fleurs-de-lys and crosses paty, four of each. The four curved

arches with plain ridge edges have beading simulating pearls spaced down the centre; they intersect beneath a plain orb and cross. The crosses paty are stylized where the customary inward curves are shaped in a somewhat straighter fashion. The "gemstone" band with alternating lozenges and beads has a twisted, rope-like border above and below.

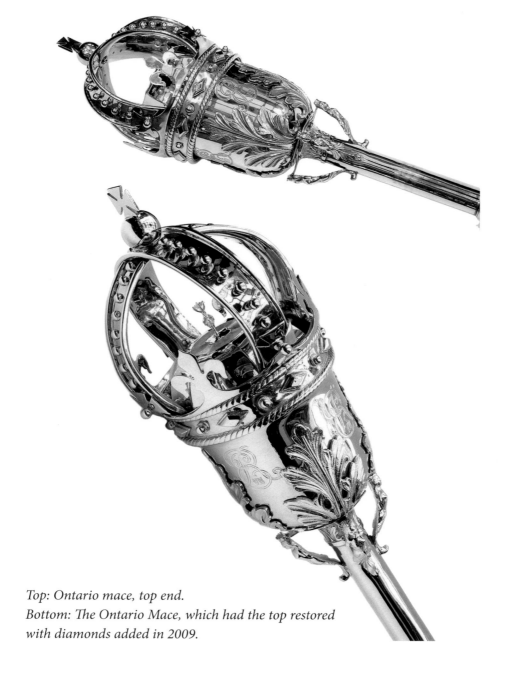

Top: Ontario mace, top end.
Bottom: The Ontario Mace, which had the top restored with diamonds added in 2009.

Cap: This is plain and does not carry any decoration or heraldic device. It is shaped as a cap of maintenance with folds around the side. In the centre of the cap two diamonds — one polished and one rough — are mounted in a platinum setting.

Head: Pronounced acanthus-type foliage in four areas ensue from the base of the cup, and in-between each within the plain fields the engraved Royal cypher of King Edward VII is replicated four times. At the change of Sovereign, from Queen Victoria to King Edward VII, the mace head underwent alteration.

Brackets: There are four armless female figureheads, each wearing a mural crown. These brackets are fixed at the top end of the shaft.

Shaft and Knops: The three sections are plain, separated by two knops along the length. Each knop flares outward with a plain middle band.

Foot Knop: The mace terminates with a bulbous knop with acanthus-like decoration.

Manufacturer and Distinguishing Marks: The mace was supplied by Charles O. Zollikoffer, Ottawa. There are no maker's marks.

QUEBEC

Lower Canada inaugurated its legislature, consisting of a legislative assembly and a legislative council, simultaneous with that of Upper Canada.

The opening occurred on 17 December 1792. Charles Huot's painting, *The Language Debate: The Sitting of the Legislative Assembly of Lower Canada on 21 January 1793*,[18] which was commissioned much later, in 1910, recording an event of the earlier period, clearly shows a mace at the foot of the table in front of the clerk. The mace is lengthwise with the crown facing the Speaker of the legislative assembly. The mace appears to have a long shaft and a medium-sized cup and crown at the head, and is quite similar in form to the mace used by Upper Canada prior to the War of 1812 and smaller in scale than the mace used by the Senate of Canada today. Whether this first mace was made of wood, as was the case in Upper Canada, or metal, is not known.

A mace for the Legislative Council of Lower Canada was manufactured in 1793 and the story of this mace can be found in the section dealing with the Senate, as it is this body that inherited the legislative council's mace in 1867 with the achievement of Confederation.

The mace used by the Legislative Assembly of Lower Canada disappeared sometime after the union of Upper and Lower Canada in 1841. Sir Allan Napier MacNab commissioned a new mace for the Legislative Assembly of the

Province of the United Canadas in 1845, and it is presumed that the mace of the Legislative Council of Lower Canada was used by the Legislative Council of the Province of Canada.

With Confederation the mace of the Legislative Council of Lower Canada was transferred to the Senate. Given that the mace of the Legislative Assembly of Lower Canada had been lost, a new set of maces had to be made for the newly created Legislative Assembly and Legislative Council of the Province of Quebec.

In 1867 the Ottawa artisan Charles Zollikoffer crafted two new maces and a black rod for the Quebec Provincial Legislature. It will be recalled that Zollikoffer produced the mace for Ontario's legislative assembly in the same year. On 19 April 1883, the Quebec Parliament buildings were ravaged by fire. The mace of the legislative council and the black rod were lost in the fire. The sergeant-at-arms, Gédéon Larocque, saved the mace of the legislative assembly. It was reported that "we saw the Sergeant-at-Arms of the Legislative Assembly, Dr. Larocque, come out, [of the building] half-dressed carrying the mace."[19]

A new mace and black rod were manufactured in 1883 for the legislative council. These were made by Cyrille Duquet and would continue to be used until 1968 when the legislative council was abolished. The *Journal de Quebec* reported in late 1884:

> Yesterday morning we had the opportunity to admire in the window of Mr. Cyrille Duquet, jeweller, watchmaker, optician and electrician, rue de la fabrique, a true work of art fashioned by this craftsman. It is a gilded bronze mace, prepared from the design of Mr. E.E. Taché, Deputy Minister of Crown Lands, who also designed the Parliament Buildings. This mace, which was ordered to replace the one which was destroyed, some two years ago, in the fire which gutted the Parliament Buildings.[20]

Quebec is the only province in Canada to still possess both its legislative council and legislative assembly maces. Despite this good fortune, the mace of the legislative assembly has not always been treated well. In 1953 the mace was altered by Henry Birks & Sons of Montreal to remove the Royal cypher of Queen Victoria and add the Royal cypher of Queen Elizabeth II.[21] Subsequently a number of clumsy repairs were made to the mace in the 1960s, and in 1967 the mace was hidden by students from the University of Montreal during their winter carnival. During this period the mace of the Legislative Council of Quebec was quietly substituted until the legislative assembly's mace could be found.

In the early 1970s, at the height of Quebec nationalist sentiment, it was suggested by procedural authority Jean-Charles Bonenfant that the mace should altogether be removed from use: "In Quebec, the mace is merely a kind of toy which students can steal without even the most serious members of parliament taking the event as a tragedy."[22] Bonenfant's assessment of the mace was clearly not shared by members of the Quebec national assembly, as the mace continues to be an important part of the proceedings of that chamber. The mace is seen as symbolizing the authority of the Speaker and the authority of the government of Quebec.

One procedural element has changed. As in other Canadian legislatures — save the Senate — the mace was traditionally placed across the end of the table that sits in front of the Speaker, with the crown of the mace pointing towards the governing party. In the late 1960s the mace of the national assembly began to be placed lengthwise down the table. The official reason given for this was on account of the lack of space on the table, although it seems more likely that this change coincided with the hiding of the mace by students in 1967. With the mace placed lengthwise down the table it would be difficult to differentiate the legislative assembly's mace from the legislative council's mace, during the period when the latter mace was in temporary use. If placed across the end of the table the difference between the two maces would have been quite obvious to an observant member.

At the first meeting of the Legislative Assembly of Lower Canada it is believed that the mace was placed upon the table in the same lengthwise fashion that it is now positioned in the national assembly.

Mace of the Legislative Council of Quebec (1884–1968)

Material: Gilded brass.

Length: 105 centimetres.

Crowned Head: The crown has four arches with prominent beads simulating pearls down their lengths, which intersect under an orb and cross finial. On the circlet there are four large stylized fleurs-de-lys.

Cap: A velvet fabric forms the cap under the arches.

Head: The head is simply decorated with a series of gadroon ribs, with sepal features ensuing beneath.

Brackets: There are no conventional brackets.

Shaft and Knop: The shaft has a spiralling ribbon effect with foliate forms, including maple leaves. At the top end there is a collar with palm-like motifs

sitting above a protruding knop. Further down the shaft it is separated along its length by two decorated protruding bands.

Foot Knop: The foot knop is encircled with a row of oval shapes, with the mace terminating in a plain button end piece.

Manufacturer: Cyrille Duquet.

Mace of the Quebec National Assembly (1867–present)

Material: Gilded copper.

Length: 106 centimetres.

Crowned Head: The crown has four arches which have plain ridge edges and beading simulating pearls along the centre; these dip down steeply at the intersection with a small plain orb and cross above. Differing from the Ontario mace made by the same maker, here there is no circlet of fleurs-de-lys or crosses paty; instead the arches are directly connected to the "gemstone" band which has alternating lozenges and beads spaced around the top of the mace, and there is a twisted rope-like border above and below.

Cap: This is plain and dome-shaped as a cap of maintenance with folds around the sides. There is no decoration.

Head: From the base of the cup, pronounced acanthus-type foliage covers most of the head, the four plain fields in between carry the applied Royal cypher E II R, which is executed in a unique decorative style, an alteration carried out in 1953. This differs from the traditional Roman-style font.

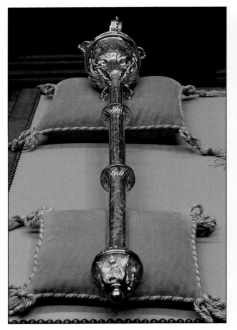

Left: Mace of the National Assembly of Quebec.
Right: Upper end of the Quebec national assembly mace.
Below: The top end of the Quebec mace.

Brackets: The four brackets immediately beneath the head of the mace consist of openwork foliate scrolls.

Shaft and Knop: The shaft, which is ornately covered in floral decoration, is separated by two knops along its length. Each knop flares outward with a plain middle band.

Foot Knop: The mace terminates with a decorated foot knop.

Manufacturer: Charles Zollikoffer.

NOVA SCOTIA

In many ways Nova Scotia is the cradle of Canadian legislative democracy. In 1758 it became the first colony in what was to become the Dominion of Canada to elect representatives, thus attaining representative government. Indeed, at this point in world history, Nova Scotians had a greater ability to participate in their political system than people anywhere in North America, being the first British colony to elect a legislature.

This made Nova Scotia the first colony in the British Empire — including what would become the United States — to attain such a high degree of control over domestic affairs. This served as a template for democratic development in Canada and throughout the Commonwealth. It has been widely observed that, unlike Upper and Lower Canada, constitutional reform in Nova Scotia "was attained not by rebellion or revolt, but through evolution and political process."[23]

After attending the 1841 opening of the legislative assembly, Charles Dickens noted that "it was like looking at Westminster through the wrong end of a telescope."[24]

While the legislature may have appeared like a miniature of the Imperial Parliament, there was one noticeable difference: Nova Scotia did not possess a mace. The sergeant-at-arms simply carried a court sword until 1930.[25]

There were repeated attempts by the House of Assembly to adopt a mace. The first came on 5 December 1785, when it was "Ordered that the Speaker do provide suitable robes for himself and the clerk of the House, as also a mace for the payment of which this House will provide."[26] While it would appear that the robes were purchased, no movement was made on the procurement of a mace. More than three decades later, on 16 April 1819, the House was again seized with the matter. On the motion of Mr. Haliburton it was resolved "that the Clerk of the House do procure against the next Session, Robes for the Speaker and himself and also a mace, for the payment of which this House will provide. And also, that a Chair be provided for the Chairman when the House is in Committee."[27] Again no action was taken on the question of adopting a mace. The topic was reintroduced on 29 January 1840, when Mr. McKim, a member of the House of Assembly, made a motion calling for the purchase of a mace. McKim's reasoning was more practical than ceremonial: "this [the presence of a mace] would relieve the Hon. Speaker — for we could proceed as a legal house whoever was in the chair, while the mace was on the table — and we would be no more than a committee, even if the Speaker was in the chair, while the mace was under the table."[28] Obviously no mace had been adopted prior to this time. The Speaker interjected that "in 1820 [sic] a similar proposition was submitted, but on making enquiries on the subject, it was discovered that the mace was a gift of the Crown to the Commons, and to produce one otherwise, would be like the Commons buying a Crown for themselves."[29]

This explanation, although not entirely correct, satisfied the honourable members and the matter was left in abeyance. An 1881 reference by Charles Clarke notes that "Nova Scotia, although following British forms in other respects, has never adopted 'the bauble,' [mace]."[30]

The present mace was received by the House of Assembly in February 1930, and was first carried by the sergeant-at-arms on 5 March 1930, prior to the speech from the throne. A brief ceremony was presided over by Lieutenant Governor James Tory before a record crowd.[31] Tory noted "the Legislature of Nova Scotia possessed for the first time in its history a mace, the symbol of authority in the British Parliamentary system."[32]

The mace was donated by the Honourable Chief Justice of Nova Scotia Robert E. Harris, although he requested that his name not be associated with the gift until after his death. Harris died on 30 May 1931, and his will stipulated that funds were to be set aside so that the mace could be engraved. This marked the first time in Canadian history that a provincial mace was given as a gift, and it started the pattern that has continued to this day. Previous colonial and provincial maces had been paid for by the treasury on the direction of the governor general or lieutenant governor.

The Nova Scotia mace in the chamber of the legislative assembly.

Sergeant-at-Arms Ken Greenham, CD, carrying the Nova Scotia mace.

Mace of the Province of Nova Scotia (1930–present)

Material: Gilded sterling silver.

Length: 130 centimetres.

Crowned Head: The crown has four arches with pronounced beaded simulated pearl ribs, and a coronet of alternating fleurs-de-lys and crosses paty, with a simulated jewelled band, all of which sits above a pierced through band of scroll shapes, separating it from the main head of the mace. The crown is surmounted by an orb and double cross paty with bead finials.

Cap: Beneath the arches is a plain round cap without decoration.

Head: The cup of the head is highly decorated with four main sections, each separated by lion mask and strap-work vertical panels. The compartments

Nova Scotia mace, upper end.

A representation of the old Great Seal of Nova Scotia displayed on the Nova Scotia mace.

are: the Arms of Nova Scotia; a representation of the Royal Crown of Scotland identified by its multiple crosses fleury and fleurs-de-lys set against a background of thistle and mayflower sprigs; a representation of the Great Seal of Nova Scotia (as used from 1839 to 1879, during the first part of Queen Victoria's reign); and a figure of St. Andrew with a saltire cross behind.

Brackets: There are two tiers of brackets. The upper one is a set of four simple scroll-supports resting on a ring, and immediately below this there are four heraldic crowned lions rampant, each bearing the shield of Nova Scotia in their paws.

Shaft and Knops: At the top end of the shaft immediately below the lion brackets is a very ornate knop covered in mayflowers and thistles, followed by two other protuberances, a knop further down the shaft with a pronounced rib around the centre, then a smaller knop. At the lower end of the shaft there is another set of four brackets made up of "C" scrolls, sitting above a ribbed protuberance.

Foot Knop: The bulbous foot knop is further decorated with four stylized mayflowers, and there is a smaller round terminal beneath this with a flattened end piece.

Engraving: Inscription above the lion brackets:

THIS

MACE

WAS

PRESENTED TO

THE HOUSE OF ASSEMBLY OF THE PROVINCE OF NOVA SCOTIA

BY

THE HONOURABLE ROBERT E. HARRIS CHIEF JUSTICE OF NOVA SCOTIA AND MRS HARRIS

MARCH 1930

Manufacturer and Distinguishing Marks: The mace carries the hallmarks "E & Co," for Elkington & Co. Ltd., Birmingham, England, 1929–1930.

NEW BRUNSWICK

Like Nova Scotia, New Brunswick was comparatively late in obtaining a mace.

There is ample evidence to indicate that a ceremonial staff, nearly two metres in length and topped with a small gilt crown, was used in place of a mace in the presence of the lieutenant governor prior to the donation of the New Brunswick mace in 1937. In some ways it is odd that New Brunswick was so late in adopting a legislative mace given that the legislative council, dating back to colonial times, had possessed a beautifully crafted black rod. Following the abolition of New Brunswick's legislative council in 1892, the black rod continued to be used in the presence of the lieutenant governor in the legislative assembly.

The ceremonial staff was carried by the sergeant-at-arms of the legislative assembly when he was required to attend the lieutenant governor of the province.[33] This usually only occurred during viceregal installations, the opening of the legislature, and Royal assent ceremonies. Charles Clarke noted "the Serjeant carries a staff, as a substitute for the orthodox mace, as he does whenever the Assembly meets the Lieutenant Governor."[34] The ceremonial staff, or "unorthodox mace," was used until the province was presented with its present mace in 1937.

The New Brunswick mace was presented to the province by Lieutenant Governor Murray MacLaren. A physician and colonel, MacLaren had served as a member of the Dominion Parliament from 1921, and was briefly the minister of pensions. MacLaren was appointed lieutenant governor in 1935, a post he would continue in until 1940. Having spent more than fifteen years in Parliament, most of which was spent in the front benches not far from

New Brunswick mace in the chamber.

New Brunswick mace being carried by Sergeant-at-Arms
Daniel Bussières.

where the House of Commons mace sits, MacLaren was well aware that New Brunswick lacked a mace. In a letter to Premier Allison Dysart, MacLaren commented that "careful search and inquiry have not shown that this Province has ever been in possession of a mace. Its acceptance would follow ancient usage and present practice in the Dominion of Canada and in the British Empire."[35] MacLaren viewed the mace as a fitting gift for the Coronation year of King George VI.

The mace was presented to the legislative assembly on 18 February 1937, on the opening day of the second session following MacLaren's delivery of the speech from the throne. MacLaren retired from the chamber following his speech and the mace was then presented to the assembly by the premier.[36] Despite entreaties from Premier Dysart, MacLaren, being a modest man, did not want to be present for the introduction of the mace. Each member of the assembly wore a purple boutonniere of violets on the day the mace was presented. This was a tribute to MacLaren, who had played a central role in the adoption of the purple violet as the provincial flower in 1936.

All partisan considerations were swept aside, despite the fact that MacLaren had been a long-serving federal Conservative politician prior to his appointment as lieutenant governor, and Premier Dysart was leader of the Liberal Party of New Brunswick.

In June 1971, a special case was built and installed in the legislative assembly to publicly display the mace when not in use.[37]

The Royal arms on the cap of the New Brunswick mace are surrounded by the collar insignia of a Knight Grand Commander of the Most Exalted Order of the Star of India. This order was created by Queen Victoria in 1861 and awarded until India's independence in 1947. The Order was only awarded for services rendered to the British Crown in the Indian subcontinent, so its inclusion on the New Brunswick mace is difficult to explain. King George VI was the Sovereign of the Order, however the Order had no direct connection with the province. The New Brunswick mace is likely the last place in the Commonwealth where the insignia of the Order of the Star of India continues to be displayed on a regular basis.

Ceremonial Staff of the Province of New Brunswick
(1867–1937)

Material: Painted wood with brass fittings.
Length: 181 centimetres.
Upper End: A small, solid St. Edward's-styled crown with four arches, orb, and

cross paty, with crosses paty and fleurs-de-lys around the band. This forms the finial attached to a cylindrical collar at the top end of a long pole.

Main Shaft: Painted black, the shaft is a simple wood-turned pole.

Manufacturer and Distinguishing Marks: None.

Other: The head of the ceremonial staff is remarkably similar to those often found on the rods of office carried by "People's Wardens" in the Anglican Church of Canada and Church of England. It is likely that the New Brunswick ceremonial staff is an improvised People's Warden rod of office, the principle difference being the length of the pole. The ecclesiastical version is usually not more than 125 centimetres in length, while the ceremonial staff is considerably longer, at 181 centimetres.

Mace of the Province of New Brunswick (1937–present)

Material: Gilded sterling silver.

Length: 133 centimetres.

Crowned Head: The crown has a coronet of alternating fleurs-de-lys and crosses paty, four of each, and a band of simulated jewels. The two semicircular main arches cross over, each have a central rib along the length of beaded simulated pearls. A beaded orb and cross paty sit above at the intersection.

Cap: The cap of maintenance is a domed area beneath the arches, and in its centre are the Royal arms of King George VI surrounded by the collar insignia of a Knight Grand Commander of the Most Exalted Order of the Star of India.

Head: The head of the mace is divided into four small rectangular shapes with the violet flower at the base of the cup forming partitions. The main motifs in sequence are the crowned arms of New Brunswick, the crowned Royal cypher of King George VI, a representation of the first Great Seal of New Brunswick (with sailing ship at anchor on the Saint John River), and a second crowned Royal cypher.

Brackets: Four brackets made up of "C" scrolls connect the head of the mace to the upper end of the shaft.

New Brunswick mace, upper end, depicting the first Great Seal of New Brunswick.

Shaft and Knops: Two main knops are positioned along the shaft. One sits just beneath the brackets and it has a pronounced rib decorated in violets, the provincial flower. The other knop is midway down and the rib is decorated with spruce boughs. The upper shaft section carries the red spruce motif, and the lower section the Canadian maple leaf motif.

Foot Knop: The mace terminates in an inverted desk-bell-shaped foot knop with a rosette button, the banded rib is decorated in violets.

Manufacturer and Distinguishing Marks: Hallmarked "G & S Co Ld" for the Goldsmiths & Silversmiths Company Ltd., London, England, 1936–1937.

PRINCE EDWARD ISLAND

The first election for the colonial legislative assembly took place in 1773, following which the sergeant-at-arms commented "this is a damned queer parliament." He was promptly fined and fired for showing such disrespect towards the honourable members.[38] Prince Edward Island (P.E.I.) was the last colony in British North America to achieve responsible government, which came in 1851. The colony played a central role in the Confederation debates which led to the creation of the Dominion of Canada in 1867, although P.E.I. did not join Confederation until 1871. The 1864 Charlottetown Conference was a pivotal event in the movement towards joining the various British North American colonies into one entity.

P.E.I. is the home to a number of peculiar developments in Canadian legislative history. It was the last province to adopt the secret ballot voting

The Prince Edward Island legislative assembly chamber.

method, which came into effect in 1913. Until 1922, employees of the Dominion Government were prevented from voting in provincial elections, as a bulwark against outside interference. These unique traits speak to the history of the Island and its desire to retain a unique character.

There is no evidence to indicate that P.E.I. had a mace prior to 1966. The province does, however, possess a ceremonial staff measuring 237 centimetres long. The staff is made of wood with a gilded top, while the remainder is painted black. It has been suggested that the staff was used in place of a mace, although there is no information to verify this.

During the American War of Independence, two American schooners, the *Hancock* and the *Franklin*, sailed into Charlottetown Harbour. On 17 November 1775, the Island's administrator (acting governor), Phillips Callbeck, along with the surveyor general, Thomas Wright, immediately

went down to the beach to meet what they assumed were two fishing vessels. To their surprise they were promptly taken prisoner by Captain John Selman and Charlottetown was sacked by the Americans.[39] Everything of value was purloined, including the island's massive Great Seal, which was made of sterling silver.[40] Callbeck and Wright were released in January 1776, and George Washington apologized for their ordeal.[41] The Great Seal, however, was never returned. Had there been a mace it would have certainly been amongst the items looted by the American raiders, however there is no mention of such an object amongst the stolen items catalogued by Callbeck.

Top: Great Seal of Prince Edward Island, obverse.
Bottom: Great Seal of Prince Edward Island, reverse.

During the 1964 Canadian conference of the Commonwealth Parliamentary Association, which took place in the legislative assembly, the Speaker of the Senate, Speaker of the House of Commons, and the Speakers of all the provincial legislatures agreed that they should present a mace to the province as a gift in honour of the centenary of the Charlottetown Conference of 1864. The gift was to be "an abiding token of goodwill between all Provinces and to commemorate the Centennial of the First Confederation

Sergeant-at-Arms Curtis Adamson carrying the Prince Edward Island mace.

Conference … as a constant reminder to future generations of Canadian goodwill, friendship and unity."[42] After deliberation by the subcommittee of the Commonwealth Parliamentary Association the various details were completed and the mace was finished by December 1965.

A special mace presentation ceremony was held on 24 February 1966, in the legislative assembly. In the presence of Lieutenant Governor Willibald J. MacDonald, the Speaker, Frank Meyers, asked the assembly for permission to allow a delegation from the Canadian Area Council of the Commonwealth Parliamentary Association to enter the chamber. The mace was draped with the Canadian flag and carried into the chamber by Mr. T.R. Montgomery, the honorary secretary-treasurer of the Commonwealth Parliamentary Association. Also in attendance were the Honourable Alan Macnaughton from the House of Commons and Senator Elsie Inman, who represented the Senate.[43] The mace was held by T.R. Montgomery and the Canadian flag was removed by Senator Inman, and the mace was then presented by Macnaughton to the sergeant-at-arms.

Mace of the Province of Price Edward Island (1966–present)

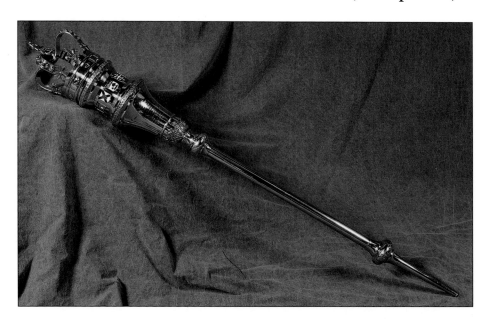

Material: Gilded sterling silver with enamel plaques applied.
Length: 135 centimetres.
Crowned Head: The crown is made up of four arches with ribs of spaced

beads simulating pearls along the centre of each. Alternating fleurs-de-lys and crosses paty, four of each, encircle the coronet section, and at the top above the crossed arches is a stylized cross paty with bead finials. Broadly spaced along the band of the crown, there are lozenges and oblong-shaped simulated jewels.

Cap: The flat circular cap is plain without decoration.

Head: The main head of the mace is made up of two sections. The upper part is a broad band, around which are attached ten coloured enamel plaques representing the arms of the provinces of Canada. Above and below is a thinner band decorated in Canadian maple leaves. The lower part is vase-shaped upon which the three main engravings occur: the arms of Canada, plus two separate inscriptions in English and in French (as detailed below), and just below all this it is embellished with the provincial floral emblem, the lady's slipper.

Brackets: There are no conventional brackets.

Shaft and Knops: The main shaft is plain and in one section, with a knop at each end, both of which carry decoration of the lady's slipper.

Foot: The foot is a tapering extension of the shaft, plain and without decoration, and terminates almost to a point.

Engraving: On the upper section below the head, in both English and French:

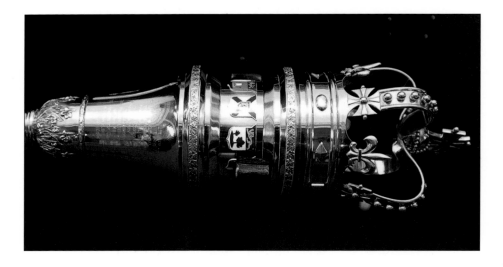

The Prince Edward Island mace, a close-up view of the crowned head with enamelled shields.

PRESENTED TO THE

LEGISLATIVE ASSEMBLY

OF PRINCE EDWARD ISLAND

BY THE FEDERAL AND THE

PROVINCIAL BRANCHES

OF THE COMMONWEALTH

PARLIAMENTARY ASSOCIATION

TO COMMEMORATE THE

ONE HUNDREDTH ANNIVERSARY

OF THE MEETING OF

THE FATHERS OF CONFEDERATION

IN 1864

***

DON DE LA SECTION FÉDÉRALE

ET DES SECTIONS PROVINCIALES

DE L'ASSOCIATION PARLEMENTAIRE

DU COMMONWEALTH

A L'ASSEMBLÉE LÉGISLATIVE

DE L'ILE DU PRINCE-EDOUARD

LORS DU CENTENAIRE

DE AL RÉUNION DER PÈRES

DE LA CONFÉDÉRATION

TENUE À CHARLOTTETOWN

EN 1864

Manufacturer and Distinguishing Marks: Manufacturer's mark, that of Henry Birks & Sons Ltd.

BRITISH COLUMBIA

British Columbia has used six different maces — that's more than any other jurisdiction in British North America. Until 1866, British Columbia was comprised of two separate Crown colonies: the colony of Vancouver Island and the colony of British Columbia. The many different maces speak to the development and expansion of the province from an island colony to Canada's third largest province. British Columbia is the only province in which the replacement of a mace became a public issue, so much so that the topic was debated over the course of three decades.

Mace of the Colony of Vancouver Island

The colony of Vancouver Island was established in 1848, and the first legislative assembly was convened on 12 August 1856. As with many frontier legislative assemblies, in British North America this first mace was fashioned out of a cane pole with the additional luxury of a silvered metal crowned head and decorative band midway down the shaft. Although it appears more like a ceremonial staff, the crowned head indicates that it was intended for use as a legislative mace, however, it may have been an adaptation of a "talking stick" of the sort presented to Aboriginal leaders by the governor. In 1866, when Vancouver Island was amalgamated with British Columbia into one colony, the Vancouver Island colony mace ceased to be used.

For many years following the dissolution of the colony of Vancouver Island the mace was owned by Judge Marsden, who bequeathed it to a Captain Guy, who in turn left it to A.F. Priestley. Priestley sent the mace to auction in December 1936. It was sold to Robert Rankin for the princely sum of $4.[44] Rankin then sold it to Mr. B.A. McKelvie, a local reporter and collector of Canadiana. The mace was subsequently presented to the Shawnigan Lake Boys' School in 1937. Eventually the mace was given to the legislative assembly, where it remains to this day.

Temporary Mace for the Colony of British Columbia

The first meeting of the British Columbia Legislative Assembly (prior to the addition of the Vancouver Island colony) took place on 19 November 1858, at Fort Langley. A makeshift mace was prepared for the opening. It was a small, crude object about a foot long, cut from a flat piece of metal, "hacked out with a pair of tin shears."[45] It is believed that this was used in place of a mace, however there is little documentation to verify the story. This mace was reportedly used at the swearing-in of Governor Sir James Douglas. Like the Vancouver Island mace it entered private hands, becoming the property of Sir Henry P.P. Crease. In 1947 it was acquired by the reeve of Langly, Noel Booth, who deposited it for safekeeping with the British Columbia Provincial Archives.[46] It is presently stored at the Legislative Building.

Mace of the Colony of British Columbia

The first British Columbia colonial mace was replaced in 1866 when

Vancouver Island was united with the mainland colonies into the colony of British Columbia. The first session of the Legislative Council of the Colony of British Columbia was opened at New Westminster on 21 January 1864, by Governor Douglas. A new mace had been crafted for this occasion, as the old temporary mace of the Colony of British Columbia was inappropriate, and it would appear that the mace from the Colony of Vancouver Island was simply not transported to New Westminster. This new mace was used until British Columbia entered Confederation in 1871. Documents related to this mace note that "this mace cannot be located," and there is no surviving description of the object.[47]

First Provincial Mace

The first session of the legislative assembly of the province of British Columbia took place on 17 February 1872. It was reported that the new mace "is a very handsome article made of wood, is gilded and about three feet long. It is surmounted by an excellently carved crown and Grecian cross."[48] This mace was carved by C. Bunting, a Victoria cabinetmaker, and the gilding and painting of the mace was executed by a Mr. Keohan. No cost was associated with this mace, although the Public Accounts for 1873 note that Mr. Keohan was paid $5 to re-gild the mace, and in subsequent years he was paid $1 to clean the object.[49]

Second Provincial Mace: The Chicago Mace

As the wealth and importance of the province grew, it was decided to construct a new legislature for the province in 1895. The magnificent structure was completed by 1898, and it was felt that a new metal mace should be completed for the opening of the new legislative building. The Chicago metalworking firm of Winslow Brothers was contracted to craft the new mace, along with a bulk lot of bronze inkwell covers. The mace was quite unconventional, being more stylistic in form than traditional. The project cost a total of $150.[50] Along with the inkwell covers, the Chicago mace would serve as a conversation piece and point of controversy for the following forty-six years. It was first put into use at the opening of the new legislature on 10 February 1898.

The Chicago mace was the source of much derision by members of the legislature and the general public almost from the moment it was adopted. The cross atop the crown became loose on a number of occasions and was reaffixed with plumbing solder. For many years a rumour circulated that the mace originated as "part of the paraphernalia of some waxwork dummy exhibited at the Chicago World's Fair in 1893, and fell into the hands of wreckers who sold it to junk dealers and eventually it passed onto Winslow Bros., who in turn disposed of it to the Provincial Government."[51] This claim is impossible to verify, and it might well have been just a clever ruse to increase support for a new mace.

The question of British Columbia acquiring a new mace was brought to a head in 1949 after the provincial government agreed to gift a mace to Newfoundland on the occasion of that province's entry into Confederation. Having just spent $4,000 on a mace for Canada's newest province, British Columbia was hardly in a position to claim it was unable to undertake a similar project for its own assembly.

The public campaign for British Columbia to obtain a new mace was led by B.A. "Pinkie" McKelvie, the very same man who purchased the mace of the Vancouver Island colony in 1936. For thirty years McKelvie, a reporter for the *Vancouver Province* (Victoria Bureau) and member of the legislative press gallery, worked to have the Chicago mace replaced. He regularly wrote articles on the subject.

Queen Elizabeth II Mace

Premier W.A.C. Bennett decided that the coronation year of Her Majesty the Queen would be a fitting occasion for the province to adopt a new mace. The Victoria silversmiths, Jefferies & Company, were commissioned to produce the new symbol of authority. The new mace was inaugurated at the opening of the 1954 session of the legislature on 16 February.

The provincial secretary, W.D. Black, gave the assembly a history of the various maces that had been used in British Columbia dating back to colonial times. On a motion made by Premier W.A.C. Bennett, it was moved "that the new Royal Mace, now resting in the Speaker's Chambers, be substituted for the present one as the emblem of Mr. Speaker's authority, and that the present one be then consigned to the Provincial Archives."[52] For the first time since 1917 a member of the general public was called to the bar of the assembly. Willard Ireland, the provincial archivist, was called and asked to deposit the Chicago mace in the provincial archives for posterity.

Sergeant-at-Arms Anthony Humphreys, CD, carrying the British Columbia mace.

Colony of Vancouver Island Mace (1856–1866)

Material: Wood cane with silvered metal mounts.

Length: 144 centimetres.

Crowned Head: A traditional Victorian crown forms the finial of this ceremonial staff, with a circlet of fleurs-de-lys and crosses paty and simulated jewels on the band. Foliate scrolls decorate the lower part of the head.

Shaft: The shaft is made of cane with a decorative metal band fitted partway down.

Manufacturer and Distinguishing Marks: None.

The Colony of Vancouver Island mace, upper end.

Province of British Columbia Mace (1872–1898)

Material: Gilded wood.

Length: 95.5 centimetres.

Crowned Head: The top of the mace is carved from a solid piece of wood, the simplified crown has four arches with simulated pearl ribs, surmounted by an orb now missing its cross finial. There are four pronounced fleur-de-lys-type forms around the circlet, alternating with four small crosses paty, and the band of the crown is plain. Beneath the crown is a carved foliate form.

Shaft and Knops: The plain slender shaft has a small turned knop at the top end, and halfway down and terminates with an acorn finial at the base.

Manufacturer and Distinguishing Marks: The mace was carved by Mr. C. Bunting, a Victoria cabinetmaker working on Yates Street, and the gilding was carried out by Mr. Keohan. No maker's marks.

The first provincial mace of British Columbia, upper end.

Province of British Columbia Chicago Mace (1898–1954)

Material: Brass.
Length: 97 centimetres.

Crowned Head: The crown has four tapering arches with beads simulating pearls, and a simple cross paty in the centre. The cap is pierced through. The circlet has alternating fleurs-de-lys and crosses paty, four of each, and these sit upon a simulated jewelled band.

Shaft and Knops: At the upper end of the plain narrow shaft is a collar with foliate-type decoration. There is a simple pierced-through knop halfway down, and the end piece is decorated.

A close-up view of the second British Columbia mace.

Manufacturer and Distinguishing Marks: No maker's marks. Made by metalworkers Winslow Brothers of Chicago.

Province of British Columbia Queen Elizabeth Mace
(1954–present)

Material: Gilded sterling silver.

Length: 103.5 centimetres.

Crowned Head: The crown of traditional form has four arches with simulated jewels along the middle and beaded outer edges. In the centre there is an orb with beading surmounted by a crowned scrolled shield with the Royal cypher E II R on both sides. The arches join a circlet of alternating fleurs-de-lys and crosses paty, four of each. The band has beaded borders.

Cap: The cap of maintenance is undecorated and dome-shaped, with concentric circles rising to a flat button in the centre.

Head: The head is divided into four parts, separated by bracket-like attachments with palm leaf tops. On two sides are the chased arms of Canada, and opposite the arms of British Columbia with an enamelled shield. The other two sides on the head of the mace have chased decoration inspired by the murals

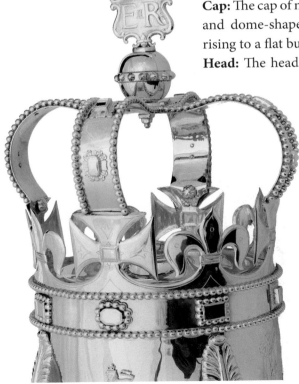

The crown on the British Columbia Queen Elizabeth II mace.

The arms of British Columbia on the British Columbia Queen Elizabeth II mace.

in the rotunda of the legislative assembly building, representing the four main industries of the province: forestry, fishing, mining, and agriculture.

Brackets: Four scroll brackets are positioned immediately below the head of the mace and they rest upon the upper knop.

The foot knop of the British Columbia Queen Elizabeth II mace.

Shaft and Knops: Positioned along the plain shaft there are three knops equally spaced apart, each having a plain pronounced rib with wave motifs on either side. An inscription is engraved on the shaft (see details below).

Foot Knop: The dogwood, the British Columbia provincial flower, is featured on the foot knop in between bracket-like attachments. Further decoration includes the wave and the palm leaf motifs. The mace terminates in a circular button end piece.

Engraving: Located on the shaft of the mace:

FIRST USED AT THE SECOND SESSION

OF THE

TWENTY-FOURTH LEGISLATIVE ASSEMBLY

OF BRITISH COLUMBIA

1954

Manufacturer and Distinguishing Marks: The mace carries the marks of Jefferies & Company, local Victoria silversmiths.

MANITOBA

Despite the "rustic quality"[53] of the early Legislative Assembly of Manitoba, the province has possessed a mace since entering Confederation in 1870. The early mace was fashioned out of wood, most likely on account of the ease with which it could be shaped into a traditional-looking mace. Indeed the first early Manitoba mace managed to incorporate a number of distinctive local and historical elements.

The original Manitoba mace was made primarily from two unique pieces of wood. The head was carved out of the wheel hub of a Red River cart by a soldier who served in General Garnet Wolsely's Red River Expedition during the Riel Rebellion of 1870. The shaft of the mace was made from a flagstaff used by the Canadian Militia during the Riel Rebellion.[54] The mace was then gilded by Henry J.H. Clarke, the province's first attorney general, who went on to become premier from 1872 to 1874.

The mace was put into use on 15 March 1871, during the opening of the first Legislative Assembly of Manitoba, which took place at the home of A.G.B. Bannatyne, a Winnipeg entrepreneur who had previously been a member of the Council of Assiniboia, the legislative body that governed Rupert's Land prior to Manitoba entering Confederation. The wooden mace escaped fire on 3 December 1873, and would go on to be used in four of the province's legislatures. Some question has been raised as to the likelihood that the original mace was really made from the hub of a Red River cart and flagstaff.[55] Upon close examination one finds that the head of the mace is indeed the same size of a Red River cart-wheel hub, and the shaft also conforms to the type and size of turned wood often used by the Canadian militia for a parade flagpole, thus the story does have validity.

A new mace was commissioned in late 1883, the project being given to the Montreal firm of E. Chanteloup Ltd., which was more noted for its manufacture of parabolic metallic reflector lanterns for lighthouses.[56] Of all the surviving Canadian maces to date, the Manitoba mace is one of the heaviest to carry. It was first carried on 13 March 1884, at the opening of the then new legislature. When the legislature moved to its fifth and current location in 1920, the original mace was placed on display and the new mace was put to use in the assembly. Purely conjectural as a point of observation, this mace, when compared with a surviving photograph, bears a close resemblance to the ill-fated House of Commons mace that perished in the parliamentary fire of 1916, which may suggest that the two were made by the same manufacturers.

Sergeant-at-Arms Garry Clark carrying the Manitoba mace in the legislative assembly chamber.

The 1871 Manitoba Wooden Mace (1871–1884)

Material: Painted wood.
Length: 86 centimetres.
Crowned Head: The head of the mace is carved from a solid piece of wood and painted gold. It was originally a Red River cart-wheel hub. At the top is a cube incised with cross paty markings on four sides, and this is positioned between two round orb shapes, one above and one below the cube. The crown is of a Victorian style, having four beaded arches ensuing from a coronet of alternating fleurs-de-lys and crosses paty, and the band is carved with simulated jewels. The cap of maintenance is a solid part of the wood block, and the head of the mace is plain upon which sits the crown.
Shaft: The shaft was taken from a flagstaff and is a straight turned wood pole painted blue at each end. The base has a round ball end piece.
Manufacturer and Distinguishing Marks: None.

The Manitoba Mace (1884–present)

Material: Gilded brass.
Length: 149 centimetres.
Crowned Head: At the top of the crown alongside the orb and cross paty there are four beaver models crouched where the four arches curve downwards at the centre. The arches are beaded with simulated pearls, and have corded borders and scalloped edges. The coronet section has alternating fleurs-de-lys and crosses paty, four of each, attached to a band with corded borders that are set with cabochon and faceted coloured stones in a variety of shades (including green, red, pale blue, and brown).
Cap: The domed cap is undecorated with a plain flat disc.

Above: The modelled beavers on the crown of the Manitoba mace.
Right: Close-up view of the crowned head of the Manitoba mace.

Head: The head has an overall elongated proportion. There are four compartments with laurel arches, separated by a bare-chested terminal figure, each wearing a feathered coronet and draped robes from the waist down. Within these sections are the Royal cypher "VR" of Queen Victoria and a crown, together with the rose, fleur-de-lys, harp, and thistle.

Brackets: These are of a traditional type, four bare-chested figures combined with openwork scrolls.

Shaft and Knops: The shaft is divided into three sections by two pronounced knops with gadroons and patterned central rib. Along the length the shaft is decorated in stylized roses and thistles, interlaced with a spiral ribbon.

Foot Knop: At the base of the mace the foot knop is an inverted vase and bell shape, decorated in five-petal roses, thistles, and fleurs-de-lys, with a patterned round ball end.

172

Manufacturer and Distinguishing Marks: Stamped on the foot knop is E. CHANTELOUP, MONTREAL.

SASKATCHEWAN

The province of Saskatchewan was quick to commission the production of a mace shortly after entering Confederation in 1905. The Saskatchewan mace is the only mace currently in use in Canada that has always borne the Royal cypher of King Edward VII[57] and not undergone any update. As one of Canada's most politically competitive and politically engaged provinces,[58] it is not surprising that the adoption of their mace in 1906 was a very public affair. On the day the mace was shipped from its Toronto manufacturer, *The Globe* noted that "A more beautiful specimen of metal-craft would be difficult to imagine."[59] When the mace arrived in Regina, *The Leader* exclaimed: "It is a massive affair and magnificently designed."[60] There was no shortage of pride in the fact that the mace had been made in Canada, and that it was of a traditional design that incorporated a variety of Canadian symbols.

The mace acquisition project was left in the charge of F.J. Robinson, the deputy commissioner of public works. Robinson was a resourceful man who was keen to see that the mace be an object of beauty and quality, but you could not just order a mace out of the Hudson's Bay Company or Eaton's catalogue. Nevertheless he did the next best thing and contacted a well-respected Toronto law firm to look after the project. E.M. Chadwick contracted the Toronto silversmiths Ryrie Brothers to manufacture the mace.[61] Given the limited budget of the project, it was decided to make the mace from gilded brass as opposed to sterling silver.

There was a slight cost overrun on account of "certain ornamentation which you [Robinson] desired to have."[62] When the mace arrived Robinson did not complain about the increased cost, remarking, "I am especially pleased with the sheaf of wheat and the beaver and also the manner in which the maple leaves were worked in with the rose, thistle and shamrock."[63] The final article cost a very reasonable $340,[64] making it one of the least expensive maces in Canada, despite its high quality. The new mace was paraded in with Lieutenant Governor Amédée Forget at the inauguration of the legislative assembly on 29 March 1906. The Saskatchewan mace includes the phrase *A Mari usque ad Mare* (From Sea to Sea), which would become Canada's official motto with the granting of the Canadian Coat of Arms by King George V in 1921. This is the first official object where the motto was used.

The Saskatchewan Legislative Assembly chamber with the mace.

On the occasion of the one hundredth anniversary of the opening of the Saskatchewan Legislative Assembly a special ceremony was held by Speaker Myron Kowalsky. A special mace runner (a small embroidered carpet-like piece of cloth) and mace cushion were presented to the legislative assembly by Chief Alphonse Bird, of the Federation of Saskatchewan Indian Nations. The two items were unveiled by Chief Bird and presented to Lieutenant Governor Linda Haverstock. The mace runner and cushion are intended to "serve as a permanent reminder of the on-going role played by First Nations in the history of the province."[65] The runner is a beaded moose hide that incorporates traditional Native symbols and craftsmanship. The mace cushion is made from a beaver pelt backed with moose hide. It was indeed a symbolic and fitting gift, as the mace, which is the symbol of the authority of the legislature, now rests on the mace runner given by the Native people of Saskatchewan, much in the same way many of the first settlers of the Canadian West had to rely upon Canada's First Nations for guidance on how to use the resources of the land to live and thrive.

Sergeant-at-Arms Patrick Shaw carrying the Saskatchewan mace.

Province of Saskatchewan Mace (1906–present)

Material: Gilded brass.
Length: 120 centimetres.
Crowned Head: A traditional crown shape is displayed, with a coronet of alternating fleurs-de-lys and crosses paty, four of each. These encircle a band with

A close-up view of the crowned head of the Saskatchewan mace.

Showing the arms plate beneath the arches of the Saskatchewan mace.

twisted rope edges and lozenge-shaped simulated jewels along the centre. The four arches have pronounced beaded ribs simulating pearls, and at the intersection there is an orb and cross paty with bead finials. On the underside of the arches where they join the coronet there is a Canadian maple leaf at each point.

Cap: The flat arms plate beneath the arches carries the Royal arms of King Edward VII.

Head: The head of the mace has four main motifs, a wheat-sheaf above a beaver on two opposite sides, alternating with the Royal cypher of King Edward VII in between. An elaborate decorated area covers the lower third of the cup, incorporating the rose, thistle, shamrock, and Canadian maple leaf.

Brackets: There are no brackets.

Shaft and Knops: The shaft is divided into thirds with two gadroon knops positioned along its length. The spiralling floral decoration along the shaft incorporates the rose, thistle, shamrock, and Canadian maple leaf.

Foot Knop: The foot knop is of medium proportion and decorated with the same symbols previously mentioned. The mace terminates in a rounded button end piece.

Manufacturer and Distinguishing Marks: Supplied by Ryrie Brothers Limited, jewellers, Toronto.

The Saskatchewan mace viewed to show the elaborate decoration on the underside of the mace head.

ALBERTA

The process by which Alberta commissioned its first mace is certainly unique in Canada, and is a reflection of the ingenuity of those settlers who travelled to the Canadian prairies to establish the provinces of Alberta and Saskatchewan. The first meeting of the Legislative Assembly of Alberta took place on 14 March 1906. Given that the legislative building was not yet complete, the assembly met in the Thistle Skating Rink in Edmonton, which had been converted to serve as a temporary legislature. As was the case in Saskatchewan, a great deal of thought was put into various details related to the meeting of the first legislature, and while the adoption of a coat of arms[66] and robes for various officials were dealt with early on, no one gave much thought to the need for a mace. This was not a unique situation. In 1901, following the federation of the Australian states into the Commonwealth of Australia, the new federal House of Representatives was without a mace for its first session and had to borrow its mace from the State of Victoria.[67]

First meeting of the Alberta Legislature, 1906. The temporary mace can be seen resting on a pillow in the middle of the clerk's table.

Little more than a week prior to the opening of the legislature the contract for manufacturing Alberta's first mace, sometimes colloquially known as the "shaving mug mace," was given to Ernest and Edward Watson of Watson Brother Jewellers who were located in Calgary. The task of building the mace was contracted out to Rufus E. Butterworth, a pattern maker and freight carpenter with the Canadian Pacific Railway. Butterworth worked in the C.P.R.'s Alyth Yard in Calgary overseeing the repair of freight cars and other rolling stock. Butterworth used materials that were not only inexpensive and durable, but those which he was accustomed to working with.

Butterworth's final product was remarkably respectable in appearance and incorporated some very unusual materials. The shaft of the mace was fashioned from iron plumbing pipe and parts of a brass bedstead. The foot knop was made from a plumbing float taken from the holding tank of a flush toilet. The small brackets made to look like mermaids were handles taken from metal shaving mugs.

It is quite likely that Watson Brothers Jewellers made a handsome profit out of the mace for this rushed job given that they charged the provincial government $150[68] for the final product, which was composed from odds and ends; however the craftsmanship was ingenious.

On the opening day of the Legislature, the *Journals* record, the clerk, having asked if there were other nominations for Speaker, put the motion forward and declared the "Ayes" had it. He then declared Charles Wellington Fisher duly elected Speaker.

The Speaker retired and re-entered the House between the premier and attorney general, who escorted him to the chair.

The Speaker, standing on the upper step, briefly thanked the House for the honour conferred upon him. The Speaker took his seat and the mace was placed on the table by the clerk.[69]

Although the shaving mug mace was only intended for temporary use it was carried by the sergeant-at-arms for fifty years. By the early 1950s it was beginning to show its age, having been repainted on a number of occasions. The provincial government began to consider the purchase of a new mace made of precious metal to honour the province's impending golden jubilee. The Civil Service Association of Alberta indicated that they would be willing to give a mace in honour of the province's golden jubilee as a token of their loyalty and devotion to the province. The magnificent new mace was presented to the legislature following the opening of the thirteenth session of the Legislative Assembly of Alberta on 9 February

Sergeant-at-Arms Brian Hodgson, CD, carrying the Alberta jubilee mace.

1956. Lieutenant Governor J.J. Bowden (having read the speech from the throne), Premier Ernest Manning, and the Leader of the Opposition Harper Prouse discharged the usual formalities that occur on an opening day and the Speaker promptly adjourned the assembly. Within a quarter hour, members of the assembly again assembled in the chamber for the mace presentation ceremony.[70] Anthony Earshaw, president of the Civil Service Association; Lieutenant Colonel Roy Harrison, the executive secretary of the association; and W.T. Aitken, who had worked as a civil servant in Alberta when it was still administered by the North West Territories Council, entered the chamber with the new mace. Earshaw explained that the new mace "will serve as a constant reminder that Governmental and Civil Servants must work hand in hand to administer and provide essential services for the people."[71] Lieutenant Colonel Harrison then presented the mace to the Speaker, the Honourable Peter Dawson.

The golden jubilee mace was designed by L.B. Blain of Edmonton, thus like the original mace it was designed by an Albertan, although the new mace was manufactured in the United Kingdom.

Province of Alberta Temporary Mace (1905–1955)

Material: A variety of unusual local materials were used, including a brass bedstead, plumbing pipe, handles of shaving mugs, and a wood block. The whole is embellished with gold and white paint and a red velvet cap.

Length: 88.5 centimetres.

Crowned Head: The notable features are four small beavers above the arches of the crown; only the orb remains, the cross having been broken off. The four arches with zigzag edgings have a single row of beads along the centre, which ensue from a coronet with crosses paty and fleurs-de-lys.

Cap: This is a dome-shaped block of wood covered in now-faded red velvet.

Head: The mace head is divided into four parts separated by armless figures wearing mural crowns connected by arches. In each compartment is the Royal cypher of King Edward VII with crown, above a rose, thistle, harp, and fleur-de-lys.

Brackets: Four mermaid-like figures as brackets support the head of the mace; these components originated from handles of shaving mugs.

Shaft and Knops: This is made from a tube of plumbing pipe with two knops along the length believed to have been taken from a brass bedstead.

Foot Knop: The bulbous end thought to be a plumbing float sits next to a round end piece.

Manufacture and Distinguishing Marks: No maker's mark. Commissioned via Watson Brothers Jewellers, Calgary, and made by Rufus E. Butterworth, a pattern maker and carpenter from the Canadian Pacific Railway.

Province of Alberta Jubilee Mace (1955–present)

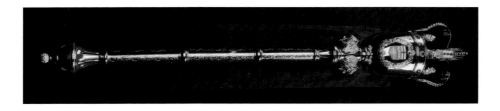

The enamelled arms of Alberta on the head of the mace.

Material: Gilded-sterling silver with enamel work on the shield, set with gemstones on the band of the crown.

Length: 129 centimetres.

Crowned Head: The four arches of the crown are beaded simulating pearls along the lengths, and curve downwards in the centre. On the top is an orb with a beaver finial. The arches ensue from a coronet with stylized Alberta emblems, alternating wheat sheaves and wild roses, four of each; the band is set with cabochon gemstones chosen to represent the word ALBERTA — amethyst, lapis lazuli, bloodstone, emerald, ruby, topaz, and agate (jasper).

Cap: On the circular cap beneath the arches are two full coats of arms side by side: the Royal arms of the United Kingdom and the Royal arms of Canada.

Head: On one side is an enamelled applied shield of the Arms of Alberta within a circular embossed wreath of wild roses and wheat; and on other side of the head of the mace is an engraved inscription (as detailed below).

Brackets: In lieu of traditional brackets, two finely-modelled bison heads are placed below the mace head at the top end of the shaft.

Shaft and Knops: The shaft, which is engraved with entwined Alberta wild roses, has two simple knops along its length.

Foot Knop: The base of the mace has a flared foot knop, and terminates with a wheat sheaf end piece.

The view of the crown on the Alberta jubilee mace.

Engraving: Engraved on the head:

THE CIVIL SERVICE ASSOCIATION OF ALBERTA

PRESENTED THIS MACE TO THE PEOPLE OF

THE PROVINCE OF ALBERTA

A close-up view of the bison heads on the Alberta mace.

TO BE HELD IN TRUST

BY THE LEGISLATIVE ASSEMBLY

AS AN EXPRESSION OF LOYALTY

AND IN COMMEMORATION OF

ALBERTA'S GOLDEN JUBILEE

1905 – 1955

Manufacturer and Distinguishing Marks: Marked with the sterling silver hallmarks "JF" Birmingham, 1955. The mace was designed by Lawrence B. Blain, who worked for the jewellers Irving Kline Ltd., Edmonton. It was then manufactured in England by the firm Joseph Fray Ltd.

NEWFOUNDLAND AND LABRADOR

Despite being the first part of Canada to be settled by Europeans, Newfoundland and Labrador, as the most recent province to join Confederation, has one of the most recently produced maces. The story of Newfoundland and Labrador's pre-Confederation wooden mace serves as the source of many amusing stories of just how free-spirited the invention of tradition and treatment of state symbols was in the early days of democratic development.

The mace used by the Legislative Assembly of Newfoundland and Labrador was presented as a gift to the province on behalf of the people and province of British Columbia. On 5 April 1950, the Honourable Herbert Anscomb, deputy premier and minister of finance of British Columbia, presented the mace to the assembly as a gift from the Dominion's westernmost province. In excerpts taken from the House of Assembly proceedings, Anscomb explained:

> A great deal of thought has been given to the designing of this Mace, which you will see for yourselves is a massive piece of furniture. It is made of sterling silver and is gold plated, both precious metals being products of British Columbia's mines.... At the top of the Mace is a replica of the British Crown complete except for the jewels, which are represented by gold plated silver insets.... Below the replica of the British Crown is a band of dogwood flowers, British Columbia's floral emblem, and maple leaves, representative of Canada as a whole.... Below the Crown, and serving as a top for the main bowl, is the Royal Coat of Arms [of the United Kingdom]. In four panels around the side of the bowl are the Coats of Arms of Canada, Newfoundland, and British Columbia and the G. R. VI. [Royal Cypher of King George VI]. Each panel is divided by lines of golden rope, symbolizing the Shipping Industry of Newfoundland and British Columbia.... Supporting the bowl on the staff are three dolphins, representing the Fishing Industry of both provinces. The rope motif is continued in ornamentation down the shaft on the Mace, while on the ball at the bottom is the official British Columbia emblem of the Thunderbird with a whale in its talons.... Whereas the thunderbird is a symbol of creation in the minds of the Aborigines [sic] of British Columbia, I think its presence on the Mace will be identified with the creation of the new province of Canada.[72]

The presentation of the new mace prompted a unique moment in the history of Canadian symbols of sovereignty. The old Newfoundland mace, which is believed to date from 1832, was retired by a motion made by Premier Joey Smallwood on the same day the new mace was presented. Usually retired maces were stored away or put on display never to be used again, but this marked the first time that an actual legislative motion was introduced to "thank" the old mace and reflect upon the history which it had endured. "It was witness to the activities of some of our greatest men.... Spare a thought for all the sentimental past represented in that Mace," said Smallwood.[73]

The original Newfoundland mace, or colonial mace, had a colourful history, which became part of the lore of the land. Newfoundland was granted representative government in 1832 and the legislative assembly immediately adopted a mace along with an "elaborately upholstered chair"[74] for the Speaker. The mace was fashioned out of wood, and gilded and painted in a respectable manner. The colony was well on its way to adopting the necessary symbols modelled on the Parliament at Westminster, aside from the fact that they did not possess a building in which to assemble the colony's legislative assembly. Thus the fifteen members of the assembly rented the house of Mrs. Mary Travers. Following the first session of the assembly Mrs. Travers was owed £103.6s.8d in rent — a rather considerable sum of money.[75] As payment was not forthcoming, Mrs. Travers listed the items left behind for sale. This included the mace, Speaker's desk, sword, and other contents of the temporary assembly. Members of the House of Assembly promptly appealed to the governor to intervene and save the various items from dispersal. Mrs. Travers agreed to return the items, although it was not for more than two decades that she was finally reimbursed.

The second significant event in the life of Newfoundland's colonial mace occurred in 1838. This incident resulted in a long legal battle and provided much amusement for the residents of St. John's and afforded them the spectacle of the mace in action outside the legislature. On the morning of August 6, John Kent, member of the legislative assembly for St. John's East, met Dr. Edward Kielly of the St. John's General Hospital in the streets of the capital. Dr. Kielly threatened and insulted Kent on account of derogatory statements that Kent had recently made about the St. John's General Hospital in the legislative assembly.[76] Dr. Kielly had called Kent a "puppy" and threatened to "pull his nose," on account of the comments made in the assembly. Kent was well aware of his privilege as a member of the legislative assembly and reported the incident to the House, which immediately took up the issue. It is worth noting that the Speaker of the legislative assembly was Dr. William Carson, who had been removed as the colony's medical officer the previous year and replaced by Kielly. Two witnesses were called to corroborate Kent's version of events, and shortly after hearing their testimony the House agreed that Dr. Kielly was in "gross breach of the privileges of this House." A Speaker's warrant was subsequently issued for the arrest of Dr. Kielly, and the sergeant-at-arms was dispatched into the streets of St. John's to "the great merriment of the following throng"[77] of onlookers.

Kielly was located in due course, and on 7 August he was brought before the bar of the House in the custody of the mace-wielding sergeant-at-arms. The clerk read the evidence to Kielly and the Speaker then offered him an opportunity to explain. Kielly immediately lost his temper and called Kent a liar and "many contumelious epithets."[78] The House ordered Dr. Kielly to leave and subsequently voted to remand him to the custody of the sergeant-at-arms, although more drastic suggestions emanated from one honourable member. By 9 August, the House decided to discharge Dr. Kielly, providing he agreed to pay all the associated expenses and to apologize. Kielly was again brought to the bar and again refused to apologize. By this point the House of Assembly had stomached enough of the irascible doctor and they sent him back to jail. On 11 August, the Speaker decided that it was time to call Dr. Kielly before the bar once again, perhaps with the expectation that his time in jail would have been cause for reflection. The high sheriff appeared before the House and informed the Speaker that Kielly had been released on a writ of *habeas corpus*, issued by Judge George Lilly, who had discharged him. The Judge had ruled that "the prisoner, having been brought before me on a writ, and after perusing the return of the sheriff hereto, I am of the opinion that the process by which the prisoner is held in custody is void."[79] The House of Assembly reacted with swift resolve and recommended that both the judge and sheriff be imprisoned for acting "in gross contempt of the Speaker's warrant."[80] The morning of 13 August 1838, brought the citizens of St. John's the spectacle of a judge of the Supreme Court being lead through the town to the jail by the assembly's sergeant-at-arms bearing the mace. High Sheriff Garrett was similarly paraded and imprisoned, although Dr. Kielly remained at large.

The entire situation was quickly spinning out of control. The House of Assembly ultimately decided to send a deputation to Canada and Lord Durham, the governor general and High Commissioner of British North America. The Speaker, Dr. William Carson, and one member, Peter Browne, were chosen to be the delegates to Lord Durham. Governor Sir Henry Prescott was not amused, and in an attempt to calm the situation agreed to pass the Revenue Bill, which the House had been considering prior to the succession of Speaker's warrants. The House saw through this thinly veiled attempt to interfere in a matter of parliamentary privilege. Governor Prescott was exasperated and quickly prorogued the House. The authority of the Speaker's warrants having expired with the prorogation, Judge Lilly and Sheriff Garrett were promptly released.[81]

The case was subsequently heard by the Supreme Court of Newfoundland, which concurred with the actions of the House of Assembly. Ultimately the decision was overruled by the Judicial Committee of the Privy Council (JCPC) in 1842. The JCPC ruled that the privileges of the British House of Commons were peculiar and inherent in the Parliament of the United Kingdom and not transferred to colonial legislatures.[82] The wooden mace was never again to be paraded through the streets of St. John's.

The most recent incident involving the wooden mace occurred following the 1917 opening of the House of Assembly. Governor Sir Walter Edward Davidson inadvertently failed to shake the hand of the sergeant-at-arms following the speech from the throne. The long-held tradition that the governor would shake hands with all members of the assembly along with the sergeant-at-arms and the clerks was not lost upon the then sergeant-at-arms, Robert Walsh. Walsh felt that the governor had failed to treat the mace with a proper amount of respect and immediately wrote him a letter demanding an apology. When Prime Minister Sir Edward Morris learned of the incident and subsequent letter to the governor he told Walsh that he had been foolish and would likely lose his job as sergeant-at-arms. This was, however, not the case. Governor Davidson issued an apology and would go on to propose a toast "to the mace and the macebearers."[83]

The Newfoundland and Labrador mace in the legislative assembly chamber.

Sergeant-at-Arms Elizabeth Gallagher carrying the Newfoundland and Labrador mace.

There has long been discussion about whether or not the wooden Newfoundland mace was the original one from 1832. Even Joey Smallwood entered into the debate in 1950, convinced that while the mace was certainly a century old, it was probably not the original one from 1832 that was saved from Mrs. Travers's eviction sale.[84] Nevertheless, there is no record that the original mace was lost or destroyed, only repainted on many occasions.

Colony/Dominion of Newfoundland Mace (1832–1950)

Material: Pine wood painted gilt, red, blue, and black.

Length: 98 centimetres.

Crowned Head: The gilt crown is carved in a simplified form, four beaded arches intersect with an orb and cross paty in the centre at the top, fleurs-de-lys and crosses paty alternate around the band, which is decorated with painted red and blue simulated gems, and the cap of maintenance is a vivid red. The crown sits upon a circular simple black cushion.

Shaft and Knops: The gilt shaft is turned into a baluster shape in two main sections: at the upper end there are three red and black rings, and halfway down a simple red and black knop.

Foot Knop: A simple round end is painted red and black.

Manufacturer and Distinguishing Marks: None.

Province of Newfoundland and Labrador Mace (1950–present)

A close-up view of the crowned head of the Newfoundland and Labrador mace.

Material: Gilded sterling silver.

Length: 121 centimetres.

Crowned Head: A large crowned head, with four beaded arches meeting beneath an orb with a pierced-through cross paty at the top. Around the circlet are alternating crosses paty and fleurs-de-lys, four of each. Above is a double band, the upper part being conventionally detailed with stylized "gems," and the lower band decorated with dogwood, the floral emblem of British Columbia, combined with Canadian maple leaves.

Cap: A flat, circular plate carrying the Royal arms of King George VI has a twisted wire border around the edge. The nautical rope and other maritime elements found on this mace symbolize the shipping industry of Newfoundland and British Columbia.

Head: The head is divided into four compartments, each framed with twisted nautical wire rope. Within these areas are the Royal cypher of King George VI and the arms of Canada, Newfoundland, and British Columbia.

Brackets: Three heraldic dolphins at the upper end of the shaft support the head of the mace.

Shaft and Knops: The shaft is divided into three sections separated by knops

Showing the arms plate under the arches of the Newfoundland and Labrador mace.

in the shape of nautical rings. An inscription is engraved on the upper section (as detailed below).

Foot Knop: At the lower end is a round bulbous shape, which has the thunderbird, a British Columbia emblem, grasping a whale in its talons.

Engraving: Inscribed on the shaft of the mace:

PRESENTED TO THE PEOPLE OF

THE PROVINCE OF THE NEWFOUNDLAND

BY THE PEOPLE OF

THE PROVINCE OF BRITISH COLUMBIA

1950

Manufacturer and Distinguishing Marks: The mace carries the punch marks of Henry Birks & Sons, and is inscribed with BIRKS STERLING. Manufactured in Vancouver, the design concept and work was organized by James Saunders.

CHAPTER TWELVE

Territorial Maces

Canada's federal structure includes territories as well as provinces. Although territorial governments do not, like their provincial counterparts, possess control over natural resources and certain types of taxation, they do include democratically elected assemblies, a premier, and a cabinet. In place of a lieutenant governor, each has a territorial commissioner. Although the post of commissioner was at one time an all-powerful federal official, in recent years the post has become increasingly ceremonial, much like that of the lieutenant governors in the provinces.

Following the Westminster tradition, each of the legislatures includes a sergeant-at-arms and a mace. There are some differences, given that in Nunavut there are no formal political parties and the legislature works on an issue-by-issue basis. In the Northwest Territories members stand for election to the territorial assembly as individuals and not as members of a particular party. These differences speak to the uniqueness of Canada's north and the ability of parliamentary democracy to be adapted to many different circumstances.

It should be remembered that six of Canada's provinces — Ontario, Quebec, Manitoba, Saskatchewan, Alberta, and British Columbia — include land that was once part of a territorial government. Manitoba, Saskatchewan, Alberta, British Columbia, the Northwest Territories, Yukon, and Nunavut were all once part of Rupert's Land — the massive parcel of land that was controlled by the Hudson's Bay Company until 1870. This land would be partitioned into part of Manitoba in 1870, the Yukon in 1898, and Saskatchewan and Alberta in 1905.

The territorial maces were not devised simultaneously, and their development mirrors that of democratic institutions in each of the regions concerned. It is easy to understand why the Northwest Territories and Yukon had little need for such symbols of parliamentary authority when one realizes that until the 1950s most of the affairs of these territories were administered by the commissioner, although territorial councils, the forerunners of territorial assemblies, did exist. Indeed, Yukon provides an interesting example: it gained an elected council in 1899, only to lose it in 1918 due to depopulation. Following protests, the council, much reduced in size, was reinstated in 1919. There was no evenness to the development of democracy in the Canadian north. Only Nunavut acquired a mace immediately upon gaining territorial status in 1999 — the other territories adopted their maces as necessary.

The territorial maces comprise some of the most unusual parliamentary instruments in the Canadian symbolic lexicon. Some of the maces include natural elements, both precious and semi-precious, and historic elements from their respective territory, while others are made of precious metals and are more traditional. Collectively these maces embody the Canadian north and are representative of the territory to which they are linked.

NORTHWEST TERRITORIES

The first mace of the Northwest Territories, made in 1955, is perhaps one of the most unusual in the Commonwealth, primarily on account of its blending of natural elements along with a traditional mace design. While a number of the maces used by African countries have included local woods and even ivory, the Northwest Territories mace incorporates a wide variety of local elements into one of the most traditional symbols of authority known in the western world. The Northwest Territories mace is also unique because of the short period of time in which it was completed, and being almost entirely fashioned by Native artisans, making it one of the most outstanding pieces of art made in Canada.

During a 1955 visit to the Northwest Territories, Vincent Massey, the first post-Confederation, Canadian-born governor general, was astonished to learn that the territorial council lacked a parliamentary mace. At once he set to commissioning a mace.

Following some initial discussions and rough design work, the fabrication of the mace commenced on 15 July 1955. Under the supervision of James Houston, a federal civil servant, nine Inuit artists crafted the mace almost entirely from local materials. This was unlike the "emergency" maces used in Alberta and Manitoba where the symbol of parliamentary authority was manufactured from odds and ends; rather, there was intent from the outset to blend local materials into a mace. Remarkably, the entire project was completed in twenty-one days.

The acute attention to historic detail and the blending of Native and historical elements is truly unique, and include the oak salvaged from the wreck of HMS *Fury*, the ship of British explorer Sir William Parry, which ran aground on Somerset Island in 1825. To extend this remarkable tapestry of Canadian

RCMP sergeant, serving as sergeant-at-arms, holds the 1955 Northwest Territory mace.

history, the oak from HMS *Fury* was recovered during the Second World War by the RCMP patrol vessel *St. Roch*. To the dismay of the craftsmen, when making the mace, the copper metal used for the crown was not annealed properly during the hammering process, causing the crosses and fleurs-de-lys to break off. Help was on hand when a woman from Cape Dorset donated a large copper kettle, which her family acquired in 1921 via reindeer herders from Lapland. Her donation of the kettle did not go unrecognized, and the governor general, upon hearing the news, dispatched a new copper kettle to the generous donor.

In some ways the Northwest Territories mace became a victim of its own fame. During the period of 1956–1957, the mace travelled across Canada and went on display in every province except Quebec. Having travelled more than 10,000 kilometres and enduring a wide variety of climate changes, the mace began to show signs of cracking and it was decided that a replica of the mace should be manufactured. The original mace is only used at the opening of the Northwest Territories Legislature and during Royal visits. The replica had been used on all other occasions from 1959–1999.

A replica of the original mace was manufactured by Breadner Company Ltd. of Hull, Quebec, predominantly of gilded brass as a more durable material. Unlike the original mace, the copy took three years to make and cost $3,263.75.

In 1999 as the Northwest Territories prepared to be partitioned into Nunavut and the Northwest Territories, the legislature decided that it was an appropriate occasion to adopt a new mace for the Northwest Territories. The mace was designed by Bill Nasogaluak, Dolphus Cadieux, and Allyson Simmie.

The mace was inaugurated at the opening of the legislative assembly on 14 January 2000. Like its predecessor the new mace is unusual, in part for its

The Northwest Territories legislative assembly chamber.

Left: The Northwest Territories 2000 mace in the legislative assembly chamber, resting on a stand in front of the Speaker's chair.
Right: Sergeant-at-Arms Brian Thagard carrying the 2000 Northwest Territories mace. His formal dress includes wearing a sash made from bison hide, with patches of beaver fur and beadwork patterns.

contemporary design, but also because of one special feature. As the mace is moved, small pebbles fall against specially positioned internal spikes, which creates a sound effect similar to a traditional rain stick.

Northwest Territories Mace (1955–1958)

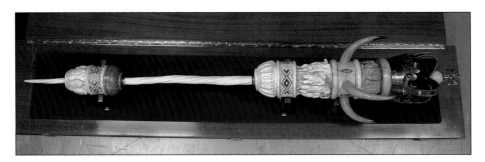

The Northwest Territories 1955 mace, showing the crowned head upper section.

Material: Made of a variety of materials, including whalebone, muskox horns, narwhal tusk, porcupine quillwork, copper, gold, and wood.

Length: 152 centimetres.

Crowned Head: The crown is fashioned of hammered Native copper from the Central Arctic and parts from an old copper kettle. It has four arches with twisted wire borders, which used to be insulated wire from an old wind charger. The circlet is of traditional form with crosses paty and fleurs-de-lys, four of each alternating. A whalebone orb sits at the top surmounted by a copper cross paty. The crown sits on a whalebone circular base.

Cap: Beneath the arches, the dome-shaped cap is made of whalebone with line markings of caribou antlers. In the centre is a hammered copper disc.

Head: The mace head beneath the crown is divided into five decorative components. The uppermost band is of whalebone and carved with a circle of eight bowhead whales. A circular ring separates the next band, which contains four majestic muskox horns from Ellesmere Island, and in between each is an applied plaque with incised markings, made of gold mined in the Mackenzie District. Farther down with a ring on either side is a whalebone

The Northwest Territories 1955 mace, showing the details of the porcupine quillwork and the whalebone carvings of Arctic fox pelts.

The Northwest Territories 1955 mace, close-up view of the whale-bone carving of figures and animals.

section carved with figures and animals of the Canadian north in the following sequence: a hunter, muskox, walrus, polar bear, mother and child, white whale, caribou, and fox. A decorative band of porcupine quillwork follows, and beneath this is a further whalebone ring and rounded section with multiple carvings of Arctic fox pelts.

Shaft: The shaft is a spiralling narwhal tusk from the Foxe Peninsula, which protrudes through the foot knop; a harpoon passes down its centre for added strength. At each end of the main shaft there is a small metal ring, and a further ring beneath the foot knop.

Foot Knop: The bulbous foot knop is in three parts. The upper domed section is an oak remnant salvaged from HMS *Fury*, the wrecked ship of the British explorer Sir William Parry. The sailing ship is drawn in black four times around the wood. In the middle part between two whalebone rings there is a band of porcupine quillwork. The lower part in whalebone is carved with six seals.

The Northwest Territories 1955 mace, a close-up view of the foot knop.

Manufacturer and Distinguishing Marks: None.

Other: Under the direction of artist James A. Houston, two main craftsmen spearheaded the project: Peter Pitseolak was the foreman and craftsman, and Oshawetuk Ipeelie was the artist and chief carver. In addition there was a team of assistants: Lukta Qiatsuk, Kovianaktuliak Parr, Nuyukshawetuk, Moses Tauki, Kavuvawak, Ashevak Ezekiel, and Kovianatuliak Ottokie. A Dene woman from Yellowknife made the porcupine quillwork belts.

Northwest Territories Replica Mace (1958–2000)

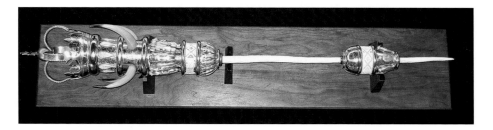

Material: Gilded brass, narwhal tusk, muskox horns, and porcupine quillwork.
Length: 153 centimetres.
Crowned Head: The crown, orb, and cross paty finial are in gilded brass.
Cap: The domed cap is gilded brass and engraved with caribou antlers; a round copper hammered disc is fixed in the centre.
Head: The head is divided into five parts and made of gilded brass, except for the protruding four muskox horns and porcupine quillwork. The decoration includes bowhead whales repeated in a band, animals of the Arctic, hunter, mother, and child, and fox pelts in the lower section.
Shaft: This is made of a narwhal tusk which extends through the foot knop. It is reinforced by a steel rod down the centre.
Foot Knop: This section is primarily of gilded brass with a band of porcupine quillwork attached around the centre. The upper hemispherical part carries engraved representation of HMS *Fury*, and the lower section seals are repeated.
Manufacturer and Distinguishing Marks: Made by Breadner Company Ltd. of Hull, Quebec, but no maker's mark.

Northwest Territories Millennium Mace (2000–present)

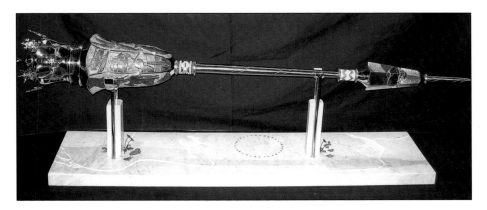

Material: Silver, bronze, marble, porcupine quillwork, beadwork, pebbles placed inside, and a single diamond set into the top.

Length: 146.5 centimetres.

Crowned Head: The stylized silver crown is a delicate construction with clever reflective qualities; a circle of six differing "snowflakes" are attached to the vertical uprights, and six smaller ones are placed between the apertures around the sides. A gilded silver orb glistens within the heart of the crown to signify the midnight sun, the circle of life, and the world, and above it there is a six-pointed cross-piece surmounted by a stylized finial combining the shapes of a tipi, an ulu (a traditional knife), and a house. There is a 1.31-carat diamond set into the very top, which was cut and polished in the Northwest Territories, and from the first Canadian diamond mine. A plain band encircles the base of the crown and this is engraved with an inscription translated into the different languages of the Northwest Territories.

Head: The head of the mace is comprised of six carved panels of stromatolitic marble from the Great Slave Lake region, with narrow silver vertical lines between each panel. The decoration represents the peoples of the Northwest Territories, with wildlife from the different regions and references to the diverse cultures.

Shaft: Shaped in the form of a narwhal tusk, the shaft is made of bronze with spiralling grooves. At the top end of the shaft, just beneath the head of the mace, is a band of beadwork in the Delta braid pattern, and at the lower end a band of porcupine quillwork. These craft skills are from Dene/Métis heritage. The stylized narwhal tusk shaft extends through and below the foot knop.

The Northwest Territories 2000 mace, detail of the crowned head.

The Northwest Territories 2000 mace, detail of the diamond set into the top.

Foot Knop: The six-sided foot knop is engraved and carved in low relief with scenes of the endless Northwest Territories landscape.

Engraving: Around the head of the mace, the words "One land, many voices" are engraved in ten different local languages.

Other: Special sound feature. Within the mace are placed small pebbles from thirty-three communities in the Northwest Territories. As the mace is moved, the pebbles fall against specially positioned internal spikes, creating a unique sound effect akin to a rain stick. A special stand for when the mace is not in use was made in white marble with references to the Mackenzie River, and the Great Slave and Great Bear lakes. The detail also incorporates the mountain aven, the Northwest Territories flower, and thirty-three nuggets of northern gold.

YUKON TERRITORY

The Yukon mace was rather late in being developed when compared with the Northwest Territories. Although the territory was older than three provinces, having been established by an act of Parliament in 1898, it was not until 1967 that the territory decided to adopt a mace. The Yukon Council decided "to adopt a mace as an outward symbol of its outward authority," on 10 January 1967.[1] This was clearly a decision taken to further assert the Yukon's growing autonomy and desire to be seen as part of the broader Canadian family — after all, every other province and territory in the Dominion possessed a mace.

Initially there was some question of how to go about obtaining a mace. The Department of Indian and Northern Affairs — which was responsible for the administration of the territory — thought that, as the mace is a symbol of Royal authority, permission from the Queen would have to be sought.[2] As the Queen had already assented to the establishment of the Yukon Council in 1899, it was decided that such permission did not have to be sought, as the adoption of a mace was viewed as part of this process. However, permission was sought from the Queen for use of the Royal Crown on the head of the mace.

On 11 February 1972, the minister of Indian Affairs, Jean Chrétien, announced that "The Yukon Territory will soon join the 10 provinces and the Northwest Territories in the possession of a mace, symbol of the authority of the Speaker of the Legislature."[3]

Since 1908 the legislative structure of the Yukon had been quite simple: the populace was represented by the Yukon Council, which was elected every four years, and from the council a Speaker was elected. Above this was the executive council, all of whom were appointed by the federal government in Ottawa. The executive council was, in essence, the cabinet of the territory. This general structure was almost an exact copy of the structures used in Upper and Lower Canada prior to the adoption of responsible government in 1841. The legislative and executive bodies were totally separate, and the executive body was not responsible to the elected legislative body.

Sergeant-at-Arms Rudy Couture carrying the Yukon Territory mace.

As the move toward responsible government became more certain, changes were made to the structure of the executive committee with the addition of two elected members from the council in 1971.

The mace was presented to the council of the Yukon Territory by Governor General Roland Michener on 6 March 1972. It was a gift given on behalf of the Canadian Crown to the territorial government. R.A. Rivett, Speaker of the council, accepted the gift on behalf of the people of the Yukon.

The design of the mace had been approved by the executive committee, in consultation with the council. The mace was designed by Sergeant James Ballantyne of the Royal Canadian Mounted Police. It was most appropriate that the principal symbol of authority in the territory was being designed by a member of the force that brought peace, order, and good government to the entire Canadian West.

The formal design work and crafting of the mace was undertaken by Henry Birks & Sons of Montreal at a cost of $8,300. Birks had a long history of producing legislative and municipal maces, and as Canada's premier silversmiths they carried out the project with a close attention to quality and detail. The noted heraldic artist and expert Alan Beddoe was consulted on the design throughout the project.

Yukon is also unique because it includes the topography of the territory under the arches of the crown of the mace.

The Yukon Territory Mace (1972–present)

Material: Gilded silver.

Length: 133.5 centimetres.

Crowned Head: The stylized crown has four arches which taper toward the circlet; each arc has a plain reed border with beading simulating pearls spaced out along the centre. The beaded orb is surmounted with a stylized cross in a textured matte finish. The circlet is formed of alternating fleurs-de-lys and crosses paty, four of each, above a band with round and oblong simulated jewels.

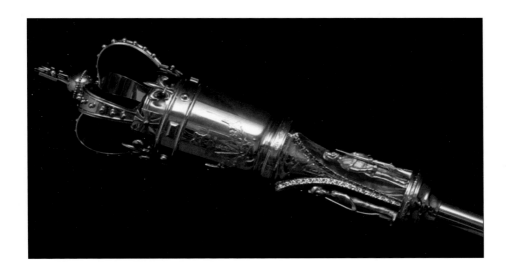

The Yukon Territory mace, close-up view of the crowned head.

Cap: The unusual cap of maintenance beneath the arches is a model of the Yukon's mountainous landscape, likely a representation of Mount Golden Horn, a dominant feature near Whitehorse.

The Yukon Territory mace, showing the topographical feature beneath the arches of the crowned head.

Head: The head is a plain cup with two armorial features, the arms of Canada on one side and the arms of the Yukon Territory on the other. Beneath this is a ring decorated with fireweed, the provincial flower.

Brackets: In lieu of conventional brackets, there are three figures standing beneath pointed maple leaf arches that represent the early settlement and development of the Yukon: a miner holding a shovel, an Aboriginal figure with a bow, and a trapper/explorer clasping a rifle. Between the figures in the three spandrels are engraved regional landscapes.

Shaft and Knops: The plain shaft tapers towards a point at the lower end, with two knops along the length. Each knop has a pronounced rib in the centre embellished with maple leaves.

Manufacturer and Distinguishing Marks: The mace was designed by Sergeant James Ballantyne of the RCMP and carries the sterling mark and the maker's stamp of Henry Birks & Sons.

NUNAVUT

As the newest territory in the Canadian federation, Nunavut has the youngest mace in the family of parliamentary symbols covered in this book. In September 1998 six artists from the soon-to-be-established territory gathered in Iqaluit to design and craft a mace for the legislative assembly. Maintaining the tradition embodied in the Northwest Territory mace of including many natural and local elements became a key goal.

It was decided that the mace would be made only from materials present in the new territory, and also the crafting of the mace should include both traditional and modern skills, thus reflecting the "cultural heritage of Nunavummiut."[4] All of the materials used in crafting the mace represent elements of importance to the inhabitants of the territory. The central role played by sea mammals for the survival of the Nunavummiut is represented in the ivory narwhal tusk that comprises the shaft of the mace. Due to the fragility of the narwhal tusk, it was decided from the outset that two maces would be produced: the heritage mace and the working mace.

The heritage mace is kept on permanent display in a glass cabinet and rests upon figurative supports made of labradorite and soapstone; these are carvings of an Elder, a man, a woman, and a child, who together hold up the mace in their hands. The working mace is used on a daily basis. This second mace is identical to the heritage mace in most respects, except two main features: for added strength the shaft of the mace is made from a synthetic material, and set into the tip of the base is a 2.25 carat diamond from the Jericho mine in western Nunavut (a quartz crystal is similarly situated at the base of the heritage mace). The heritage mace is used primarily for display and during Royal tours.

The mace was first used on 1 April 1999, at the opening of the Nunavut Legislative Assembly. The Speaker, Levi Barnabas, noted:

> I would finally like to recognize the artists who created the mace. We are honoured that they are with us today. Inuk Charlie, Joseph Suqslaq, Paul Malliki, Mariano Aupilardjuk, Mathew Nuqingaq and Sam Pitsiulak — thank you. The mace, which will shortly be presented to the House, is itself a reflection of the rights and authority of a democratically elected Assembly. It is a gift from the Qikiqtaaluk Corporation and seven other Inuit organizations. It speaks eloquently for itself in the way it embodies the soul of our land, this Assembly and our people.[5]

Nunavut Territory Heritage Mace (1999–present)

Material: Narwhal tusk, silver, various semi-precious stones, soapstone, and granite.

Length: 150 centimetres.

Crowned Head: Encircled around the head of the mace — made in silver from the high Arctic — are four stylized common loons with heads bowed down towards the centre, their long necks forming graceful arches meeting at the intersection upon which there is a cross finial. Beneath the cross within the crown is an orb of lapis lazuli mined from Kimmirut, Nunavut. The circlet of the crown is a simple soapstone band set with seven semi-precious gemstones: quartz, amethyst, garnet, black quartz, citrine, lapis lazuli, and white marble. Four simple brackets connect the crown to the shaft.

The Nunavut heritage mace, close-up view of the upper end.

Shaft and Knop: The shaft is made from a single narwhal tusk, and attached along the length are three seals made from granite, marble, and lapis lazuli. Two-thirds of the way down is a knop made of granite. Set into the tip of the shaft is a quartz crystal.

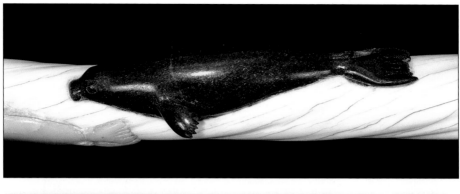

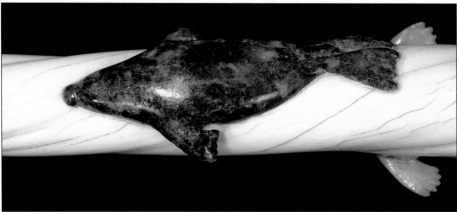

*Top: A carved granite seal on the shaft of the Nunavut Territory heritage mace.
Middle: Close-up view of the narwhal tusk shaft with carved lapis lazuli seal.
Bottom: A quartz crystal set into the tip at the base of the Nunavut Territory
heritage mace.*

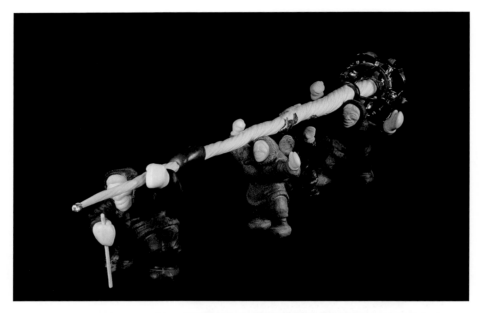

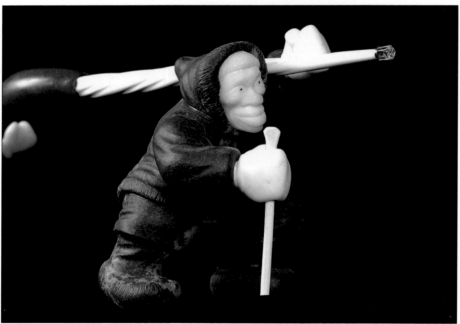

Top: Carved figurines support the Nunavut Territory heritage mace.
Bottom: An Elder figure holding the end piece of the Nunavut Territory
heritage mace.

Above Left: A woman is positioned in the middle section.

Above Right: A child reaches up towards the mace.

Left: A figure of a man carries the head of the mace.

*In front of the Speaker's chair the Nunavut Territory working
mace is placed on a stand with two figure supports to hold it.*

Manufacturer: Designed and created by six Nunavut artists:
- Mariano Aupilardjuk — Rankin Inlet
- Inuk Charlie — Cambridge Bay
- Paul Malliki — Repulse Bay
- Mathew Nuqingaq — Iqaluit
- Simata Pitsualak — Kimmirut
- Joseph Suqslaq — Gjoa Haven

Other: For display, the mace is resting on three figurine supports made from
labradorite and soapstone: an elder, a man, and a woman with a child. Together
they hold up the mace in their hands.

Nunavut Territory Working Mace (1999–present)

Material: Silver, a diamond, various semi-precious stones, soapstone, and
granite with a man-made synthetic shaft.
Length: 150 centimetres.
Crowned Head: Predominantly in the same style as the heritage mace, with
common loons in silver and a lapis lazuli orb. The band of the crown is set
with various semi-precious gemstones. Four simple brackets connect the
crown to the shaft.

Sergeant-at-Arms Simanuk Kilabuk wearing the traditional silaapak, he is carrying the Nunavut Territory working mace.

Shaft and Knop: The shaft is made of a synthetic man-made material (to imitate narwhal tusk), and attached along the length are three seals made from granite, marble, and lapis lazuli. Two-thirds of the way down is a bulbous knop made of granite. Set into the tip of the shaft is a solitaire 2.25-carat diamond.

Manufacturer: Designed and created by the six Nunavut artists that created the heritage mace.

Other: The mace stand in front of the Speaker's chair is made up of two stone figures representing Nunavummiut (the people of Nunavut). The people of Nunavut are embodied in these two sculptures and hold the power granted to the legislative assembly as symbolized by the mace.

CHAPTER THIRTEEN

Municipal and Academic Maces

The use of maces is not limited to Canada's various legislatures. A number of other institutions and organizations also possess maces of various descriptions. These maces can be divided into three categories: civic/municipal, academic, and societal.

In England, Wales, and Ireland there has long been a tradition of municipalities and town councils possessing a mace. The first real inventory of these symbols of authority was undertaken in 1874. It was discovered that of the 204 boroughs and municipalities surveyed, 174 had at least one mace — some, such as Hereford, had four maces.[1] The City of Galway, Ireland, possesses a mace crafted in Dublin in 1710 that is a fine example of a Great Mace. This mace was presented to the town by Major Edward Eyre and later came into the possession of the Heart Foundation, which returned the mace to Ireland in 1960.[2]

Simon Fraser University, McMaster University, Renison University College, and a number of other institutions possess academic maces. Royal Roads Military College also possessed an academic mace that was retired when the college was decommissioned in 1995. There are relatively few societal maces in Canada. The Royal Society of Canada, unlike its British counterpart, never adopted a societal mace.[3] The Royal Heraldry Society of Canada uses a heraldically rich mace fashioned from pewter and wood.

The most impressive non-legislative mace in Canada is the City of Vancouver mace. The Vancouver mace was presented by the City of London on the occasion of Vancouver's golden jubilee in 1936. An elaborate ceremony was arranged at the Hotel Vancouver in the Crystal Ballroom on 20 August 1936. The mace is a near exact replica of the City of London mace which dates from 1735. The Vancouver mace was made from 304 ounces of Canadian silver.[4]

In presenting the mace, the Lord Mayor of London Sir Percy Vincent reflected:

The mace of the Corporation of London has, throughout the centuries, been the emblem of its power and jurisdiction, and similar practice is followed in the great legislatures of the world, including the Imperial House of Parliament. Here today it is my privilege to hand into your safekeeping, Mr. Mayor, an exact replica, but bearing the cipher of His Majesty King Edward VIII, the Maple Leaf and the Arms of Vancouver, made in London of Canadian silver. May it ever remain your jealously-guarded possession and an unbreakable link between the capital city of the Empire and this great city of the West.[5]

The mace was first carried by Constable Alex MacKay of the Vancouver Police Department. The mace of the Corporation of the City of London and the Lord Mayor's chain of office were brought to the centennial celebrations, marking the first time these objects had ever been transported outside the United Kingdom.[6]

The Mace of the City of Vancouver

Material: Gilded sterling silver.

Length: 160 centimetres.

Crowned Head: The crown has a coronet of alternating fleurs-de-lys and crosses paty, four of each, above a band with simulated jewels. There are four half arches which have beaded ribs simulating jewels and pearls. These are surmounted at the intersection by an orb, also beaded, and a cross paty with bead finials.

Cap: The arms plate beneath the arches carries the Royal arms of King Edward VIII, within a circular wreathed border surrounded by foliate decoration.

Head: Divided into four sections, containing the Royal cypher of King Edward VIII, a natural maple leaf, the arms of the City of Vancouver, and the arms of the Corporation of London.

Brackets: There are four ornate scroll brackets at the top of the shaft supporting the head of the mace.

Shaft and knops: In the centre of the shaft are a group of ornate baluster-shaped knops.

Foot knop: The foot knop is flared with multi-shaped bulbous protrusions.

Engraving: The foot knop is engraved, "Presented by the Corporation of the City of London to the City of Vancouver, on the occasion of the visit of the Lord Mayor, Sir Percy Vincent, and a deputation from the Corporation of London,

The Vancouver mace.

CHAPTER FOURTEEN

Insignia and Chains of Office of the Canadian Orders

The Canadian honours system is a relatively new institution when compared with the other symbols of authority that have come to represent the Canadian state. Yet the honours system is perhaps the most visible and widely recognized of all the symbols examined in this book. Since 1967, more than 350,000 Canadians have been recognized with the various Canadian orders, decorations, and medals that make up our modern honours system.

Prior to 1967, Canada periodically used the British honours system to recognize meritorious service and lifetime achievement. This included awards such as the Order of the Bath, the Order of St. Michael and St. George, the Order of the British Empire, and the Imperial Service Order.

Every national order has a titular head. In the case of countries with monarchical systems of government, it is the Sovereign; in the case of republics, it is the president. As Canada is a constitutional monarchy, it is natural that the Queen serve as the Sovereign of the Order of Canada — it is, after all, from the Crown that all official honours flow.

In addition to the Sovereign there are a number of other officials charged with administering the various Canadian orders. These include the chancellor, who is the governor general of Canada; the secretary general, who is the secretary to the governor general and herald chancellor of Canada; and the registrar, who has traditionally been the director of honours for the Chancellery of Canadian Honours.

In addition to these administrative posts, at present only the chancellors of the various Canadian orders, and the principal commanders of the Order of Military Merit and Order of Merit of the Police Forces, possess distinctive chains of office. When the Order of Canada was established in 1967 it was expected that special chains of office would be made for the registrar of the order and the secretary general of the order, but these plans have yet to be fulfilled. The Most Venerable Order of the Hospital of St. John of Jerusalem, more commonly known as the Order of St. John, has operated in Canada since 1883. The order is an important part of the Canadian honours system, and both the prior of the order, who is the governor general, and the chancellor of the order, who is an official of the order, have unique chains of office. It is only in 2004 that chains of office for the Order of St. John were adopted in Canada.

In many ways the Sovereign's insignia of the Order of Canada and Order of Military Merit constitute the Canadian Crown jewels.

THE ORDER OF CANADA, SOVEREIGN'S BADGE

Origins: It has long been a tradition that the Sovereign of an order possess special insignia to denote his or her position. These insignia are usually encrusted with precious stones and different in some way from those awarded to the general membership of the order. The Order of Canada follows this tradition, and in 1967 it was decided that a special Sovereign's insignia should be commissioned and presented to the Queen. The design was complete in 1968, and was presented to the Queen by Governor General Roland Michener on 23 June 1970, at Buckingham Palace.

Insignia: A six-armed cross of 18-carat gold, enamelled white, with a large square diamond set between each of the arms. In the centre there is a maple leaf surrounded by an annulus, both with pavé-set, calibré-cut rubies. On the annulus is the motto in pierced gold. Above the cross there is a gold St. Edward's Crown with the cap of maintenance enamelled red and the ermine enamelled white. The arches are set with twenty-one diamonds, with a larger one in the orb. The base is set with a sapphire, two emeralds, and two rubies. The reverse is plain, aside from the word CANADA in gold.

Other: The Sovereign's insignia was manufactured by Garrard & Co. Ltd., under the supervision of Crown Jeweller William Summers.

Sovereign's insignia of the Order of Canada.

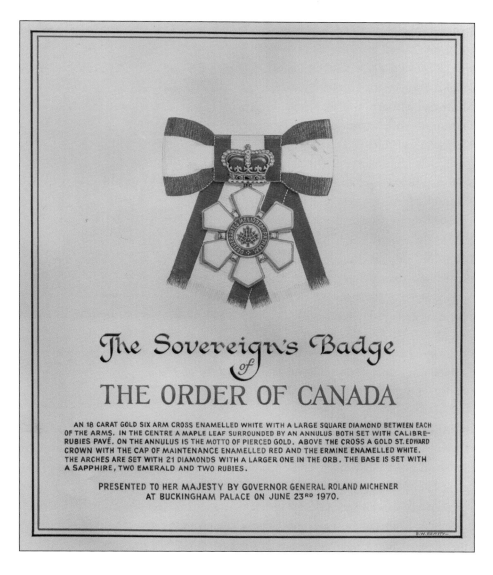

The Sovereign's Badge
of
THE ORDER OF CANADA

AN 18 CARAT GOLD SIX ARM CROSS ENAMELLED WHITE WITH A LARGE SQUARE DIAMOND BETWEEN EACH OF THE ARMS. IN THE CENTRE A MAPLE LEAF SURROUNDED BY AN ANNULUS BOTH SET WITH CALIBRE-RUBIES PAVÉ. ON THE ANNULUS IS THE MOTTO OF PIERCED GOLD. ABOVE THE CROSS A GOLD ST. EDWARD CROWN WITH THE CAP OF MAINTENANCE ENAMELLED RED AND THE ERMINE ENAMELLED WHITE. THE ARCHES ARE SET WITH 21 DIAMONDS WITH A LARGER ONE IN THE ORB. THE BASE IS SET WITH A SAPPHIRE, TWO EMERALD AND TWO RUBIES.

PRESENTED TO HER MAJESTY BY GOVERNOR GENERAL ROLAND MICHENER AT BUCKINGHAM PALACE ON JUNE 23RD 1970.

Painting of the Sovereign's insignia of the Order of Canada.

Numbers: There has been one Sovereign of the Order of Canada: Her Majesty Queen Elizabeth II.

THE ORDER OF MILITARY MERIT, SOVEREIGN'S BADGE

As with the Order of Canada, the Queen is Sovereign of the order and she wears a special jewelled Sovereign's insignia. The Sovereign's badge was presented to the Queen in July 1973 by Governor General Roland Michener aboard the Royal yacht *Britannia* while it was anchored off Kingston, Ontario. The governor general is chancellor of the Order and usually wears the Order of Military Merit (CMM) on a ribbon around his neck, or, in the case of ladies, on a bow worn on the left shoulder. A special chancellor's chain also exists, but it is usually only worn during investiture ceremonies.

Sovereign's insignia of the Order of Military Merit.

Origins: As with the Order of Canada and most national honours, the Sovereign is presented with a special insignia.

Insignia: An 18-carat gold, four-armed cross, enamelled over scalloped machine work in translucent blue. Between each of the arms, a rectangular diamond is set between two cushion-shaped diamonds. In the centre of the cross, there is a maple leaf surrounded by an annulus, both of which are set with calibré-cut rubies. On the annulus the words *Merit — Mérite — Canada* appear in finely pierced gold. Above the cross there is a gold St. Edward's Crown with seven diamonds set in the ermine, three in each of the fleurs-de-lys and a larger one in the orb. On the arches are twenty-one pearls. The base is set with a sapphire, two emeralds, and two rubies. The cap is enamelled red.

Other: The Sovereign's insignia was manufactured by Garrard & Co. Ltd., under the supervision of Crown Jeweller William Summers. It has a blue leatherette case lined with white satin and blue velvet. The insignia was designed by Bruce Beatty.

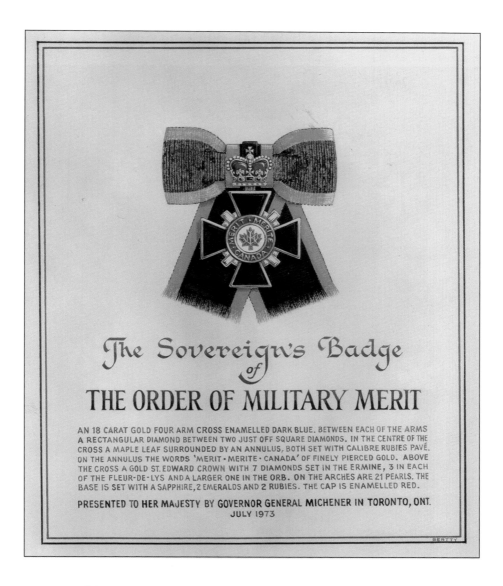

The Sovereign's Badge of

THE ORDER OF MILITARY MERIT

AN 18 CARAT GOLD FOUR ARM CROSS ENAMELLED DARK BLUE. BETWEEN EACH OF THE ARMS
A RECTANGULAR DIAMOND BETWEEN TWO JUST OFF SQUARE DIAMONDS. IN THE CENTRE OF THE
CROSS A MAPLE LEAF SURROUNDED BY AN ANNULUS, BOTH SET WITH CALIBRE RUBIES PAVÉ.
ON THE ANNULUS THE WORDS 'MERIT · MERITE · CANADA' OF FINELY PIERCED GOLD. ABOVE
THE CROSS A GOLD ST. EDWARD CROWN WITH 7 DIAMONDS SET IN THE ERMINE, 3 IN EACH
OF THE FLEUR-DE-LYS AND A LARGER ONE IN THE ORB. ON THE ARCHES ARE 21 PEARLS. THE
BASE IS SET WITH A SAPPHIRE, 2 EMERALDS AND 2 RUBIES. THE CAP IS ENAMELLED RED.

PRESENTED TO HER MAJESTY BY GOVERNOR GENERAL MICHENER IN TORONTO, ONT.
JULY 1973

Painting of the Sovereign's insignia of the Order of Military Merit.

THE ORDER OF MERIT OF THE POLICE FORCES, SOVEREIGN'S BADGE

Unfortunately at the moment there is no Sovereign's badge of office for the
Order of Merit of the Police Forces. Although there is no official reason for
this, it is likely that Rideau Hall was reluctant to pay for such an insignia to
be manufactured.

Chancellor's Chain of the Order of Canada

Origins: While every order has a titular head, tradition has also called for there to be a senior official known as either a grand master or a chancellor. Prime Minister Lester Pearson decided that the term "grand master" was a little grandiose for

Reverse of the Chancellor's chain of the Order of Canada.

Canada, thus the term "chancellor" was chosen. Given that the governor general is the Queen's representative in Canada, it was decided that he or she should also serve as the chancellor of the order and perform most of the ceremonial and administrative duties relating to certain aspects of the order. The chancellor of the Order of Canada is also styled the "Principal Companion of the Order of Canada."

When a governor general's term expires, he or she ceases to be chancellor of the Order of Canada but remains a companion of the order.

Insignia: The chancellor's chain was produced by the Royal Canadian Mint. Like the other insignia of the order, it was designed by Bruce Beatty. Marvin Cook and Argo Aarand made the various parts of the chain from gold, and Aarand enamelled them in a small kiln in the basement of his home. The chain is made of twenty-three devices linked together by a double row of small gold links. Twelve of these devices are miniature replicas of the white snowflake. Alternating with these are ten devices, each in the form of a red maple leaf on a white background, encircled by the red annulet bearing the motto of the order. The chain is completed by a centre device in the form of the shield from the arms of Canada ensigned by the Royal Crown, each in their proper colours. The governor general's companion's insignia is hung from this device. The insignia of the Order of Canada that hangs from the chancellor's chain was manufactured by Garrard & Co. Ltd., the Crown jewellers. The reverse is the same as that of a regular companion's insignia, although a small box that usually contains a three-digit number bears the legend "-C-." The chain — made over a nine-month period, during which

Aarand and Cook devoted their lunch hours to the project — was presented to Governor General Michener by E.F. Brown, the acting master of the Royal Canadian Mint, on 22 December 1968.

Other: The companion's insignia is detachable from the chancellor's chain, although this is rarely done. The chancellor's chain is worn primarily on special occasions, such as investitures and sometimes the opening of Parliament. The chain is housed in a large red leatherette case whose lid is embossed with the insignia of the order in gold. The chancellor's chain is returned to the government upon retirement.

Numbers: There have been seven chancellors of the Order of Canada:

Jeanne Sauvé wearing the chancellor's chain of the Order of Canada.

- Roland Michener, PC, CC, CMM, CD, QC, 1967–1974
- Jules Léger, PC, CC, CMM, CD, 1974–1980
- Edward Schreyer, PC, CC, CMM, CD, 1980–1985
- Jeanne Sauvé, PC, CC, CMM, CD, 1985–1990
- Ray Hnatyshyn, PC, CC, CMM, CD, QC, 1990–1995
- Roméo LeBlanc, PC, CC, CMM, CD, 1995–2000
- Adrienne Clarkson, PC, CC, CMM, COM, CD, 2000–2005
- Michaëlle Jean, CC, CMM, COM, CD, 2005–2010
- David Johnston, CC, CMM, COM, CD, 2010–present

Chancellor's Chain of the Order of Military Merit

Origins: As with the Order of Canada and most national honours, the senior official is presented with insignia of office.

Insignia: A chain of ten maple leaves alternating with four naval crowns (rep-

resenting the navy), four mural crowns bearing a maple leaf (representing the army), and four aerial crowns composed of wings (representing the air force). The chain is completed by a centre device in the form of the shield from the arms of Canada ensigned by the Royal Crown, each in their proper colours. The governor general's commander's insignia is hung from this device. The entire chain was made of 9-carat gold and bears hallmarks for London, 1972. The chancellor's chain was made by Spink & Son Ltd. of London. It is housed in a large blue leatherette case whose lid is embossed with the insignia of the order. The interior of the case is lined with white satin and red velvet.

Other: As the governor general only wears the chancellor's chain on special occasions, such as investitures, the insignia of the Order of Military Merit is detachable so that the governor general can wear his or her commander's insignia from a ribbon. The chancellor's chain is returned to the government upon retirement. The chain, like the other insignia of the order, was designed by Bruce Beatty.

Numbers: There have been seven Chancellors of the Order of Military Merit.

- Roland Michener, PC, CC, CMM, CD, QC, 1972–1974
- Jules Léger, PC, CC, CMM, CD, 1974–1980
- Edward Schreyer, PC, CC, CMM, CD, 1980–1985
- Jeanne Sauvé, PC, CC, CMM, CD, 1985–1990
- Ray Hnatyshyn, PC, CC, CMM, CD, QC, 1990–1995
- Roméo LeBlanc, PC, CC, CMM, CD, 1995–2000
- Adrienne Clarkson, PC, CC, CMM, COM, CD, 2000–2005
- Michaëlle Jean, CC, CMM, COM, CD, 2005–2010
- David Johnston, CC, CMM, COM, CD, 2010–present

Chancellor's Chain of the Order of Merit of the Police Forces

Origins: While every order has a titular head, it has also been a tradition for there to be a senior official known as either a grand master or chancellor. As the governor general is the Queen's representative in Canada, it was decided that he or she should also serve as the chancellor of the order and perform most of the investiture and administrative duties relating to certain aspects of the order. Following the precedent set by the Order of Canada, it was decided that the term "chancellor" should be used for the second-highest official of the order.

When a governor general retires from the office, he or she ceases to be chancellor of the Order of Merit of the Police Forces, but remains a commander of the order.

Insignia: A neck chain composed of fourteen gold natural maple leaves and thirteen silver shields, alternating and joined by gold chain links. Each of the silver shields features a provincial or territorial flower in gold. The chain is completed by a centre device in the form of the shield from the arms of Canada ensigned by the Royal Crown, each in their proper colours. The governor general's commander's insignia is hung from this device. The chancellor's chain of the Order of Merit of the Police Forces was made by Pressed Metal Products of British Columbia.

Other: As the governor general only wears the chancellor's chain on special occasions, such as investitures, the insignia of the Order of Merit of the Police Forces is detachable so that it can be worn from a ribbon. The chancellor's chain is returned to the government upon retirement.

Numbers: There have been two chancellors of the Order of Merit of the Police Forces:

- Adrienne Clarkson, PC, CC, CMM, COM, CD, 2000–2005
- Michaëlle Jean, CC, CMM, COM, CD, 2005–2010
- David Johnston, CC, CMM, COM, CD, 2010–present

Principal Commander's Chain of the Order of Military Merit

Origins: In most national military orders, the chief of the armed forces is usually an ex officio member. In Canada this means that the chief of the defence staff (CDS) serves as the principal commander of the Order of Military Merit. Most chiefs of the defence staff have been either officers or commanders of the Order of Military Merit prior to their appointment as CDS; nevertheless, they are presented with a special insignia for wear during investitures and state occasions.

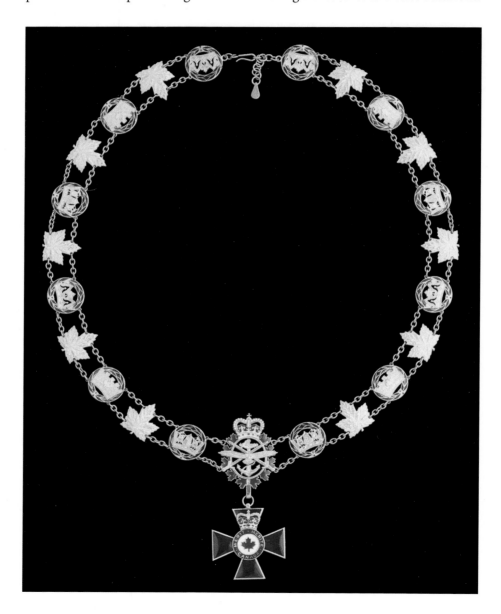

General Walter Natynczyk CMM, MSC, CD, wearing the Chain of Principal Commander of the Order of Military Merit.

Insignia: A chain of ten maple leaves alternating with four naval crowns (representing the navy), four mural crowns defaced with a maple leaf (representing the army), and four aerial crowns composed of wings (representing the air force). The chain is completed by a centre device in the form of the arms of the Canadian Forces in their proper colours. The principal commander's insignia is hung from this device. The entire chain was made of

9-carat gold and bears hallmarks for London, 1972. The principal commander's chain of the Order of Military Merit was made by Spink & Son Ltd. It is housed in a large blue leatherette case whose lid is embossed with the insignia of the order. The interior of the case is lined with white satin and red velvet.

Other: As the chief of the defence staff only wears the principal commander's chain on special occasions, such as investitures and sometimes the opening of Parliament, the insignia of the Order of Military Merit is detachable so that the commander's insignia can be worn from a ribbon. The chain is returned to the government upon retirement. The chain, like the other insignia of the order, was designed by Bruce Beatty.

Numbers: There have been thirteen principal commanders and one acting principal commander.

- General F.R. Sharp, CMM, DFC, CD, 1972
- General J.A. Dextraze, CC, CBE, CMM, DSO, CD, 1972–1977
- Admiral R.H. Falls, CMM, CD, 1977–1980
- General R.M. Withers, CMM, CD, 1980–1983
- General G.C. Theriault, CMM, CD, 1983–1986
- General P. Manson, CMM, CD, 1986–1989
- General A.J.G.D. de Chastelain, OC, CMM, CD, CH, 1989–1993
- Admiral J. Anderson, CMM, CD, 1993–1994
- General A.J.G.D. de Chastelain, OC, CMM, CD, CH, 1994–1995
- General Jean Boyle, CMM, CD, 1995
- Vice Admiral L.E. Murray, CMM, CD (acting), 1996–1997
- General M. Baril, CMM, CD, 1997–2001
- General R.R. Henault, CMM, CD, 2001–2005
- General R. Hillier, CMM, MSC, CD, 2005–2008
- General Walter Natynczyk, CMM, MSC, CD, 2008–present

Principal Commander's Chain of the Order of Merit of the Police Forces

Origins: The Order of Merit of the Police Forces is almost entirely based on the Order of Military Merit. Thus, following this pattern the head of the national police force (the Royal Canadian Mounted Police) is ex officio, the principal commander of the Order of Merit of the Police Forces.

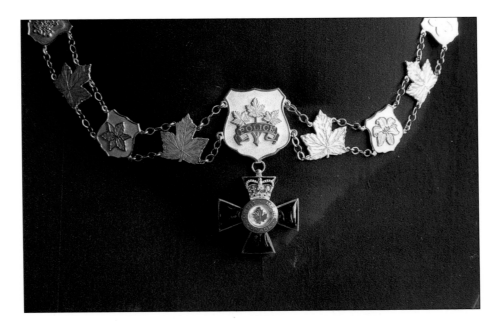

Insignia: A neck chain composed of fourteen gold natural maple leaves and thirteen silver shields, alternating and joined by gold chain links. Each of the silver shields is defaced with a provincial or territorial flower in gold. The chain is completed by a centre device made up of a police shield, defaced with three maple leaves surmounted by a crown with the word POLICE at the base, from which the commander's insignia is hung from this device. The principal insignia of the Order of Military Merit was made by Pressed Metal Products of British Columbia.

Other: As the commissioner of the RCMP only wears the principal commander's chain on special occasions, such as investitures and sometimes the opening of Parliament, the insignia of the Order of Merit of the Police Forces is detachable so it can be worn from a ribbon. The chancellor's chain is returned to the government upon retirement.

Numbers: There have been two principal commanders of the Order of Merit of the Police Forces.

- Commissioner Giuliano Zaccardelli, COM, 2000–2006
- Commissioner William J.S. Elliott, COM, QC, 2007–present

THE MOST VENERABLE ORDER OF ST. JOHN OF JERUSALEM

Prior's Chain of the Most Venerable Order of the Hospital of St. John of Jerusalem

The Right Honourable Michaëlle Jean wearing the prior's chain of the Most Venerable Order of the Hospital of St. John of Jerusalem.

Origins: Modelled on the chancellor's chain of the Order of Canada, the chain was developed to afford the prior an insignia of office to denote his or her position as the senior official of the Order in Canada aside from the Queen. The chain is intended to be worn at investitures.

Insignia: A chain composed of two separate rows of gold chain, joined in the centre by the shield of Canada, surrounded by the motto of the Order of Canada, surmounted by a Royal Crown. From this hangs a gold eight-pointed cross in white enamel, defaced with the shield of the Priory of Canada in red and white enamel. On the chain are the thirteen shields of the Canadian provinces and territories in gold with enamels, alternating with gold and white enamel eight-point crosses. Each side of the chain bears the shield of the Priory of Canada in gold with red and white enamels, at the point where the chain affixes to the shoulder.

Other: The chain is made of gilt sterling silver and enamel and was manufactured by J.R. Gaunt & Son in the United Kingdom. The badge of the chain carries London hallmarks for 2002.

Numbers: Two priors have worn the chain since its inception:

- Michaëlle Jean, CC, CMM, COM, CD, 2005–2010
- David Johnston, CC, CMM, COM, CD, 2010–present

Chancellor's Chain of the Most Venerable Order of the Hospital of St. John of Jerusalem

Origins: Like the chain worn by the prior of the Order, this chain was developed for use during investiture ceremonies and other Order of St. John events where decorations are worn.

Insignia: A chain of office comprised of two separate rows of gold chain, joined together in the centre by the shield of Canada surrounded by the motto of the Order of Canada, surmounted by a Royal Crown. From this hangs a gold eight-pointed cross in white enamel, with the shield of the Priory of Canada in red and white enamel superimposed. On each side of the shield of Canada is a natural gold maple leaf.

Other: The chain is made of gilt sterling silver and enamel and was manufactured by J.R. Gaunt & Son in the United Kingdom. The badge of the chain carries London hallmarks for 2002. There is also a past chancellor's chain of the order which is identical to the chancellor's chain except it does not have the two maple leaves on each side of the Canadian coat of arms. It is engraved on the reverse GIFT OF ROGER ALEXANDER LINDSAY KSTJ, 2007.

Numbers: Four chancellors have worn the chancellor's chain since its inception in 2003:

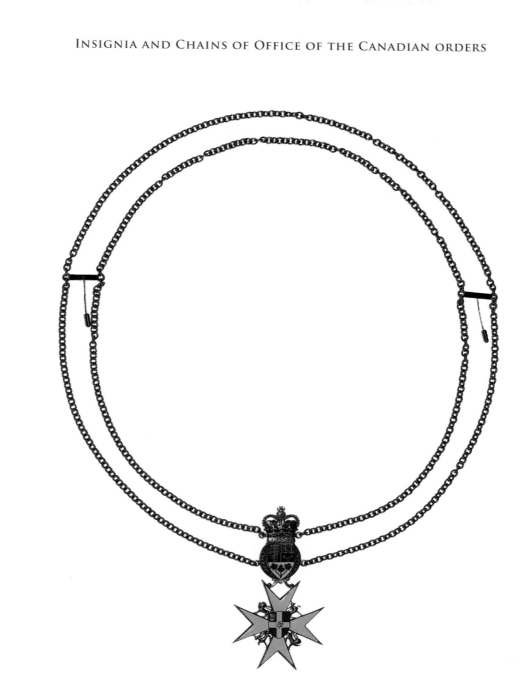

- Jeffrey G. Gilmour, KStJ, CD, 2003–2005
- Commodore René Marin, CM, OMM, O.Ont, KStJ, CD, QC, 2005–2007
- John Mah, GCStJ, CD, QC, 2007–2009
- Richard Bruce, MOM, KStJ, AdeC, 2009–present

The Honourable Justice René Marin, CM, OMM, O.Ont, KStJ, CD, QC, wearing the chancellor's chain of the Most Venerable Order of the Hospital of St. John of Jerusalem.

CHAPTER FIFTEEN

Uniforms and Badges of Civil Authority

The Court Uniforms and the Viceregal and Territorial Commissioners Recognition Badge

The use of court uniforms in Canada provides an interesting window into the official and public perception of symbols of authority.[1] This section may seem out of place, as the focus of this book has primarily been on batons, maces, chains, and badges of office; however, court uniforms are in every respect akin to a badge of office. The uniform itself denoted a certain position; that the wearer was a servant of the Crown and an office-holder at the federal or provincial level. While military uniforms are worn by all members of the military, not all persons who were servants of the Crown — that is household staff, civil servants, or political office holders — were entitled to wear a court uniform. There were different types of court uniforms: the civil uniform, household uniforms, consular uniforms, and dress for gentlemen who otherwise did not have a uniform (court dress, old and new style). The type of court uniform that became most common in Canada was the civil uniform. Although originally intended for wear in the presence of the Sovereign "at court," in Canada and throughout the Commonwealth the civil uniform grew to become part of state events, not only in London, but in every Commonwealth country which composed the old British Empire. The wearing of the civil uniform became a potent symbol of the state's authority and the then-exalted position of the Crown.[2]

Uniforms were seen as both a badge of office and an honour to wear, as permission came directly from the Sovereign. Their purpose was much more than simply an attempt to project authority as they imbued the wearer with not only the authority of the Sovereign, but also provided a spectacle of honour.

The use of court and civil uniforms in Canada dates back to the French regime. By a Royal edict issued by King Louis XV in 1744, the governor general of New France was given authority to wear the uniform of a French lieutenant general, with minor differentiation.[3] It was a blue coat with gold embroidery in the form of lace, two rows on the cuff, and no epaulettes.[4] As we have seen in the section dealing with batons, French governors general are also recorded to

Left: Sir Edward Peacock, GCVO, wearing court dress (new style), circa 1937. Above: Consular coat, 1840.

have carried a French marshal's baton, most likely capped with a gold top and bottom, the shaft covered in light blue velvet.

Like the French, the British also possessed court uniforms, many of which would come to be worn in Canada. These uniforms were not limited to the use of the governor general alone, but would come to encompass all government officials down to mid-level bureaucrats.[5] From the time of Confederation until recently, it was customary for lieutenant governors to wear the United Kingdom civil uniform. This uniform is often referred to as "Windsor Court Dress"[6] or "Windsor uniform," on account of the fact that the civil uniform found its initial beginnings in the Windsor uniform. The original version of the Windsor uniform was designed by King George III in 1777 for use by male members of the Royal household. By the end of the nineteenth century the Windsor uniform was "only worn at Windsor Castle by the Royal family and certain officers of the Household."[7] There is evidence to suggest that it was the

Prince Regent (the future George IV) who first ordered civil and household uniforms to be worn.[8] While the Windsor uniform had some similarities with the civil uniform, the two modes of dress were different, the civil uniform being a descendant of the Windsor uniform. Sometime after the Prince of Wales became Prince Regent in 1811 the civil uniform was developed, "heavily influenced by the costume of marshals in the French Army."[9]

By the reign of Queen Victoria the civil uniforms were being worn by senior civil servants both in the United Kingdom and throughout the British Empire. While the use of court uniforms in Canada was of a highly limited scope,[10] the civil uniform was used on a much broader basis and would come to be inexorably linked with viceregal office-holders, although it was also worn by other officials of the Crown.

Until the 1980s lieutenant governors wore civil uniforms on state occasions, such as the opening of the provincial legislature, the New Year's levee, and during Royal tours. It is important to examine how lieutenant governors and the governor general became the last and only officials in Canada to wear civil uniforms, for there was a time when every prime minister, premier, member of the federal cabinet, Canadian diplomat, and deputy minister of the federal civil service was entitled to wear a civil uniform.

The origin and use of the first standardized civil uniforms widely used in Britain and Canada were developed out of the court uniforms that were designed and instituted by King George III in 1777. George III had taken the idea from Augustus III, Count of Saxony and King of Poland, who developed a court uniform in 1751. It was a relatively "simple sporting costume [dark blue with scarlet cuffs and facings] into a dark blue coat embroidered with gold but still with scarlet cuffs and facings, worn with a buff waistcoat and breeches."[11] Sweden and Prussia followed suit shortly thereafter.[12] The Windsor uniform ushered in "the beginnings of court uniforms in Britain."[13] Court uniforms were most commonly worn in the presence of the Sovereign at formal state events. Outside of the Royal court it was the civil uniform that came to be frequently worn by British diplomatic and consular officials. By the outbreak of the Great War the diplomatic services of every major power possessed a gold-embroidered civil uniform of some sort, except the United States.[14]

Use of the civil uniform was not limited to mainland Britain. There is an early reference to a version being worn by Ninian Home, who, "appointed Governor of Grenada in 1793 had his tailors, Douglas and Lambert of St. Martin's Lane, London, make up a coat of the Windsor uniform in thin cloth suitable for tropical wear."[15]

Lord Aylmer in governor's uniform, 1830.

Lord Aylmer, governor general of British North America from 1830 to 1835 is believed to be the first Canadian governor general to wear a civil uniform.[16] The regulations for this uniform were promulgated in 1824. The civil uniform worn by colonial governors was the same as that worn by Lord Lieutenants of English counties, the only difference being that the body of the uniform was blue with red lapels and gold embroidery.[17] The body of a Lord Lieutenant's uniforms was red. All of the embroidery and epaulettes were the same for both the Lord Lieutenants' uniform and the civil uniform worn by colonial governors. Provision was also made for a civil uniform to be worn by superior civil officials. This was a blue coat, but with no epaulettes or lapels, with buttons on the cuffs and collar only, the overall pattern being the same as that worn by Lord Lieutenants.[18]

In March 1825 it was clarified that the civil uniform to be worn by superior civil officials in the colonies was to be "worn only by members of H.M. Executive and Legislative Councils, by Chief Justices and the Speaker of the House of Assembly in the province under your Lordships Government."[19]

Shortly after the accession of Queen Victoria in 1837, a new set of civil uniform regulations were adopted. These regulations served as the foundation for future augmentations.[20] The regulations set out:

> Governors of Colonies — The same as the present Lord-Lieutenants of counties in England, only in blue with silver embroidery and scarlet collar and cuffs [the Lord-Lieutenant's Uniforms were made of red fabric]
>
> Superior Civil Officials — The same silver embroidery as the English Deputy-Lieutenants of counties, only blue coats with scarlet cuffs and collars, single breasted, cut the same as a Minister's Coat, white Kersimere linings and no turnbacks, buttons under the flaps, nine holes in front, no epaulets.
>
> The Superior Civil Officers entitled *ex-officio* to wear the uniform are;
>
> - Members of the Executive Council,
> - Members of the Court of Policy in British Guiana,
> - Speaker of the House of Assembly,
> - Members of the Legislative Councils,
>
> And Colonial Secretaries, who may not be members of the Executive Councils.
> All other superior civil servants must obtain Her Majesty's special permission to entitle them to wear the uniform.[21]

As most of Canada's pre-Confederation governors and governors general were military men, there was no real demand for a civil uniform in Canada until the latter part of the nineteenth century. The governors simply wore their military uniform for the opening of the legislature. The few who did not hold military rank simply wore a tailcoat with trousers, not unlike a modern-day morning suit.

In 1869 a new design of civil uniform was introduced. The old style of uniform was replaced with a more Victorian ensemble, as the old design was highly unpopular. One observer noted: "So hated was this absurd travesty that men too refuse from its soldier-like deputy-lieutenants uniform … it is not a dress but a costume."[22] The change caused quite a stir in the British press and it even merited inclusion in the *Morning Post*: "Lord Sydney has, by Her Majesty's permission, issued a notice which virtually abolishes the old dress, although that is still to be allowed at Court if any one sufficiently eccentric can be found to wear it."[23] There is little evidence that Canadians had the same distain for the pre-1869 civil uniform; obviously it was used in a much more limited fashion in colonial British North America.

Civil Uniform Types

Although not simultaneously introduced, five different types of civil uniforms were used in Canada (see Chart I). Each of these will be examined individually, as they were used in different periods and for different purposes.

The full dress civil uniform, which was descendent from that designed by King George III, was an impressive affair that was richly embroidered with gold metallic thread on midnight blue fabric and worn with white silk stockings. When worn with blue trousers the full dress civil uniform was known as half dress. The silk stockings became an issue for many Canadians, as they were not suitable for wear in the winter.

The levee civil uniform was a slightly toned-down version of the full dress civil uniform, in that it had much less gold embroidery and was worn with midnight blue trousers. The full dress and levee dress uniforms were worn with a cocked hat.

King Edward VII introduced the Government House evening dress uniform, which was a traditional evening waistcoat with light blue lapels. This uniform was worn only by members of the governor general's and lieutenant governor's staff. For a very brief period between 1908 and 1910, governors general were authorized to wear it, although there is no evidence that it was worn by a governor general in Canada. During the reign of King Edward VII, governors general throughout the empire were permitted to wear "a coat based on the frock coat worn in undress by general officers."[24] Although this was not worn in Canada, Canadian governors general preferred to wear the first class civil uniform.

Left: The Right Honourable Sir Robert Borden, PC, GCMG, in full dress civil uniform, Privy Councillor class.
Above: The Honourable Henry Bell-Irving, OC, DSO, OBE, OBC, ED, CD, wearing the second-class half dress civil uniform.

In 1910 the governor general's dress civil uniform was introduced.[25] It was a double-breasted affair of midnight blue material with silver embroidery and scarlet coloured facings. This was in every sense the most senior and formal civil uniform worn anywhere in the Commonwealth. The governor general's dress civil uniform was worn with a bicorn hat very similar to that worn by admirals in the Royal Navy, with the exception that the trimmings were silver, not gold. The overall uniform was largely based on that worn by Lord Lieutenants in the United Kingdom.

Lastly, and much less common in Canada, was the tropical dress civil uniform. This was a simple white cotton drill jacket with a high collar and gorgets (collar tabs). To complete the tropical flavour of this uniform the headdress was a white pith helmet with white feathers. For obvious reasons this uniform was very rarely worn in Canada. One of the only governors general to do so was Roland Michener, who added gold shoulder boards and personally redesigned the hat worn with the outfit.[26]

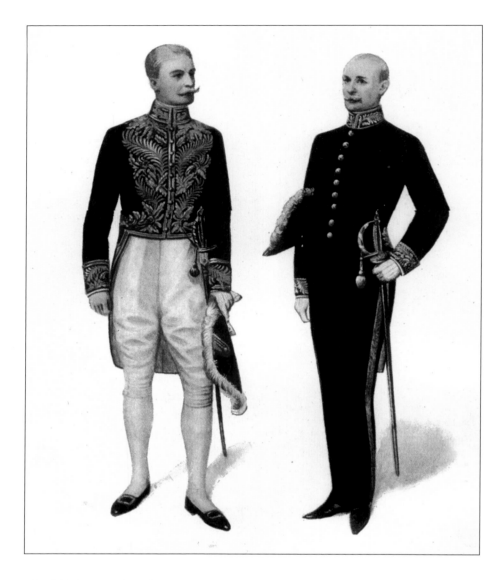

The full dress civil uniform and levee dress civil uniform, Privy Councillor class.

With the full dress, levee dress, and tropical dress civil uniforms there were six different ranks (see Chart II); Privy Council being the highest and fifth class being the lowest. The governor general's civil uniform had a single class, as it was worn by the governor general alone. Only a minor differentiation was made between the uniform worn by governors general of the senior Dominions and the uniform worn by governors of Crown colonies, even those as small as

Bermuda.[27] Governors and governors general were all equal in the eyes of the Colonial office, even if the breadth of their respective responsibilities were vastly different. The Sovereign's representative, no matter where he served, was to be an exalted figure, and this was reflected by the uniform he wore at state events.

The evening dress civil uniform made no differentiation in rank; from the governor general to the lowliest official of the viceregal household they were attired in the same fashion when at evening events. Of course the governor general could be easily spotted by the impressive array of decorations and breast stars worn on his chest and orders around his neck.

The Full Dress Civil Uniform to Canada

One of the first official references to the use of civil uniforms in Canada came in a *Colonial Office Circular* sent to all colonies on 15 February 1859. The circular outlined that whereas "it is Her Majesty's wish to mark in some distinctive manner the service of the Crown in the Colonies, as being in every respect on an equality with that of the mother country, Her Majesty has been, therefore, graciously pleased to confer on Her Majesty's Civil Servants in the Colonies, the right to wear the Civil Uniform prescribed for Her Majesty's Servants in Great Britain."[28] The program, if it can be called that, was administered by the Lord Chamberlain, who is head of the Royal household. Although it was the colonial office which was charged with publicizing the regulations, the governor general was required to work through the Lord Chamberlain.

The first class of uniform was to be worn by the governor of Canada and the governors of a number of other colonies. The second class uniform was to be worn by lieutenant governors, administrators (acting in place of a governor), and the governors of less significant colonies. The third class of uniform was reserved for members of the executive councils (colonial cabinets), "in Colonies having responsible Governments, this Class [third] will include only the Members of the Provincial or Colonial Cabinet."

Civil servants who were heads of departments got to wear the fourth class of uniform, and deputy heads of departments wore the fifth class of uniform. A provision was included to allow the governor general to promote any holder of the fifth class uniform to the fourth class uniform.

It was very clearly delineated that only those holding an office serving the Crown could wear the uniform. Thus members of the legislative assembly were not entitled to wear a civil uniform, although members of the legislative council and later the Senate were entitled to wear the civil uniform. There was a desire not to see civil uniforms politicized.

René Kimber in the court dress uniform of the Gentleman Usher of the Black Rod of the Senate of Canada. The head of the pre-1916 black rod can be seen at Kimber's right hand.

René Edouard Kimber wearing the third-class levee dress civil uniform. The pre-1916 black rod can be seen on the table.

In 1859 the full dress civil uniform was originally intended to be worn on state occasions in the United Kingdom, such as any occasion when an individual was in the presence of Queen Victoria. The levee dress civil uniform was worn on all other appropriate formal occasions. It was this uniform that was intended for use in Canada, it being "presumed that the Levee Dress only would be preferred for colonial use."[29] Shortly after Confederation this convention was abandoned, and the full dress civil uniform entered much wider usage in Canada.

The regulations were revised in 1860 to allow people who resigned from office to retain their civil uniform, provided they "upon their resignation request through you [the Governor] Her Majesty's permission to do so."[30] Although this question was raised in the context of former members of the executive council of New South Wales, it was applicable throughout the Empire. This decision was in part reversed in 1864: "the Queen is adverse in principle to the continuance of the Civil Uniform generally beyond the tenure of Office." Applications were still sent through the governor and now stated "length or merit of service would appear to render it desirable that the privilege should continue."[31]

Augmentations to the uniforms were made in 1905. Given the weight of the garments themselves it was decided necessary to adopt a tropical dress civil uniform.[32] The tropical uniform was adopted to provide members of the "Colonial Service with a simple and inexpensive uniform that shall be more convenient for wearing in hot climates than the ordinary Civil Uniform."[33] The full dress and levee dress civil uniforms were extremely expensive and far too heavy to wear in tropical climates at a time when air conditioning was unknown.

The question of the civil uniform was a particularly acute one following each change of government. Because of the rule that only those currently in the service of the Crown were permitted to wear the civil uniform, when a government was voted out of office all of the members of the defeated federal cabinet were no longer permitted to wear the civil uniform — "the right of a particular officer to wear the civil uniform attached to a particular office must cease when he has ceased to hold that office."[34] However, the King would grant special permission for some to continue to wear their civil uniforms. Following the 1911 general election, the Liberals were swept from power and replaced by Sir Robert Borden's Conservatives. There was a flurry of applications by almost the entire Liberal cabinet to retain the right to wear their second-class civil uniforms.[35] This spectacle was repeated in 1921 after the Conservatives were voted out of office.[36] The King invariably granted permission to former members of the cabinet to wear their civil uniforms. This was in part because

The Right Honourable Vincent Massey in the second-class full dress uniform with winter overcoat, taken outside the White House, Washington, D.C., circa 1927.

in the United Kingdom all members of cabinet who were members of the His/Her Majesty's Most Honourable Privy Council (also known as the Imperial Privy Council) were permitted to continue to wear their Privy Council rank civil uniforms after leaving office, as they remained members of the Privy

Council. In Canada all members of cabinet were members of the King's Privy Council for Canada, and thus the logic used by the King was that Canada should follow the British precedent in this regard.

As seen in Chart II, lieutenant governors were initially only permitted to wear the second-class civil uniform, while members of the King's Privy Council for Canada were entitled to the third class and deputy ministers the fourth class.[37] This general pecking order was never changed in Canada. In 1928 the Lord Chamberlain proposed to allow lieutenant governors and members of the King's Privy Council for Canada to wear the first class of uniform, and deputy ministers were greatly promoted to the second-class uniform, however Canada was slow to adopt the regulations.[38]

The issue of civil uniforms was again introduced on the eve of the 1939 Royal tour of King George VI and Queen Elizabeth. The governor general, Lord Tweedsmuir, noted, "it is true to say that generally speaking there is no real demand for the wearing of Civil Uniform in the Dominion."[39] The impending Royal tour brought up a host of questions about who would wear what class of uniform. Canadian officials had little interest in opening up the question, in part because of difficulties a number of lieutenant governors were having with their premiers. Thus in 1939, Canada was still using the 1904 civil uniform ranking schedule, while the rest of the Commonwealth was using the 1929 schedule. "The Secretary of State expressed the hope that this whole matter may be allowed to stand in abeyance for a further short period."[40] It was explained to British officials that following the 1939 tour the issue would probably be reopened. Of course the 1939 Royal tour provided the last series of large-scale state occasions where all lieutenant governors, the governor general, prime minister, members of the federal cabinet, provincial governments, and senior civil servants wore their civil uniforms.

Canadian diplomats did, however, continue to wear the uniforms throughout the war at official functions. The Canadian High Commissioner to London, Vincent Massey, wore the first-class uniform while provincial agents and general and trade commissioners wore the second and third classes, respectively. Future Prime Minister Lester Pearson frequently wore a fourth-class civil uniform while working at the Canadian embassy in Washington, D.C., in the 1930s, and later wore the third class of civil uniform when he was posted to the Canadian High Commission in London. As in most European countries, the Commonwealth and Japan had civil uniforms; Canadian diplomats seemed to have worn them to fit into the diplomatic world.

The Right Honourable Roland Michener in the levee dress uniform, second class, accompanied by Major General George R. Pearkes, following an investiture.

Evening Dress Civil Uniform

In 1908 King Edward VII determined that a special evening dress uniform should be worn by Dominion/colonial governors and their staff. It was an evening dress tailcoat of dark blue cloth (it appears black), with a dark blue velvet collar and light blue silk facing. The buttons were gilt, bearing the Royal cypher and a crown. The waistcoat was white pique with no collar, joined by four small gilt buttons, the entire affair worn with black trousers.[41] Thus, both governors general and their staff wore exactly the same uniform for evening dress. This order of dress did not survive long, and in 1910, King George V, who is said to have never liked this uniform, decided that governors general would no longer wear this evening dress uniform. After 1910 only viceregal staff wore the civil evening dress uniform. This uniform was also used by a number of provincial government houses. There was even some discussion that the uniform should have different coloured facings for provincial viceregal staff to help differentiate them from their federal counterparts.[42]

The evening dress civil uniform had a very long life in Canada. It had fallen out of use at Government House in Ottawa following the end of the Second World War, but Lord Alexander examined the issue, and in 1950 the uniform was reinstated: "an evening dress coat, of blue cloth, with dark blue collar and St. Patrick's blue silk facing and linings."[43] This was to enable "their Excellencies and the public to identify them [staff] more readily."[44] There had been some difficulty and embarrassing moments caused when Lady Alexander was unable to differentiate staff from guests. The old standby of merely examining the number of medals on a person's chest was no longer sufficient, given that a number of the Rideau Hall staff had served in the Second World War, returning with four or five medals each. This uniform was last worn by non-military male members of the Rideau Hall household staff in 1985 shortly after the departure of Esmond Butler, the long-serving secretary to the governor general, who is said to have very much liked the evening dress civil uniform. Jeanne Sauvé, who had little time for many Canadian traditions, greatly disliked the evening dress civil uniform, and following Esmond Butler's departure its wear was discontinued. The evening dress worn by non-military members of the Rideau Hall staff is a simple dinner jacket with a gold viceregal lion pin in the lapel.

Governor General's Dress Civil Uniform

In 1910 King George V decided that governors general and colonial governors required a new, more distinctive uniform. A governor general in the Dominions could not be differentiated from his prime minister in those cases where the prime minister was a member of the Imperial Privy Council, which was the case in both Canada and Australia, as both were entitled to the Privy Councillor class civil uniform.

The *Colonial Office Circular* of 1 September 1910, specifically stated that the new colonial governor general's uniform was not to be worn by lieutenant governors. The governor general's civil dress uniform had a distinctively naval flair, being roughly modelled on that worn by members of the Royal Navy and by Lord Lieutenants in the United Kingdom. One of the chief differentiations was that the governor general's uniform had silver wire trim with scarlet background and not gold wire trim with white background which the navy wore.

Governors general holding the rank of rear admiral, major general, or above were entitled to wear their military dress uniform. This was the reason that General Vanier often wore his military uniform in place of the governor general's dress civil uniform.[45] In 1938 an undress version of the governor general's civil dress uniform was created, although no Canadian governor general ever wore it. Further augmentations to the regulations governing the governor general's dress civil uniform came in 1959, although by this point Canadian officials did not feel inclined to follow them — Canada was an independent country, and the governor general was empowered to make his own regulations. Of course, Massey, Vanier, and Michener continued with tradition and made no significant changes.

Above: The Right Honourable Lord Tweedsmuir, GCMG, GCVO, CH, wearing the governor general's uniform.

Left: Lord Tweedsmuir laying a wreath at the Tomb of the Unknown Solider, Arlington National Cemetery.

The full dress governor general's uniform.

With the retirement of Roland Michener as governor general in 1974, the use of the governor general's civil dress uniform came to an end, as did the use of the tropical civil uniform.[46] Upon taking office, Jules Léger refused to wear the governor general's civil dress uniform, referring to it as a "colonial uniform." In fairness to Léger, the uniform was colonial in its origins. He referred to the

Major General the Right Honourable Georges Vanier, PC, DSO, MC, CD, wearing the uniform of a major general in the Canadian Army.

outfit as the "jaquette noir,"[47] and wanted nothing to do with it.[48] A special commander-in-chief's uniform was created for Jeanne Sauvé in 1986. It was quite simply a modified Canadian Forces uniform, with special shoulder and cuff insignia. Ray Hnatyshyn cut an impressive figure in the uniform, and is said to have quite liked it, as it took him back to his days in the Royal Canadian

The Right Honourable Jeanne Sauvé wearing the commander-in-chief's army summer uniform.

The Right Honourable Ramon Hnatyshyn wearing the commander-in-chief's air force uniform.

The Right Honourable Michaëlle Jean wearing the commander-in-chief's navy uniform.

Air Force. During the 2009 visit of Their Royal Highnesses the Prince of Wales and the Duchess of Cornwall, the Prince wore the uniform of a Canadian Forces lieutenant general, while then-Governor General Michaëlle Jean wore the army uniform of commander-in-chief. Subsequently, in May 2010, Jean wore the navy uniform of commander-in-chief during the consecration of the Queen's colour for the Royal Canadian Navy, which took place on the garrison grounds in Halifax.

The Tropical Dress Civil Uniform

The tropical dress civil uniform had a very limited existence in Canada, with Roland Michener being the only Canadian official known to have worn it. Michener made some augmentations to the original design, adding gold wire shoulder boards and replacing the pith helmet with an admiral's peak cap bearing the Royal arms of the United Kingdom on the badge. No Canadian governor general before or since has worn this uniform.

The Right
Honourable Roland
Michener, PC,
CC, CMM, CD,
QC, wearing the
governor general's
tropical uniform.

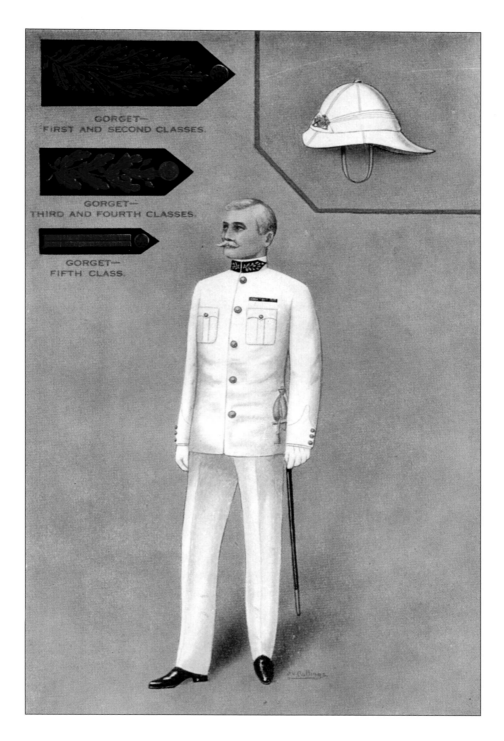

GORGET—
FIRST AND SECOND CLASSES.

GORGET—
THIRD AND FOURTH CLASSES.

GORGET—
FIFTH CLASS.

The tropical uniform.

Lieutenant Governors and the Full Dress Civil Uniform

At Confederation, lieutenant governors in Canada were entitled to wear the second-class full-dress civil uniform. In 1929 the regulations changed, and lieutenant governors — as representatives of the Sovereign — were permitted to upgrade their uniforms to the first-class version. This was enacted on a sporadic basis. In fact, the difference between the first- and second-class uniforms is almost indistinguishable, and thus the change was not seen as necessary. As lieutenant governors started ordering new uniforms in the 1950s and 1960s a few replaced the old second-class full-dress civil uniform with the first-class version. That this change took more than forty years to take hold was a result of how rarely new uniforms were ordered.

The office of the lieutenant governor in British Columbia had the longest continuous tradition of wearing the civil service uniform, and it was used there from 1861 to 1991. After a number of questions from the public, then lieutenant governor, the Honourable David See-Chai Lam, commented:

> I would beg your indulgence to allow me to make a few comments. Some of you may have noticed that I am not wearing the traditional civil uniform that has been used these past years to open the legislative sessions of the parliaments of British Columbia. Our world is changing; and traditions, while being honoured and respected, must also change to make institutions relevant in today's time. This may be the last throne speech I read to you, as my term of office is due to end this coming autumn. I feel that on this very special occasion it is time to look forward and to begin a new custom that my successors may wish to follow. I will trust that you will understand my decision and join with me in moving forward in harmony, preaching established ideals with contemporary reality.[49]

The decline of the civil dress uniform in British Columbia was lamented in some quarters, but its absence did not cause great public discussion.[50] In 2008 the newly installed lieutenant governor of British Columbia, Stephen Point, resumed the practice of wearing the civil uniform at formal functions.

The most recent Canadian lieutenant governors to wear the full-dress civil uniform are Myra Freeman, lieutenant governor of Nova Scotia from 2000–2006, and her successor, Mayann Francis. Iona Campagnolo is believed to have been the first woman to wear the civil uniform. The civil uniform has been worn

by the Crown's representative in Nova Scotia almost uninterrupted since Confederation. In 1907, Lieutenant Governor Duncan Fraser opened the legislature in morning suit, although his successor, David MacKeen, and subsequent lieutenant governors have worn the civil uniform.[51]

There was heavy criticism of the civil uniform, and some commentators noted that the custom of wearing the civil uniform was "foreign to this democratic land and contrary to the spirit of our people."[52] In the 1930s there were further attempts to reduce the ceremonial aspect of the legislative opening, however this was blocked by Premier Macdonald, who went on at great length about the importance of tradition and ceremony.

While the traditional civil uniform is rarely used in Canada today — or in the United Kingdom for that matter — the concept of a civil uniform that could be worn by representatives of the Crown has not disappeared. In Alberta, viceregal robes were designed and adopted by Helen Hunley, who served as lieutenant governor of the province from 1985 to 1991.

The Honourable Mayann E. Francis, ONS, wearing the full civil dress uniform.

The Honourable Iona Campagnolo, PC, OC, OBC, in civil uniform.

The robes were styled along the lines of academic regalia — purple in colour edged with gold wire and bearing the shield of the province surmounted by a Royal Crown on the left breast. As the first woman to hold viceregal office in Alberta, Hunley felt that she required some sort of formal attire to wear during Royal assent ceremonies and other legislative events where the full civil dress uniform would be worn by male holders of the viceregal office. Hunley remains the only Alberta lieutenant governor to have worn the robes. In 2001, shortly after presiding over her first official function as lieutenant governor, Iona Campagnolo — British Columbia's first female lieutenant governor — made it a priority to develop a new civil uniform, to be styled as a viceregal uniform. Her goal was to create a garment that was not only appropriate for a woman to wear, but a garment that would reflect the symbols and character of the province of British Columbia.

The British Columbia viceregal uniform consists of a midnight blue, single-breasted military doeskin jacket with a high collar, featuring an embroidered yoke of silver dogwood flowers (the provincial flower). The dogwood flowers are coupled with two silver-embroidered aboriginal figures, one placed on each side of the upper chest below the collar. These denote the First Nations names that have been accorded to Campagnolo. On the left is a Haida whale, and on the right an eagle of Haida design. In place of the traditional embroidered gold oak and palm clusters of the civil uniform, the cuffs and collar of the B.C. viceregal uniform are embroidered with the image of the great Pacific red cedar. An ankle-length, midnight blue skirt with an open seam is worn with the uniform. Finally, there is a hat with a rounded top and a round brim that is bent upwards on the right hand side. White ostrich plumes extend backwards from the right-hand side of the hat.

Although only Mayann Francis in Nova Scotia has followed Campagnolo's lead, it is easy to see how this sort of modern and province-specific (with local symbols and elements) uniform could be adapted for all of Canada's provinces.

The Civil Uniform in the Political World

Changing attitudes towards the civil uniform are difficult to trace, although taking the example of William Lyon Mackenzie King, we can track the demise of the civil uniform in the political world. Mackenzie King was appointed deputy minister of labour in 1900, and in 1906 he received his fourth-class civil uniform. He spent a good deal of time reflecting on the uniform in his famous diary. After Mackenzie King became a full cabinet minister in 1909, he commented: "my regret is I have not a Minister's full uniform, only a deputy."[53] Mackenzie King received his full minister's (third-class) uniform in 1911 just before the Laurier Liberals were voted out of office. Nonetheless, he was quick to apply for special permission to continue to wear the uniform. He and other members of the recently defeated government obviously felt that retention of the civil uniform was a necessary status symbol. Mackenzie King would continue to wear the uniform as prime minister at openings of Parliament and other senior state occasions. The last public occasion where Mackenzie King wore the civil uniform, by now that of the Privy Council class, was during the 1939 Royal tour.

Left: The Right Honourable William Lyon Mackenzie King wearing the third-class levee dress civil uniform.
Right: The Right Honourable William Lyon Mackenzie King wearing the cape and cocked hat that accompany the civil dress uniform, wearing the Privy Council class half dress civil uniform underneath.

By this time, Mackenzie King's attitude towards the uniform had changed. He commented: "I should never wish to have myself perpetuated in public memory, either in painting or drawing in uniform or in court dress of any kind."[54] At future state functions he simply wore a morning suit or three-piece suit. We can only speculate why he came to dislike the uniform, however it may well have had something to do with his growing girth and the fact that the uniform could make a stout person look even more portly. Mackenzie King's refusal to wear the uniform after 1939 had a great deal to do with its demise.

Those senators and members of Parliament who had served in the Laurier and Borden cabinets steadfastly refused to cease wearing their civil uniforms, but newer members took little interest in the matter. Sir William Mullock and Senator Raoul Dandurand wore them well into the 1940s.

The final blow to the civil uniform at the federal level for non-viceregal officials came in 1957, just prior to the Queen's 1957 Royal tour. The cabinet of John Diefenbaker considered the issue of what order of dress should be worn for formal occasions in the presence of Her Majesty. During the cabinet's deliberations, "doubt was raised as to the desirability of the use of the civil uniform in present day Canada and it was suggested that while the solemnity of the occasions should be recognized, excessive formality of dress might bring undesirable public criticism."[55] Fear of adverse public reaction to ministers wearing the civil uniform brought the issue to a final close. In the United Kingdom, the last politician to wear the civil uniform was Jeremy Thorpe, in 1973, who wore it at the signing ceremony where Britain acceded to the European Union.[56]

In Canada no subsequent government has examined the possibility of ministers returning to wearing a civil uniform of any type. Indeed the wearing of even a traditional morning suit at federal state functions has begun to wane on account of a fear that ministers will look like they are not dressed "to work." The last time morning attire was worn by the prime minister was Paul Martin's first speech from the throne in 2004. Canadian state functions now lack formality, as even at the most important events participants wear everyday clothes. Ceremonies are very much state theatre; they require a stage, actors, a scenario, and also costumes. The demise of formal dress has removed the sense of occasion from our state events. Some lieutenant governors and their private secretaries continue to wear morning suits, but this remains the last refuge of formality at state events.

Aside from changing style and attitudes towards formality, one of the main factors in the demise of the civil uniform in Canada was the cost of having such garments manufactured. Civil uniforms were quite costly and the Crown bore none of the expense for their purchase. Most of the civil uniforms worn by Canadians were made in London, and it was not until the 1950s that a Canadian firm was able to tailor civil uniforms in Canada. William Scully Ltd. of Montreal is the only firm in Canada that ever managed to produce a civil uniform. The project undertaken in the 1950s "involved two women in hand gold embroidery work for eight months."[57] By the early 1970s, most lieutenant governors — the last remaining office in Canada to make regular use of civil uniforms — were simply recycling the uniforms worn by their predecessors. Indeed there was a long tradition of altering and reusing civil uniforms. Vincent

Left: Lord Bessborough wearing the governor general's uniform.
Right: Lord Bessborough in the Senate Chamber, 1931.

Massey wore Lord Tweedsmuir's governor general's uniform, and General Vanier wore that which had belonged to Lord Bessborough. The quoted cost in 1970 for a new civil uniform was $3,000, a significant amount during a time when lieutenant governors were earning less than $30,000 a year.

The Lieutenant Governor and Territorial Commissioners Recognition Badge

While a number of lieutenant governors have continued wearing the civil uniform well into the twenty-first century, the majority of the Queen's representatives in Canada have not. One of the distinct advantages of the uniform was that in a large group of people it was easy to recognize just who the lieutenant governor was; there was no mistaking the midnight blue tunic embroidered with gold wire.

Following the establishment of the Order of Canada in 1967, a number of lieutenant governors sought to be made ex officio members of the Order of Canada, as a way to help members of the public identify them as representatives of the Crown. The federal government rejected this idea and no solution was found to the "identification" problem that was often experienced by lieutenant governors and territorial commissioners.

The issue of a badge of office was routinely brought up at the annual lieutenant governors' and territorial commissioners' conferences. The concept for a badge

Top Left: The Honourable Hilary M. Weston, CM, O.Ont, wearing the viceregal recognition badge on a red bow and the Order of Ontario below.
Top Right: Lady Jennifer Gretton, Lord Lieutenant of Leicestershire.
Bottom: Lord Lieutenant's badge as worn by female Lord Lieutenants in the United Kingdom.

of office was finally resolved at the June 1995 conference in Charlottetown, Prince Edward Island. It was agreed that a badge should be developed which would "visually signal the presence of an incumbent Lieutenant Governor or Territorial Commissioner."[58]

The concept for a badge of office was not entirely unique. In the United Kingdom, female Lord Lieutenants (in some ways equivalent to a Canadian lieutenant governor) began wearing an insignia of office in place of the Lord Lieutenant's uniform in 1975. There are four different varieties of insignia: a version for English counties (a Tudor rose enamelled in red and white), Scottish counties (a thistle), Northern Irish counties (a sprig of shamrocks enamelled in green), and Welsh counties (the Prince of Wales's plume enamelled in white). The badge is only worn by women and is made from 18-carat gold and hung from a plain white ribbon containing two thin stripes of maroon. Men continue to wear the Lord Lieutenant's uniform.[59]

The first detailed proposal for the Canadian badge of office was developed by the deputy secretary of the Chancellery of Honours, Lieutenant-General James Gervais, while the form and symbolic elements of the badge were developed by the then Chief Herald of Canada Robert Watt, and the artistic designs were drawn by Fraser Herald Cathy Bursey-Sabourin.

The proposal for a badge of office was presented at the November 1996 lieutenant governors' and territorial commissioners' conference held at Rideau Hall in Ottawa. This proposal underwent some additional fine-tuning at the 1998 lieutenant governors' and territorial commissioners' conference held in Whitehorse, Yukon, on 30 October 1998.

Quite simply, the purpose of the badges was to give lieutenant governors, territorial commissioners, and their spouses a symbol by which they could be easily identified, and also to provide recognition of service as a representative of the Crown during the lifetime of the recipient.

The badges were established by a viceregal warrant on 26 January 1999. Her Majesty the Queen approved the insignia design in July 1998. The insignia is usually presented to a newly installed lieutenant governor or territorial commissioner by an official from Rideau Hall.[60] The first presentation of badges was made by Governor General Roméo LeBlanc on 3 October 1999.

The badge is intended to be worn on the left breast, above the general area where orders, decorations, and medals are worn. The lapel badge is to be worn on the left lapel, or left side in the case of ladies attire that lacks a lapel. Former lieutenant governors and commissioners are only supposed to wear the lapel badges upon leaving office, and not the full-size badge.

Top Left: Viceregal and commissioner's recognition badge.
Top Right: Viceregal and commissioner's recognition pin.
Bottom Left: Reverse of the viceregal and commissioner's recognition badge.

Origins: Intended to replace the need for court uniforms and to serve as an easily identifiable symbol that would help Canadians better recognize their lieutenant governors and territorial commissioners.

Insignia for Lieutenant Governors and Territorial Commissioners: A silver-gilt insignia 38 milimetres in diameter that is composed of four stylized maple leaves in red and white enamel. The centre has a circle with a thin border of red, containing a gold maple leaf in the centre and surmounted by a crown.

Insignia for the Spouses: A silver-gilt insignia 38 milimetres in diametre that is composed of four stylized maple leaves in red and white enamel. In the centre is a circle with a thin border of red, containing a silver maple leaf in the centre surmounted by a crown.

Left: Spouses viceregal and commissioner's recognition badge.
Right: Spouses viceregal and commissioner's recognition pin.

Lapel Badge: In addition to the full-size badge, lieutenant governors, territorial commissioners, and their spouses are given a lapel badge for regular wear. This badge is circular with a thin border of red enamel, measuring 20 millimetres in diameter. In the centre is a maple leaf, and the entire insignia is surmounted by a crown. As with the full-size badges, a gold maple leaf denotes a lieutenant governor or territorial commissioner, while a silver maple leaf denotes a spouse.

Other: The badge is worn on the left shoulder above decorations. Upon retirement, recipients of these badges are permitted to retain and wear them to denote their service as a representative of the Crown. The badge is not intended for wear on either the court uniform or a Canadian Forces uniform.

Numbers: Every lieutenant governor, territorial commissioner, and spouse since 1999 has been presented with a badge. Each badge is individually numbered, and a register of recipients is retained by the Chancellery of Honours.

Chart I
Types of Civil Uniforms Worn in Canada

Civil Uniform	Jacket	Trousers	Hat	Court Sword
Full Dress	Dark blue tailcoat embroidered with varying degrees of gold thread, depending upon rank.	White silk breeches, later changed to dark blue trousers with gold trim. When worn with dark blue trousers, it was known as "half dress."	Cocked hat with white feathers and gold trim.	Yes
Levee Dress	Dark blue tailcoat embroidered with varying degrees of gold thread on the collar and cuffs only.	Dark blue with gold trim.	Cocked hat with white feathers and gold trim.	Yes
Governor General	Dark blue, double-breasted frock coat embroidered with silver thread on the red collar and cuffs.	Dark blue with silver trim.	Bicorn hat with silver trim and white feathers.	Yes
Tropical Dress	Plain white drill jacket with a high collar. Gorgets embroidered with gold worn on the collar, and gold shoulder boards and buttons on the sleeve (number varying by rank).	Plain white.	Pith helmet with white feathers or forage cap, modified by Roland Michener to consist of a Royal Canadian Navy flag officer's forage cap with gilt Royal arms as the cap badge.	Yes

Evening Dress	Black wool tailcoat with light blue "St. Patrick" blue lapels.	Plain black.	None.	No

Chart II
Rank and Office of the Full Dress and Levee Dress Civil Uniforms

Rank	1859	1904	1929 Proposal
Privy Councillor	Members of the Imperial Privy Council	Members of the Imperial Privy Council	Members of the Imperial Privy Council
First Class	Governor general (if not a member of the Imperial Privy Council)	Governor general (if not a member of the Imperial Privy Council)	Prime minister of Canada, lieutenant governors, and members of the King's Privy Council for Canada (federal cabinet)
Second Class	Administrators (acting for a governor general) and lieutenant governors	Administrators (acting for a governor general) and lieutenant governors	Deputy ministers
Third Class	Members of the executive council (colonial cabinet), administrators (acting for a lieutenant governor), and members of provincial cabinets	Members of the King's Privy Council for Canada (federal cabinet), and members of provincial cabinets	The secretary to the governor general

Fourth Class	Heads of departments (deputy ministers), and auditors general	Deputy ministers, and auditors general	
Fifth Class	Assistant heads of departments (assistant deputy ministers)	Assistant deputy ministers and the secretary to the governor general	

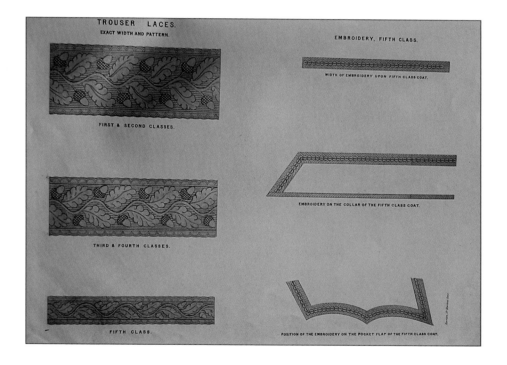

Civil uniform patterns for the first- to fifth-class civil uniforms.

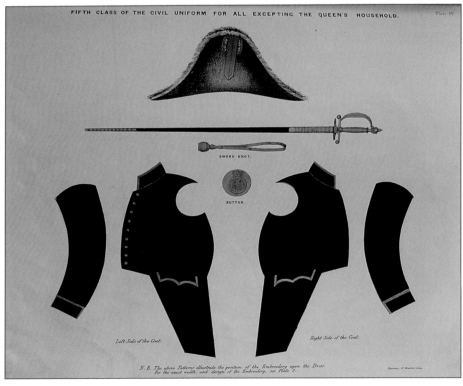

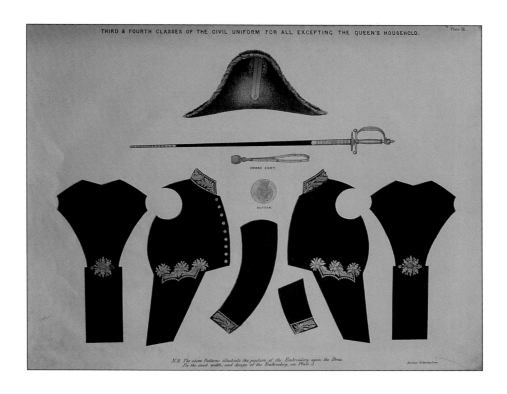

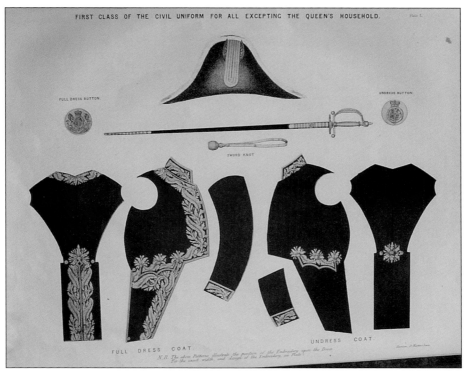

COLLAR, PRIVY COUNSELLORS.

COLLAR, FIRST CLASS.

COLLAR, SECOND CLASS.

CUFF, PRIVY COUNSELLORS.
First Class, same design, slightly narrower, and with wavy edge.
Second-Class, same design, narrower than First Class, and with saw edge.

POCKET FLAP, PRIVY COUNSELLORS.
First Class, same design, with wavy edge.
Second Class, same design, with saw edge.

EMBROIDERY FOR PRIVY COUNSELLORS, FIRST AND SECOND CLASSES.
CIVIL UNIFORM.

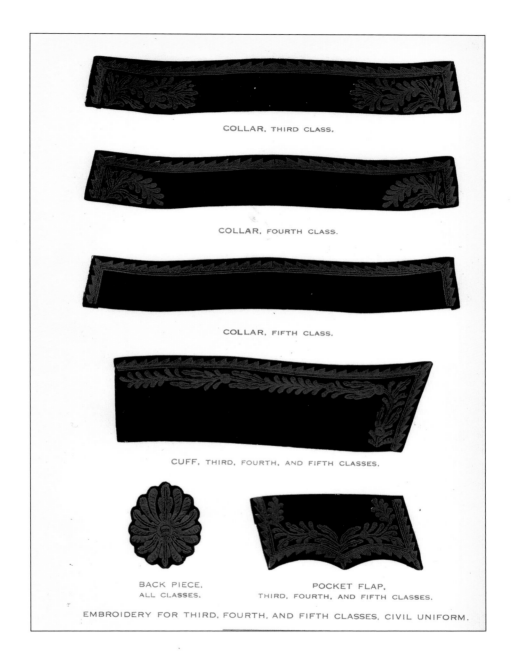

COLLAR, THIRD CLASS.

COLLAR, FOURTH CLASS.

COLLAR, FIFTH CLASS.

CUFF, THIRD, FOURTH, AND FIFTH CLASSES.

BACK PIECE,
ALL CLASSES.

POCKET FLAP,
THIRD, FOURTH, AND FIFTH CLASSES.

EMBROIDERY FOR THIRD, FOURTH, AND FIFTH CLASSES, CIVIL UNIFORM.

CHAPTER SIXTEEN

Collar of the Sergeant-at-Arms of
the House of Commons

The origins of the collar of Ss that the sergeant-at-arms of the House of Commons wears can be traced back to the twelfth century and the Savoyard Order of the Collar.[1] In England, the collar of Ss became an official ornament worn on various state occasions by Kings of Arms, Lord Chief Justices, and the Lord Mayor of London, and the tradition was transplanted in part to Canada. There are a number of differing theories as to the meaning of the letter Ss and there is no definite answer. One theory states that they stand for *Sanctus Spiritus* (Holy Spirit) and another that it represents the word *Sovereygne*, the motto of King Henry IV.[2] Earlier accounts suggest that "it was the custom of those persons to wear about their necks silver collars, composed of double S's, which noted the name of Saint Simplicus: between these double S's the collar contained 12 small plates of silver, which were engraved with 12 Articles of the Creed, together with a single Trefoyle."[3] The seventeenth-century historian of honours, Elias Ashmole, noted in 1672 that "how long since the collar of S's came to use here in England, we no where find."[4] However, he does note that the collars have been worn by women as well as men.

This type of collar was worn by Cardinal Wolsey and Sir Thomas More. King Henry VIII of England bestowed it as a mark of honour and it has not always directly connected with a specific state office.[5] The use of this type of collar in Canada seems to have originated in the Parliament of the Province of Canada in 1844. The collar currently worn by the sergeant-at-arms is made of sterling silver and was manufactured by William Chapman, a London silversmith, in 1859. Today the collar is only worn during the opening of Parliament. The daily wearing of the collar while the House of Commons was sitting was phased out in the early 1970s.

Origins: In Canada, the collar of Ss has come to be one of the principal symbols of the sergeant-at-arms of the House of Commons. It has been worn for state occasions continuously by sergeants-at-arms since Confederation.

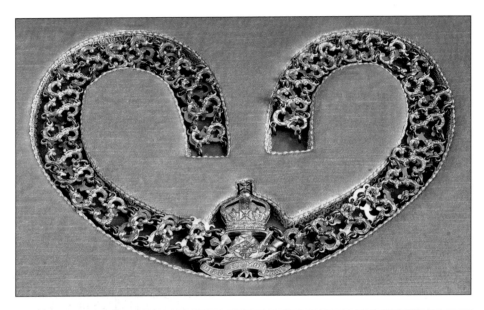

Top: The collar of Ss in its case.
Bottom: Close-up detail of the collar of Ss.

Insignia: A sterling silver chain composed of seventy-four stylized *S* links. There are two silver-gilt badges, one at the front and one at the back, which consist of a conjoined shamrock, rose, and thistle, surmounted by a large crown, with a scroll bearing the motto DIEU ET MON DROIT. The chain bears the maker's mark "W.C" for William Chapman, and silver hallmarks for London 1859.

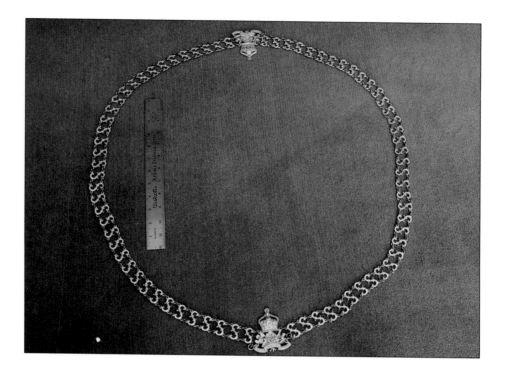

Sergeant-at-arms collar of Ss.

Former Sergeant-at-Arms Major General Gaston Cloutier, CMM, CVO, CD, wearing the collar of Ss and carrying the mace of the House of Commons.

Central badge of the collar of Ss.

House of Commons assembled in its temporary location, March 1918, with sergeant-at-arms Lieutenant Colonel Henry R. Smith, CMG, ISO, VD, wearing the collar of Ss.

Other: This chain was rescued from the 1916 parliamentary fire that destroyed the original House of Commons mace. The Sergeant-at-Arms Lieutenant Colonel H.R. Smith, CMG, ISO, VD, was in the House of Commons when the fire started and simply rose with Deputy Speaker Edgar N. Rhodes and the other twenty members of Parliament present in the chamber when the seriousness of the fire had been discovered. During the fire, Smith returned to the building to help retrieve furniture and documents. There is no indication as to whether or not he continued to wear his chain of office during the rescue operation.

The famous photograph of the House of Commons in 1918 clearly shows the sergeant-at-arms wearing the collar of Ss.

Chain of the Usher of the Black Rod

In the United Kingdom, the Gentleman Usher of the Black Rod, along with possessing the black rod as his symbol of office, has a chain of office as well. Composed of three rows of gold chains joined at the back by a Tudor rose, the pendant of the chain contains the garter knot, circumscribed by the motto of the Order of the Garter, surmounted by a crown.

In 1966, C.R. Lamoureux, Gentleman Usher of the Black Rod of the Senate, visited the Crown jewellers, Garrard & Co. Ltd., in London. Lamoureux inquired about the creation of a chain of office for the Gentleman Usher of the Black Rod of the Senate. The insignia was to be a 22-carat gold triple chain, 73 centimetres long, from which a pendant was to be hung. In place of the garter knot, a simple gold maple leaf was proposed. The entire insignia had a projected cost of £685, or $2,740 Canadian.[6] The quotation was obviously too great for Lamoureux to proceed, and although he was quite pleased with the design, he informed Garrards: "I regret to inform you that it has been decided to dispense with the purchase of this Chain of Office."[7]

Although not an insignificant cost, such an addition to Canada's symbols is something that could still be made. It would be only fitting for the Usher of the Black Rod to have a chain of office similar to that worn by the sergeant-at-arms of the House of Commons.

Chain of office worn by the Gentleman Usher of the Black Rod in the House of Lords.

Proposed design for chain of office for the Gentleman Usher of the Black Rod of the Senate, 1966.

CHAPTER SEVENTEEN

Collars of Office of the Canadian Heraldic Authority

L
ike the Canadian honours system, the Canadian Heraldic Authority (CHA) is a recent creation, yet one that is imbued with a great deal of history and a special connection to Canada's symbolic development. Most heralds around the world wear some insignia of office, and in both Britain and Spain the custom is for heralds to wear a tabard, which is a short cloth smock embroidered with the coat of arms of their Sovereign. Heralds also wear a collar of office on official state occasions or when presenting a grant of arms, and this tradition can, like the wearing of the collar of Ss, be traced back to the fourteenth century.

When the Canadian Heraldic Authority was created in 1988, little attention was given to what insignia the Chief Herald or the Heralds of Arms should wear. The main focus was on creating a Canadian body capable of granting arms and badges on behalf of the Canadian Crown. Government officials were afraid that if the new institution was accompanied by a wide array of insignia and accoutrements, that the new institution would be ridiculed for its almost instant "invention of tradition."[1]

Former Chief Herald of Canada Robert Watt noted: "for many centuries, heralds have worn ceremonial collars of office."[2] As the success and notoriety of the Canadian Heraldic Authority grew, questions arose as to why the Chief Herald did not have some sort of insignia to denote his position. Being that this is the norm in most other countries, it seemed a natural extension of Canada's heraldic sovereignty that such an insignia should be developed.

In Canada, all grants of arms and badges are made as grants of honour on behalf of the Queen. The governor general acts as the Queen's representative and thus presents many grants, while the Chief Herald is the chief administrative officer of heraldry in Canada. Given that there is such a special relationship between the Crown and heraldry, it was natural that two collars of office were designed: one for the governor general as the Queen's representative — in whose name all grants are made — and one for the Chief Herald of Canada, the person ultimately responsible for the administration of heraldry in Canada.

Ceremonial collar of the governor general as head of the Canadian Heraldic Authority.

The concept was devised by Robert Watt, whose initial idea was for a collar of Cs, similar to the collar of Ss worn by English heralds and the Canadian sergeant-at-arms. He envisioned a collar that would be worn when presenting grants and on special state occasions.

The design of the collar of Cs was drawn by Fraser Herald Cathy Bursey-Sabourin, who modified the original idea of interlinked Cs by adding a small

Ceremonial collar of the Chief Herald of Canada.

blank white escutcheon (shield) between the opening of the *C*. This blank shield represents the CHA's role in granting arms.

The project and designs were approved by Governor General Adrienne Clarkson in November 2003. This was followed by the long process of manufacturing the chains of office. The chains were manufactured under the direction of Alan Tramrell of Pressed Metal Products and were donated to Canada by Dr. Helen Mussallem, CC, the noted Canadian nurse and philanthropist.

The governor general's collar was first worn on 28 September 2004, when Governor General Adrienne Clarkson presented personal arms to Lieutenant Governor Chiasson of New Brunswick and Lieutenant Governor Roberts of Newfoundland and Labrador. The Chief Herald wore the Chief Herald's heraldic collar for the first time on 4 October 2004, when he presented arms to the city of Leduc, Alberta. Both collars have been worn with increasing regularity at heraldic functions since the initial use.

Origins: The general concept for a collar was taken from the collar of *Ss*. The letter *C* was chosen because it is the first letter in "Canada."

Insignia of the Governor General's Collar: A chain composed of sixty interlinked letter *C*s, each holding a blank white escutcheon (shield) between the arch of the letter. The collar is made from gilt sterling silver with white enamel and measures 90 centimetres long. An enamel pendant bearing the full Royal arms of Canada surmounted by a crown is hung from the chain; from this, another pendant is hung bearing the arms of the Canadian Heraldic Authority.

Insignia of the Chief Herald's Collar: A collar composed of sixty interlinked letter *C*s, each holding a blank white escutcheon (shield) between the arch of the letter. The collar is made from sterling silver with white enamel and measures 90 centimetres long. Hung from the chain is an enamel pendant bearing the arms of the Canadian Heraldic Authority. A second pendant is hung that bears the arms of the office of the Chief Herald.

Other: The reverse of the shields hung from each chain bears two small enamelled shields: one of Adrienne Clarkson, the governor general when the chains were instated, and one of Dr. Helen Mussalem, CC, who donated the chain.

Insignia of the Herald's Collars

With the success of the collar of *C*s, the project was expanded to included collars for all of the Heralds of the Canadian Heraldic Authority. The CHA is served by seven Heralds of Arms, two Heralds Emeritus, and six Heralds

Top Left: The Right Honourable Michaëlle Jean, CC, CMM, COM, CD, wearing the collar of the Canadian Heraldic Authority.
Top Right: Chief Herald Dr. Claire Boudreau, wearing the Chief Herald's collar and holding the Chief Herald's baton.
Bottom Left: Reverse of the Canadian Heraldic Authority collar.

Extraordinary.[3] In addition to collars for the Heralds, collars were also created for the Herald Chancellor (secretary to the governor general), Deputy Herald Chancellor (deputy secretary chancellery), and Deputy Chief Herald. Thirteen of the Herald's collars were unveiled in May 2009 by then Governor General Michaëlle Jean at Rideau Hall following a reception celebrating the twentieth anniversary of the establishment of the Canadian Heraldic Authority. The remaining collars are presently in production.

Insignia: Each of the herald's collars consist of three rows of interlinked chain, connected at equal intervals by ten blank enamelled escutcheons, the entire insignia is joined together at the bottom by the shield of the Canadian Heraldic Authority, below which is hung a sprig of four maple leaves. From this device the heraldic badge of the enamelled herald in question is hung with a loop. The collars worn by the Herald Chancellor and Deputy Herald Chancellor are gold in colour, while the collars worn by each of the other Heralds are silver.

Other: The collars worn by the Herald Chancellor, Deputy Herald Chancellor, Deputy Chief Herald, and all of the other Heralds were manufactured by Bond Boyd of Toronto. These collars were paid for through a donation made by the Weston Foundation.

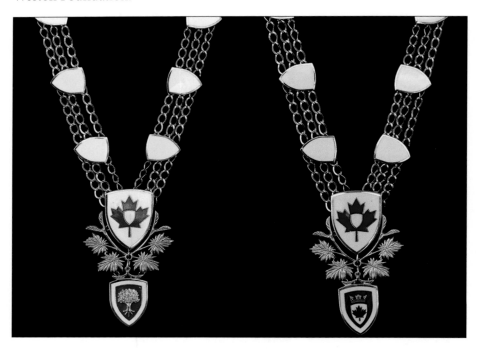

Left: Collar of the Deputy Herald Chancellor. Right: Collar of the Deputy Chief Herald of Canada.

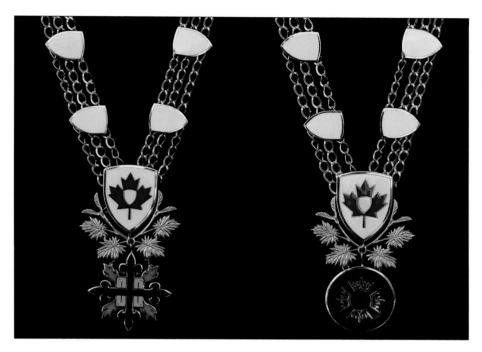

Left: Collar of the Saint-Laurent Herald. Right: Collar of the Saguenay Herald.

Left: Collar of the Assiniboine Herald. Right: Collar of the Mirimichi Herald.

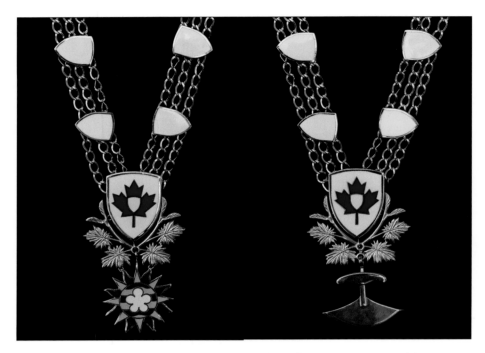

Left: Collar of the Fraser Herald. Right: Collar of Coppermine Herald.

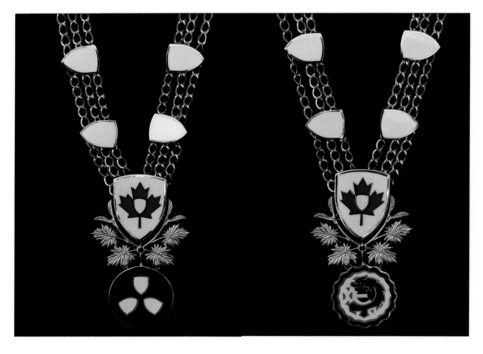

Left: Collar of Outaouais Herald Emeritus. Right: Collar of Dauphin Herald Extraordinary.

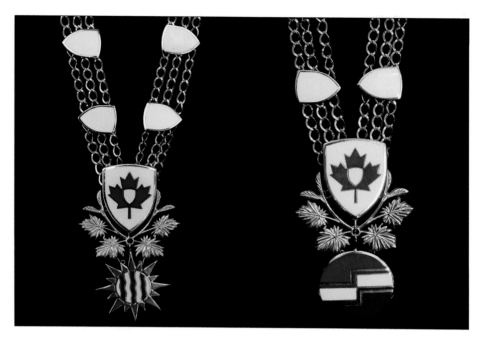

Left: Collar of Niagara Herald Extraordinary. Right: Collar of Albion Herald Extraordinary.

Left: Collar of Capilano Herald Extraordinary. Right: Collar of Rouge Herald Extraordinary.

IV

FUTURE PROSPECTS

CONCLUSION

Additions and Changes

The question of what additions and changes need to be made to Canada's symbols of authority is a sensitive one. While the inclination might be to ensure that every office-holder throughout the land be entrusted with a chain or badge of office, there is the risk that such additions will bring the existing symbols into ridicule. There is a razor's edge to be walked so that additions are not hastily added or done in such a way that such symbols of office become a joke.

The most significant badge of office currently missing from Canada's symbols of authority is a Sovereign's insignia for the Order of Merit of the Police Forces. Established in 2000, the Order of Merit of the Police Forces is awarded to police officers from across Canada. While the governor general as chancellor has a chain of office, and the commissioner of the Royal Canadian Mounted Police has a chain of office as the order's principal commander, no thought was given to the necessity for a Sovereign's insignia. This was partly due to the anticipated cost of such an insignia, not to mention the fact that the insignia of the Order of Merit of the Police Forces is identical to that of the Order of Military Merit. The only physical difference between the two orders is the ribbon from which they are hung. At the very least, a separate bow made of the ribbon of the Order of Merit of the Police Forces should be provided to the Queen.

In terms of Canada's parliaments and legislatures, one addition could be that of a baton for the Speaker of the Senate. Currently only the Speaker of the House of Commons possesses a ceremonial baton, and it would seem only fitting that his counterpart in the upper chamber also be endowed with such a symbol of office. The baton could be used during the opening of Parliament and while foreign Heads of State and Heads of Government are speaking before Parliament. In 1966 the Senate considered commissioning the production of a chain of office for the Usher of the Black Rod, similar to that worn by his counterpart in the United Kingdom. The creation of such a chain would be a fitting addition, would afford the Usher of the Black Rod a chain of office, and provide a symbolic balance with the sergeant-at-arms of the House of Commons who wears the chain of Ss.

Another baton that could be created would be for the Herald Chancellor of Canada. The person who holds this post is the secretary to the governor general and, as with the baton used by the Speaker of the House of Commons, a baton could be used during openings of Parliament and the installation of a new governor general. The Herald Chancellor's baton already exists in art form, having been included in the grants of arms given to successive secretaries to the governor general in their capacity as Herald Chancellor of Canada. Such a baton could easily be "brought to life" much as the Chief Herald's baton of office was.

Although the chief of the defence staff (CDS) is entrusted with a sword of office upon being appointed, there is no reason that a particularly illustrious CDS could not be presented with a baton of office similar to that given to French and British field marshals. In 1967, in honour of the centennial, the federal cabinet considered making Governor General Georges Vanier a field marshal in recognition of his outstanding services to the Crown. Had he lived to be appointed a field marshal, he would have almost certainly been presented with a baton. Such gifts should not be automatic, but should serve as recognition for the outstanding service.

All of the provinces now possess their own orders, and it would be fitting for their respective lieutenant governors to be presented with chancellor's chains. To date, only Saskatchewan's lieutenant governor has a chancellor's chain, and this is certainly something that other provinces should consider. A design similar to the chancellor's chain of the Order of Canada would be a good model to follow — the respective provincial flower interspersed amongst the armorial bearings of the province joined in the centre by the shield of the province and a crown, from which the insignia of the order would be hung.

An addition that is presently being produced is a tabard for the Chief Herald of Canada. There has been some debate in the heraldic community as to whether or not the creation of tabards would be a worthwhile addition. Many European heralds possess tabards, as do the South African heralds. The Chief Herald's tabard will likely be used during ceremonies at which arms are granted and heraldic letters patent presented. It could also be worn at the installation of governors general, as they have a very direct link with the Canadian Heraldic Authority.

Symbols enrich the nation's patrimony and help to form a more developed identity beyond simply the national flag, maple leaves, and the beaver. Additions should be considered with caution and undertaken with the greatest care in a non-partisan manner. When one considers how well the Order of Canada and Canadian heraldry have been accepted by the citizenry as elements of the nation's character, it is obvious that with proper explanation and prudent expansion there is room for dignified additions to Canada's symbols of authority.

APPENDIX I

Ushers of the Black Rod of the Senate

René Kimber	1867–1875
René Edouard Kimber	1875–1901
Molyneux St. John	1902–1904
Lieutenant Colonel Ernest John Chambers, VD	1904–1925
Major Andrew Ruthvern Thompson, VD	1925–1946
Major Charles Rock Lamoureaux, DSO, ED	1947–1970
Major A. Guy Vandelac, MC, CD	1970–1979
Lieutenant Colonel Thomas Guy Bowie, CD	1979–1984
Claude G. Lajoie	1984–1985
Major René M. Jalbert, CV, CD	1985–1989
Lieutenant General Rene Gutknecht, CMM, CD	1989–1990
Colonel Jean Doré, CD	1990–1997
Mary C. McLaren	1997–2001
Blair Armitage (acting)	2001–2002
Lieutenant Commander Terrence J. Christopher, OMM, LVO, CD	2002–2008
Kevin Stewart MacLeod, CVO, CD	2008–present

APPENDIX II

Sergeants-at-Arms of the House of Commons

Lieutenant Colonel Donald William Macdonell	1867–1892
Lieutenant Colonel Henry Robert Smith, CMG, ISO, VD	1892–1917
Lieutenant Colonel Henry William Bowie, VD	1918–1930
Lieutenant Colonel Henry Judson Coghill, VD	1930–1934
Major General The Honourable Milton Fowler Gregg, VC, PC, OC, CBE, MC, ED, CD	1934–1944
Lieutenant Colonel William John Franklin, MC, VD	1945–1960
Lieutenant Colonel David Vivian Currie, VC, CD	1960–1978
Major General Maurice Gaston Cloutier, CMM, CVO, CD	1978–2005
Audrey Elizabeth O'Brien (acting)	2005–2006
Chief Superintendent Kevin M. Vickers	2006–present

APPENDIX III

Maces Currently in Use — Reference Chart

Legislatures	Materials	Manufacturers	Presented By	Dates
Senate of Canada	Gilt brass	Parts likely made by François Baillaragé	Legislative council of Lower Canada at a cost of £40	Parts date as early as 1793
House of Commons	Gilt sterling silver	Goldsmiths & Silversmiths Co. Ltd.	The Lord Mayor of London, United Kingdom, Sir Charles Wakefield	1916
Ontario	Gilt copper	Charles Zollikoffer	Provincial treasury at a cost of $200	1867
Quebec	Gilt copper	Charles Zollikoffer	Provincial treasury at a cost of $200	1867
Nova Scotia	Gilt sterling silver	Elkington & Co. Ltd.	Chief Justice Robert E. Harris	1930
New Brunswick	Gilt sterling silver	Goldsmiths & Silversmiths Co. Ltd.	Lieutenant Governor Murray MacLaren	1937
Prince Edward Island	Gilt sterling silver with enamelled shields	Henry Birks & Sons	Commonwealth Parliamentary Association	1966
British Columbia	Gilt sterling silver with an enamelled shield	Jefferies & Company	Provincial treasury	1954

Manitoba	Gilt brass with semi-precious gemstones on the crown	E. Chanteloup	Provincial treasury	1884
Saskatchewan	Gilt brass	Ryrie Brothers	Provincial treasury at a cost of $340	1906
Alberta	Gilt sterling silver with an enamelled shield	Joseph Fray Ltd.	Provincial Civil Service Association	1955
Newfoundland & Labrador	Gilt sterling silver	Henry Birks & Sons	Province of British Columbia Provincial Civil Service Association $4,000	1950
Northwest Territories	Silver, bronze, marble, quillwork, and set with a diamond	Various artists	Territorial treasury	1999
Yukon Territory	Gilt sterling silver	Henry Birks & Sons	Federal treasury at a cost of $8,300	1972
Nunavut Territory	Heritage mace: narwhal tusk, silver, and semi-precious gemstones. Working mace: shaft of man-made material, and set with a diamond	Various artists	Territorial treasury	1999

NOTES

Chapter One: Canadian Symbols of Authority and Traditions of Ceremonial Protocol in Canada

1. Sir David Smith, *Head of State: The Governor-General, The Monarchy, The Republic and the Dismissal* (Sydney: Maclean Press, 2005), p. 149.

Chapter Two: Historical Roots of the Black Rod

1. Peter Begent and Hubert Chesshyre, *The Most Noble Order of the Garter: 650 Years* (London: Spink and Son, 1999), p. 132.
2. Elias Ashmole, *The Institution, Laws and Ceremonies of the Most Noble Order of the Garter* (London: Frederick Muller, 1672), p. 256.
3. Maurice Bond and David Beamish, *The Gentleman Usher of the Black Rod* (London: HMSO, 1976), p. 1.
4. Alastair Bruce, Julian Calder, Mark Cator, *Keepers of the Kingdom* (London: Cassel Press, 2002), p. 109.
5. *Ibid.*
6. Maurice Bond and David Beamish, *The Gentleman Usher of the Black Rod* (London: HMSO, 1976), p. 15.
7. Wiesinger, Véronique, *Chefs-d'oeuvre du Musée National de la Légion d'honneur et des Ordres de Chevalerie* (Paris : Carte Segrete, 1994), p. 34.
8. The Usher of the White Rod (1393) attended the King of Scotland at Parliament, general councils, and feasts. The other state orders of the United Kingdom also have "ushers." The Order of the Thistle has an Usher of the Green Rod (1714); the Order of the Bath has an Usher of the Scarlet Rod (1725); and the Order of St. Patrick used the Gentleman Usher of the Black Rod (1783) from the Irish House of Lords. After Ireland became part of the United Kingdom, Gentleman Ushers of the Black Rod of the Order of St. Patrick were appointed. This continued until the last in 1918.

The Order of St. Michael and St. George has a Gentleman Usher of the Blue Rod (1911); The Order of the British Empire has a Gentleman Usher of the Purple Rod (1917).

9. A definition of the official position and duties of "Black Rod" in England.

Chapter Three: The Black Rod of the Senate of Canada

1. Robert Christie, *A History of the Late Province of Lower Canada; Parliamentary and Political* (Quebec: Cary Publishers, 1848), p. 139.
2. *Journals, The Senate of Canada*, 1867–68, p. 68.
3. *Debates, House of Commons Canada*, 26 November 1867, p. 32.
4. *Journals, The Senate of Canada*, 1867–68, 25 November 1867, p. 90.
5. *The Canadian Parliamentary Guide*, 1897, p. 54. Also see Bournoit p. 205, 206.
6. LeMoyne's appointment as sergeant-at-arms was not formalized until 9 February 1884, when letters patent under the Great Seal of Canada were issued appointing him to be the sergeant-at-arms of the Senate. *Journals, The Senate of Canada*, 1884, p. 76–77.
7. *National Standard*, 1 October 1934. Reference to the death of the Senate's sergeant-at-arms who died in 1932 and the fact that no new officer had been appointed to this position.
8. Alcide Paquette, *The Senate Mace* (Library of Parliament Document 1970), p. 2A.
9. LeBlanc served as deputy sergeant-at-arms from 1991–1994.
10. Pennsylvania's House of Representatives possesses a mace which is carried by a person styled mace bearer.
11. Sir Barnett Cocks, *Erskine May's Treatise on the Law, Privileges, Proceedings and Usage of Parliament, 18th Edition* (London: Butterworth Ltd, 1971), p. 222.
12. *Keepers of the Kingdom*, p. 109.
13. Jane Varkaris and Lucile Finsten, *Fire on Parliament Hill!* (Erin: Boston Mills Press, 1988), p. 44.
14. *Debates, The Senate of Canada*, 28 February 1919, p. 66.
15. See engrossed certificate "Subscription List" located in the Black Rod's office, the Senate of Canada.
16. *Ibid*.
17. *Debates, The Senate of Canada*, 28 February 1919, p. 67.
18. *Debates, House of Commons Canada*, 6 November 1867, p. 1.
19. Bond and Beamish, p. 5.

Chapter Four: Black Rods in the Provinces

1. For a brief period between 1856 and 1862, members of the Legislative Council of Canada were elected.
2. *Journals of the Legislative Council, Province of Nova Scotia*, 25 January 1838, p. 7.
3. *Annals of the North British Society, 1768–1903*. Appointed 11 March 1874, *Canadian Parliamentary Companion 1887* (Ottawa J. Durie and Son, 1887), p. 273. There is no mention of the position after 1886.
4. *Journals of the Legislative Council of Upper Canada*, 1 July 1800.
5. Frédérick Starr Jarvis was appointed Gentleman Usher of the Black Rod, a post he had held while serving the Legislative Council of Lower Canada. Oliver Vallerand was appointed sergeant-at-arms of the Legislative Council of the Province of Canada. *Journals of the Legislative Council of the Province of Canada*, 24 August 1841.
6. *Journals of the Legislative Council of the Province of Manitoba*, 15 March 1871.
7. See both the *Journals of the Legislative Council* and *Journals of the Legislative Assembly for the Province of Manitoba, 1871–77*. Entries for 15 March 1871, 16 January 1872, 18 January 1876, 4 February 1876.
8. *Year Book and Almanac of Newfoundland*, 1932, p. 18. *Encyclopedia of Newfoundland*, Volume II, p. 479.
9. Section IX of the Quebec Act, 1774.
10. Section XIII of the Quebec Act, 1774. William Houston, *Documents Illustrative of the Canadian Constitution* (Toronto: Carswell Press, 1891), p. 95.
11. *Journals of the Legislative Council of Lower Canada*, 31 October 1792.
12. *Journals of the Legislative Council of Lower Canada*, 17 December 1791.
13. The Ushers of the Black Rod for the Legislative Council of Lower Canada and the Legislative Council of the Province of Canada were:

William Boutillier	1791–1823
Robert-Anne D'Estimauville	1823–1831
John St. Alban Sewell	1831–1839
Frédérick Starr Jarvis	1839–1852
René Kimber	1852–1867 (Served in the Senate from 1867–1875)
Samuel Staunton Hatt	1867–1901
Frank Pennee	1901–1904
Arthur Saint-Jacques	1904–1948
Pierre Gelly	1948–1968

14. *Journals of the Legislative Council of New Brunswick*, 1786–1937.

15. *The Journals* for 15 February 1787, note that "Mr. Winslow and Mrs Hazen" were instructed by the lieutenant governor that he required members of the legislative assembly to attend him in the council chamber.

16. *Debates, The Legislative Assembly of the Province of Alberta*, 27 January 1998, p. 1.

17. It was not until the legislative assembly was created in 1773 that the Legislative Council of Prince Edward Island began functioning as an upper house. See A.B. Warburton's *A History of Prince Edward Island* and J.M. Bumsted's *Land, Settlement and Politics on Eighteenth Century Prince Edward Island*.

18. See *Journals of the Legislative Council of Prince Edward Island*, 24 January 1843. Henry Palmer was appointed Black Rod to replace George Wright, who had resigned his position as such.

Chapter Five: Baton of the Speaker of the House of Commons

1. Du Verdier, *Le Vrai et Nouveau Estate de la France* (Paris, 1656), p. 77.

2. François Gaston Duc de Lévis was made a marshal of France on 13 June 1783. Lévis had one of the most remarkable military careers of the period and after leaving New France went on to a successful career as governor of Arras. *Dictionary of Canadian Biography*, Volume III.

3. *Mercure Galant*, October 1684, p. 12.

4. AC, C11A, 70, File 217. Dennis de St. Simon au Ministre, Quebec, 2 November 1738.

5. *Keepers of the Kingdom*, p. 184.

6. Bruce Hicks, "The Baton of the Speaker of the House of Commons," *Canadian Parliamentary Review*, Vol. 24, No. 4, 2001.

7. *Public Register of Arms, Flags and Badges of Canada*, Vol. II, p. 213.

8. Letter from Bruce Patterson, Saguenay Herald, to Corinna Pike, 18 September 2006.

Chapter Seven: Tipstaffs and Batons of Canadian Police Forces

1. The tipstaff currently used in England is 30 centimetres in length and made of ebony. The top is decorated with a silver crown, and three bands of silver are set into the wood. These are engraved with the Royal arms at the top, and engraved with "Amos Hawkins, Tipstaff Courts of Chancery,"

and the bottom band is engraved "Appointed 14th January 1884 by the Right Honourable The Earl of Selborne, L.C." and another engraving of the Royal arms is present.

2. C.O. Ermatinger, *The Talbot Regime* (St. Thomas: Municipal Press, 1904). Also see C.W. Jeffreys' *The Picture Gallery of Canadian History* (Toronto: Ryerson Press, 1941), p. 243.

3. *RCMP Quarterly* (January 1971), p. 4.

4. *The Quarterly; RCMP Veteran's Association* (Fall 2002), p. 33.

5. *La Sûreté du Québec de 1870 à 1995* (Quebec: Sûreté du Québec, 1995), p. 3.

6. *Sûreté*, "le magazine de la Sûreté du Quebéc," No. 12, 1983.

Chapter Eight: Origins and Development of Parliamentary Maces

1. W.L. Morton, *The Critical Years: The Union of British North America, 1857–1873* (Toronto: McClelland and Stewart), 1964, p. 10

2. *Erskine May's Treaties on the Law and Privileges, Proceedings and Usage of Parliament* (London: Butterworth Press, 1971), p. 225.

3. L.A. Abraham and S.C. Hawtey, *A Parliamentary Dictionary* (London: Butterworths Press, 1964), p. 117.

4. Fred Burgess, *Silver, Pewter, Sheffield Plate* (New York: Tudor Publishing, 1957), p. 142.

5. John McDonough, "The History of the Maces of the British and Canadian Parliaments," *Canadian Parliamentary Review*, Vol. 2. No. 2., 1979.

6. Thorne, p. 1.

7. Charles Clarke, "The Mace and Its Use," *Rose-Belford's Canadian Monthly and National Review*, August 1881, p. 2.

8. Some historians believe that another origin of the mace can be traced back to the ancient Romans. Following the fall of the first empire and the establishment of the Roman Republic, the fasces became an outward symbol of authority. Two patrician magistrates called consuls were elected annually and entrusted with all the powers of a monarch. These consuls were attended by twelve servants called lictors, who were essentially bodyguards and attendants. Each lictor carried an axe bound in a bundle of rods or fasces, which served as the symbol of the consul's authority to order a flogging or death. Provincial magistrates in the Roman Republic were also attended upon by lictors bearing fasces. The lictors used their fasces to maintain order in courts of justice and at large assemblies. There is little evidence to suggest that the fasces borne by lictors became

maces. Given that parts of pre-Revolutionary America used maces and the attraction many of the Founding Fathers had toward things Roman, it seems likely that the maces were adopted to reflect the Roman symbol of authority, while, in a curious way, maintaining a connection to the British tradition of having a mace present at meetings of a legislature.

9. Yigael Yadin, *The Art of Warfare in Biblical Lands* (Weidenfield and Nicholson, 1963), see introduction.

10. Peter Thorne, *The Royal Mace* (London: HMSO, 1990), p. 4.

11. Frank Warren Hackett, *The Gavel and the Mace* (New York: McClure Phillips, 1902), p. 52.

12. Lewis Thorpe, *The Bayeux Tapestry and the Norman Invasion* (London: Folio Society, 1973), p. 18–19.

13. Peter Thorne, "Maces: Their Use and Significance," *Journal of the Parliaments of the Commonwealth*, Vol. XVII, No. 1. 1963, p. 25.

14. Alfred T.P. Byles (ed.), *The Book of the Order of Chivalry* (Oxford University Press, 1926), p. 80–81.

15. *Ibid.*, p. 23.

16. Thorne, p. 5.

17. *Ibid.*, p. 8.

18. T.F. Tout, *Chapters in the Administrative History of Mediaeval England Volume II* (Manchester: Manchester University Press, 1920), p. 136.

19. Clarke, p. 4.

20. Thorne, p. 17.

21. From the time of Edward I, it was tradition that sergeants-at-arms received an annual grant to cover the cost of their robes. Chris Given-Wilson, *The King's Affinity* (New Haven: Yale University Press, 1986), p. 21.

22. Norman Wilding and Philip Laundy, *An Encyclopedia of Parliament* (London: Cassel Press, 1972), p. 849.

23. *Calendar of Patent Rolls, Henry V, 1413–1416* (London: HMSO, 1911), p. 196.

24. John McDonald, "The History of the Maces of the British and Canadian Parliaments," *Canadian Parliamentary Review*, Vol. 2, No. 2, 1979., p. 28.

25. Thorne, p. 28.

26. *Ibid.*, p. 28. This may have been one of the reasons why Cromwell treated the instrument with such contempt, because it was a gift from the Commons to itself.

27. H.D.W. Sitwell, "Royal Serjeants at Arms and the Royal Maces," *Society of Antiquity of London*, 1969, p. 214.

28. E. Alfred Jones, *The Burlington Magazine for Connoisseurs*, Vol. 71, No. 416 (November 1937), "The Old Plate of the Corporation of Retford," p. 237.

29. Thorne, p. 29.

30. T.F. Tout, p. 136.

31. Thorne, p. 25.

32. Abraham and Hawtey, p. 116.

33. Thorne, p. 38.

34. In the Irish House of Commons, which existed prior to union with Great Britain in 1801, the mace was placed lengthwise on the table with the head pointing towards the Speaker's left hand. Thus, there is a very old Commonwealth precedent for placing a mace lengthwise with the head facing the Speaker's chair. Thorne, p. 34.

35. Erskine May, p. 225.

36. Abraham and Hawtey, p. 116.

37. Canadian authorities never seem to have followed the British practice of covering the mace with a cloth bag (usually of red velvet) when the Sovereign or the governor general is in the chamber. This is done in Britain because with the Queen present there is no need for an additional symbol of Royal authority.

38. *Record of the South Carolina General Assembly*, 116th Session, 30 May 2006.

39. The mace was manufactured by Fuller White, an English silversmith who was active between 1744 and 1775. It is sterling silver with a wood core and measures 105.4 centimetres in length.

40. The original mace and one of the replicas can be found on display at the Chrysler Museum of Art in Norfolk, Virginia.

41. Clarke, p. 11.

42. Jonathan T. Matias, "The Mace: A Symbol of Parliamentary Authority," *Parliamentary Journal*, Vol. XLV, No. 1., January 2004. p. 4.

43. Joseph Callahan, *The Mace of the House of Representatives of the United States*, 4th edition (Washington DC: Government Printer, 1950), p. 5.

44. Callahan, p. 6.

45. *Journal of the Legislative Assembly of the Province of Prince Edward Island 1966*, p. 17. Also see *Debates, House of Commons Canada*, 3 February 1981, p. 6815.

46. The story of the New Zealand Parliamentary fire is remarkably similar to that of the 1916 Canadian Parliamentary fire. Both fires started in parts of the building located between the upper and lower houses, and in both cases the parliamentary libraries were saved on account of iron doors being closed.

47. Carolyn A. Young, *The Glory of Ottawa: Canada's First Parliament Building* (Montreal: McGill Queen's Press, 1995), pp. 97, 99.
48. *The National Parliament Building, Papua New Guinea* (Boroko: Government Press, 1984).
49. Maxwell Owusu, "Politics Without Parties: Reflections on the Union Government Proposals in Ghana," *African Studies Review*, Vol. 22., No. 1, April 1979, p. 94.
50. Victor T. Le Vine, *The Journal of Modern African Studies* 35, 2 (1997), "The Rise and Fall of Constitutionalism in West Africa." p. 185. A number of these continue to be used. One amusing episode saw Sir Ahmadu Bello, premier of Northern Nigeria, pick up "the mace during a recess and swing it several times like a golf club to emphasize a conversational point."
51. K.S. MacLeod, *A Crown of Maple* (Ottawa: Department of Canadian Heritage, 2008).
52. Thorne, p. 38.
53. *Beauchesne's Rules and Forms of the House of Commons of Canada*, fifth edition (Toronto: Carswell Company, 1978), p. 34.

Chapter Nine: The Mace of the Senate of Canada

1. A term coined by Sir John A. Macdonald.
2. David E. Smith, *The Canadian Senate in Bicameral Perspective* (Toronto: University of Toronto Press, 2003), p. 8.
3. Quoting Lord Carnarvon, 19 February 1866. W. L. Morton, *The Critical Years* (Toronto: McClelland and Stewart, 1966), p. 213.
4. Arthur Meighen, "The Canadian Senate," *Queen's Quarterly*, No. 44, 1937, p. 162.
5. *Journals of the Legislative Council of Lower Canada*, 17 December 1792.
6. Alcide Paquette, *The Senate Mace*, Library of Parliament Document, 1970, p. 3-C.
7. *Ibid.*, p. 3-B.
8. What would become the Legislative Council of the Province of Quebec until the body was dissolved in 1968.
9. Sir J.E.G. Bourinot, *Parliamentary Procedure and Practice* (Montreal: Lawson Brothers, 1892), p. 271.
10. Sir Conrad Swan, *Canada: Symbols of Sovereignty* (Toronto: University of Toronto Press, 1977), p. 55.

11. Alcide Paquette, Extract from a memorandum written by Mr. Auguste Vachon, Historical Research Officer of the Picture Division of the Public Archives of Canada, sent to Mr. Spicer, Parliamentary Librarian, 14 April 1970.

12. LAC, RG 4 A1, Vol. 55, pp. 18171–18173. The Great Seal of Lower Canada is described as "A Representation of a flourishing Oak, growing on the Bank of a large River covered with Shipping — a distant view of a Town on an Eminence — at the Foot of the Oak and around it, some vigorous Branches cut off — a pruning Hill in the Ground — the Legend *Ab ipso Ducit opes animumque ferro* — the inscription round the Circumference, Sigill: Prov: Nos: Can: Inf:"

13. Some have claimed that the Senate mace was manufactured after 1840, although there is little evidence to support this theory. John McDonald, "The History of the Maces of the British and Canadian Parliaments," *Canadian Parliamentary Review*, Vol. 2, No. 2, 1979, p. 28.

14. Swan, p. 107.

15. H. Hickl-Szabo, curator of the European department, Royal Ontario Museum to the Speaker Deschatelets, July 1969.

16. Officials at the Royal Ontario Museum suggested in 1968 that the "plaque of crown" bearing the Royal arms of King George III and part of the knop dated were earlier than other parts of the mace, being of "slightly finer workmanship than other parts." It was the ROM's opinion that these two parts were of an earlier date than the rest of the mace and that they formed "some part of an earlier object." This still does not explain the presence of the Great Seal of Lower Canada, which was used between 1794 and 1841. Surely if the seal part of the mace was manufactured after 1841, it would have represented the Seal of the United Provinces of Canada, and not that of Lower Canada.

17. Thorne, p. 33.

18. Bourinot, pp. 205–206.

19. *Journals of the Legislative Council of Lower Canada*, 31 October 1792.

20. See *Canada's Parliament* (Ottawa: Lawson Graphics, 1977), p. 85.

Chapter Ten: The Mace of the House of Commons

1. House of Commons Archives D 292.

2. Clarke, p. 12.

3. Clarke, p. 9.

4. This is equivalent to $67,000.00 in 2006.

5. Sadly the *Journals of the Legislative Assembly of the Province of Canada* do not contain a reference to precisely when the mace was delivered or who manufactured it. Indeed the public accounts records contain no information in this regard either.

6. Clarke, p. 9.

7. A pre-1916 photo of the House of Commons clearly shows the presence of a cushion on which the mace was rested. It was only with the 1916 mace that special brackets were made to hold it on the table. The photo can be found in Carolyn A. Young, *The Glory of Ottawa: Canada's First Parliament Building* (Montreal: McGill Queen's Press, 1995), p. 96.

8. Jake Varkaris and Lucile Finsten, *Fire on Parliament Hill* (Erin: Boston Mills Press, 1988), p. 51. Wilfrid Eggleston, *The Queen's Choice* (Ottawa: Queen's Printer for Canada, 1961), p. 14.

9. In parliamentary terms, when a member is speaking in the Senate or House of Commons, it is custom not to refer to the other body by name, but rather to simply call it "the other place."

10. House of Commons Archives, D 292. The Ontario mace was delivered to the House of Commons on 24 February 1916.

11. The Ontario Legislature could only lend its mace to the House of Commons until 29 February 1916, as this was the day the legislature was set to open. *The Canadian Parliamentary Guide 1917* (Ottawa: Mortimer Company, 1917), p. 257.

12. *The Ottawa Citizen*, 24 February 1916.

13. *Ibid.*

14. House of Commons Archives, D 291. Mace Dedication Pamphlet. Also see The House of Commons *Debates*, 14 February 1916, p. 762.

15. LAC, MG 24-H, Borden Papers, Sir George Perley, Canadian High Commissioner to Britain to Sir Robert Borden, 20 July 1916, p. 37709.

16. LAC, MG 24-H, Borden Papers, Sir Robert Borden to Sir George Perley, 31 July 1916, p. 37712.

17. LAC, MG 26-H, Papers of Sir Robert Borden, Borden to Sophia Countess of Albemarle, 7 May 1916, p. 37548.

18. *Dominion of Canada: The New Mace; Presentation at the Guildhall*, London, 28 March 1917, p. 8.

19. *Debates, House of Commons Canada*, 16 May 1917, p. 1469.

20. *Debates, House of Commons Canada*, 16 May 1917, p. 1470.

21. House of Commons Archives, D 295, D.H. Lonogman (Birks) to R.G. Donohue, 5 March 1952.
22. Ontario altered its mace following the accession of Edward VII to the throne. Quebec and the House of Commons altered the Royal cyphers on their maces following the coronation of Elizabeth II. The Senate mace is a composite mace, and we do not know the exact reason for its augmentation. No description of the original mace of the Legislative Council of Lower Canada exists, although parts of the mace date from different periods.

Chapter Eleven: Provincial Maces

1. List of maces bearing Royal arms or Royal cyphers.

Jurisdiction	Royal emblems
The Senate	King George III
The House of Commons	Queen Elizabeth II (originally King George V)
Ontario	King Edward VII (originally Queen Victoria)
Quebec National Assembly	Queen Elizabeth II (originally Queen Victoria)
Quebec Legislative Council	Queen Victoria
Nova Scotia	Crown of Scotland
New Brunswick	King George VI
Prince Edward Island	Queen Elizabeth II
British Columbia	Queen Elizabeth II
Manitoba	Queen Victoria
Saskatchewan	King Edward VII
Alberta "Jubilee"	Queen Elizabeth II
Newfoundland	King George VI
Northwest Territories "Millennium"	None
Nunavut	None
Yukon	Arms of Canada

2. J.M. Bliss, *Canadian History in Documents, 1763–1966* (Toronto: Ryerson Press, 1966), p. 10.

3. Bliss, p. 14.

4. Read, D.B, *The Life and Times of General John Graves Simcoe* (Toronto: George Virtue Publishing, 1890), p. 148. Also see speech of Major General Milton F. Gregg, VC, Sergeant-at-Arms, to the Maritimes Women's Club of Montreal, 17 November 1934.

5. *Public Papers and Addresses of Franklin D. Roosevelt*, Vol. 3, 1934, p. 215. *The Statutes at Large of the United States of America*, Vol. XLVIIII, Part 1, p. 978. Message to Congress Requesting Authority to Return a Mace to Canada, 4 May 1934.

6. *Public Papers and Addresses of Franklin D. Roosevelt*, Vol. 3, 1934, p. 215. Message to Congress Requesting Authority to Return a Mace to Canada, 4 May 1934.

7. *The Toronto Mail and Empire*, 2 July 1934.

8. Leahy would later serve as the U.S. Ambassador to France and rise to the rank of Admiral of the Fleet during the Second World War.

9. *The Toronto Mail and Empire*, 5 July 1934.

10. Herbert A. Bruce, *Our Heritage and Other Addresses* (Toronto: Macmillan, 1934), p. 329.

11. *The Toronto Globe and Mail*, 9 April 1938.

12. MacNab was a veteran of the War of 1812 and although only fourteen years old at the start of the war, he saw action on five occasions during the conflict. He would go on to become chief minister (premier) of the United Canadas from 1852 to 1854. He would later become Speaker of the Legislative Council of the United Canadas and was the first Canadian to become an honorary Aide de Camp to Queen Victoria. *The Encyclopedia of Canada*, Vol. IV (Toronto: University Associates of Canada, 1948), p. 216.

13. The public accounts for 1868 indicate that Todd was reimbursed $64.25 for travelling expenses.

14. $200 to Charles E. Zollikoffer, *Ontario Public Accounts*, 17 December 1867, p. 232.

15. Carolyn A. Young, *The Glory of Ottawa: Canada's First Parliament Building* (Montreal: McGill Queen's Press, 1995), p. 79.

16. The Dorrien Plating and Manufacturing Company charged $33 for the new crown and cup, $25 for re-plating the mace, and $10 for repairs to the staff of the mace. *Ontario Public Accounts*, 1902, p. 15.

17. Library of the Legislative Assembly of Ontario. Letter from the Provincial Archivist to W.J. Hanna, Provincial Secretary, 2 February 1906.

18. This massive painting, 3.9m x 8.7m, is on display in the Legislative Assembly Chamber of the National Assembly of Quebec.

19. *Le Journal de Quebec*, 20 April 1883.

20. *Le Journal de Quebec*, 20 November 1884.

21. House of Commons Archives, D 295, D.H. Lonogman (Birks) to R.G. Donohue, 5 March 1952.

22. Quoting a letter from Jean-Charles Bonenfant, Chief Librarian of the Quebec Legislative Assembly to the Parliamentary Library in Ottawa, 15 March 1967. Alcide Paquette, *The Senate Mace*, Library of Parliament Document 1970.

23. Gary Levy and Graham White, *Provincial and Territorial Legislatures in Canada* (Toronto: University of Toronto Press, 1989), p. 140.

24. Charles Dickens, *American Notes* (Wilson and Company, 1842), p. 21.

25. The body was composed of the House of Assembly and Legislative Council. The latter was abolished in 1928, and there are even records indicating the employ of a Gentleman Usher of the Black Rod between 1838 and 1874.

26. *Journals and Proceedings of the House of Assembly of Nova Scotia*, 5 December 1785.

27. *Journals and Proceedings of the House of Assembly of Nova Scotia*, 16 April 1819.

28. *The Nova Scotian*, 30 January 1840, p. 37.

29. *Ibid.*

30. Clarke, p. 10.

31. *The Herald*, 6 March 1930.

32. *Journals and Proceedings of the House of Assembly of the Province of Nova Scotia*, 5 March 1930, p. 2. Speech from the throne.

33. Clarke notes that until 1879 the sergeant-at-arms carried a silver court sword. After 1879 the sword was changed to a gilt-silver court sword.

34. Clarke, p. 10.

35. New Brunswick Legislative Library. The Hon. Murray MacLaren to The Hon. A.A. Dysart, 15 February 1937.

36. *Journals of the Legislative Assembly of the Province of New Brunswick*, 18 February 1937, p. 9.

37. *The Daily Gleaner*, 19 June 1971, New Brunswick mace on public display.

38. Wayne E. Mackinnon, *The Life of the Party* (Summerside: Prince Edward Island Liberal Party, 1973), p. 7.

39. Gardner W. Allen, *A Naval History of the American Revolution* (Boston: Houghton, 1913), p. 45, also see Russell W. Knight, "The Headers In Life and Legend," *Marblehead Magazine*, 1996.

40. The seal was engraved by the Royal Mint, London, in 1769. It contained 50 ounces, 1 pennyweight of sterling silver. The total cost of the seal matrices and a special case was £85.8s.6d. Royal Mint Record Book 1/12, pp. 111–113. This would be worth in the region of $17,000 Canadian dollars in 2006. House of Commons Research Paper 99/20 Inflation: *The Value of the Pound*, 1750–1998.

41. *Dictionary of Canadian Biography*, Phillips Callbeck.

42. *Journal of the Legislative Assembly of the Province of Prince Edward Island*, 1966, p. 15.

43. Inman was also the first woman to represent Prince Edward Island in the Senate.

44. The mace of the Colony of Vancouver Island was owned by a number of individuals, although it is not entirely clear how it came to leave government hands. *Victoria Colonist*, 2 December 1936.

45. *The Province*, 11 January 1950.

46. British Columbia Legislative Assembly Library, *Maces of British Columbia*, 1950.

47. *Ibid.*

48. *The Victoria Standard*, 17 February 1872. Also see the *British Colonist*, 17 February 1872.

49. *Public Accounts of the Province of British Columbia*, 1873.

50. *Public Accounts of the Province of British Columbia*, 1896–97, p. 112.

51. *The Province*, 17 March 1953, by B.A. McKelvie.

52. *Journals of the Legislative Assembly of the Province of British Columbia*, 1954, 16 February 1954, p. 5.

53. Levy and White, p. 91.

54. H.S. Bennett, *The Mace* (Winnipeg: Legislative Assembly Library, 1954), p. 10.

55. Frank Hall, "Take Away the Fools Bauble: The Story of the Manitoba Mace," *The Bison*, 1967, p. 24.

56. One of these lamps survives at the Cabot Head Lighthouse on Georgian Bay in Ontario.

57. Ontario's mace bears the Royal cypher of King Edward VII, "E VII R," although the original post-Confederation Ontario mace bore the Royal cypher of Queen Victoria "V.R."

58. Levy and White, p. 48.

59. *The Toronto Globe*, 20 March 1906.

60. *The Regina Leader*, 26 March 1906.

61. Ryrie Brothers was amalgamated with Birks in 1917 to form Ryrie-Birks, which later became Ryrie-Birks-Ellis but has colloquially always remained just Birks.

62. Library of the Legislative Assembly of Saskatchewan, E.M. Chadwick to F.J. Robinson, 9 March 1906.

63. Library of the Legislative Assembly of Saskatchewan, F. J. Robinson to E.M. Chadwick, 26 March 1906.

64. Library of the Legislative Assembly of Saskatchewan, Ryrie Brothers Jewellers to F.J. Robinson, 3 April 1906.

65. Margaret A. Woods, *Canadian Parliamentary Review*, "The 100th Anniversary of the First Opening of the Saskatchewan Assembly," Summer 2006, p. 33.

66. The Public Accounts reveal that the College of Arms in London billed $122.24 for the Alberta Coat of Arms. *Province of Alberta Public Accounts, 1907*, p. 20.

67. A.R. Browning, *The Mace* (Canberra: Australia Government Printer, 1970), p. 5.

68. *Province of Alberta Public Accounts*, 1907, p. 20.

69. *Journals of the Legislative Assembly of the Province of Alberta*, 15 March 1906, p. 12.

70. *Journals of the Legislative Assembly of the Province of Alberta*, 9 February 1956, p. 10.

71. *Alberta Civil Service Bulletin*, April 1956, pp. 16–18.

72. *Proceedings of the House of Assembly of Newfoundland*, 5 April 1950, pp. 567–68.

73. *Ibid.*, p. 571.

74. "Aspects," *Journal of the Newfoundland Historical Society*, February 1968, Vol. 2., No. 1., p. 14.

75. Approximately $14,000 in 2006 Canadian dollars.

76. *Journals of the House of Assembly*, 6 August 1838, p. 60.

77. Gertrude Gunn, *The Political History of Newfoundland, 1832–1864* (Toronto: University of Toronto Press, 1966), p. 55.

78. *Journals of the House of Assembly*, 7 August 1838, p. 67.

79. *Journals of the House of Assembly*, 10 August 1838, p. 73.

80. *Ibid.*

81. In January 1839 Governor Prescott submitted his resignation in the hopes of returning to service in the Royal Navy. The legislative assembly refused his request, and he remained governor of the colony until 1841.

82. John Courage, "Parliamentary Privilege in Newfoundland: The Strange Case of Kielly *v.* Carson," *The Canadian Parliamentary Review*, Vol. 4, No. 3, 1981.

83. "Aspects," *Journal of the Newfoundland Historical Society*, February 1968, Vol. 2, No. 1, p. 15.

84. *Proceedings of the House of Assembly of Newfoundland*, 5 April 1950, p. 571.

Chapter Twelve: Territorial Maces

1. LAC RG 85, File 510-15, The Mace Yukon, J.F. Delaute to Commissioner J. Smith, 10 January 1967.

2. LAC RG 85, File 510-15, The Mace Yukon, F.B. Fingland to J. Smith, 19 January 1967.

3. Department of Indian Affairs Press Release, 11 February 1972, 1-7179X.

4. *Legislative Assembly of Nunavut*, "History of the Mace," 2006.

5. *Hansard of the Legislative Assembly of Nunavut*, Thursday April 1, 1999.

Chapter Thirteen: Municipal and Academic Maces

1. William Kelly, "The Great Mace and other Corporation Insignia of the Borough of Leicester," *Transactions of the Royal Historical Society*, Vol. III, London, 1874, pp. 295–345.

2. Proceedings of the Dáil Éireannan, Vol. 184, 9 November 1960, question 25.

3. The Mace of the Royal Society traditionally "laid upon the table before the president when the meetings were convened, was an emblem of the source of order. Again, as in the Commons, the mace indicated that the ultimate source [or authority] was royal." Steven Shapin, "The House of Experiment in Seventeenth-Century England," *Iris*, Vol. 79, No. 3 (September 1988), p. 383.

4. The silver was obtained from Messrs Hicklenton and Sydal of Queen Street, Vancouver.

5. *The Daily Province*, Vancouver, 20 August 1936. Also See City of Vancouver minutes of Council, 20 August 1936.

6. Vancouver City Archives, MSS 177, 513-C-4 File 2, "Vancouver Golden Jubilee Society Fonds."

Chapter Fifteen: Uniforms and Badges of Civil Authority

1. Civil uniforms are a type of court uniform. Presently the only officials in Canada who continue to wear a traditional court uniform (new style) are the Usher of the Black Rod of the Senate of Canada, the sergeant-at-arms of the House of Commons, the Speakers of the two houses of parliament, clerks, and a number of the Speakers, clerks, and sergeants-at-arms of the provincial legislatures.

2. The focus of this section will be primarily on the use of civil uniforms in Canada. Given that they were used around the Commonwealth, a truly exhaustive examination would be lengthy.

3. The governor general's uniform was worn without epaulettes.

4. Marquis de La Jonquiere, *Le Chef d'Escadre de La Jonquière*, Paris: n.d., p. 131 (circa 1749).

5. By 1869 the hierarchy of uniforms included five different classes.

6. First worn in Canada in 1859 by Governor General Sir Edmund Walker Head, Bt, LAC, RG 7, File 1590A, Circular from the British prime minister's office.

7. *Dress and Insignia Worn at Court*, 1929 edition, p. 9.

8. See *The Annual Register 1817*, "all his state and household officers [should] wear costly dress of home fabrication ... to be made in three classes of uniforms ... the coats are of dark purple, with crimson velvet collars richly ornameneted all over with gold." With thanks to Nigel Arch for this information.

9. Nigel Arch and Joanna Marschner, *Splendour at Court: Dressing for Royal Occasions since 1700* (London: Unwin Hyman, 1987), p. 83.

10. The court uniform had a much more limited existence in Canada, being worn primarily by officials of the colonial, provincial, and Dominion legislatures. The Usher of the Black Rod in the Senate of Canada and the Speakers of both houses of parliament and the Speakers of a number of the provincial legislatures continue to wear a modified version of the court uniform. The viceregal household of Lord Tweedsmuir was the last where pages and staff wore court uniforms. The practice was not reinstated following the end of the Second World War.

11. Arch and Marschner, p. 81.

12. Alan Mansfield, *Ceremonial Costume: Court, Civil and Civic Costume from 1660 to the Present Day* (Totowana: Barnes and Noble Books, 1980), p. 167.

13. Arch and Marschner, p. 81.
14. Arch and Marschner, p. 92.
15. Nigel Arch and Joanna Marschner, *Splendour at Court: Dressing for Royal Occasions since 1700*, p. 81.
16. See Portrait of Lord Aylmer circa 1830, LAC C4809 and also the portrait of Sir Charles Metcalfe circa 1844, LAC C142188.
17. The only difference was that the epaulettes on the Lord Lieutenants' uniforms carried a rose, thistle, or shamrock to denote an English, Scottish, or Irish county. No such device was worn on the epaulettes used in Canada.
18. LAC RG 7 G1, Vol. 13, Lord Bathurst to Earl Dalhousie, governor general of Canada, 20 November 1824.

> Downing Street, London, 20 November 1824
> My Lord,
> I have the honour of enclosing an order which the King has been graciously pleased to direct should be transmitted to Governors & Acting Lieutenant Governors, for a Uniform which they are permitted to wear. By this order your Lordship will observe that there is also a Uniform which Superior Officers of each Colonial Government will be permitted to wear — Your Lordship will therefore notify to me the names of those superior officers within your Government who may appear to you most deserving of this distinction; & it must be understood that none but those whose names you shall have transmitted to me for His Majesty's Approval shall be at Liberty to wear this Uniform.
> George R.
> The Uniform for Colonial Governors the same as that worn by the Lord Lieutenants of English Counties, only the body of the uniform to be blue with red lapels — the Epaulettes and Embroidery to be also the same as the Lord Lieutenants of Counties.
>
> Superior Civil Officers Blue Coats, but no epaulettes nor lapells [*sic*] Button Holes upon the Cuff & Collar only; but the same pattern as the Lord Lieutenants. 9 November 1824.

19. LAC RG 7 G 1, Vol. 14, Lord Bathurst to Earl Dalhousie, Governor General of Canada, 1 March 1825.

20. *British Consular Service; General Instructions for Her Majesty's Consular Officers* (London: Harrison and Sons, 1879), pp. 51–52.
21. The 1847 *Quebec Directory*.
22. "Court Dress Reform," *Morning Post*, 15 February 1869.
23. "Court Dress Reform," *Morning Post*, 15 February 1869.
24. This order of dress was introduced in 1903. Arch, p. 87.
25. George Titman, *Dress and Insignia Worn at His Majesty's Court* (London: Harrison and Sons, 1937), pp. 80–82. In 1938 an *undress* version of the governor general's uniform was introduced, although it was never used in Canada. The undress governor general's uniform was to be worn when full dress or plain clothes were inappropriate.
26. Realizing that a pith helmet with plume was a bit unusual for Canada, Michener personally designed a headdress for wear with the tropical uniform. The chapeau consisted of a Royal Canadian Navy flag officer's forage cap (with two rows of oak leaves on the brim) and in place of the RCN Cap badge he wore a gilt version of the Royal arms of the United Kingdom. The buttons on the chinstrap also bore the Royal arms of the United Kingdom. While it may seem odd that the U.K. arms were used, as opposed to the Royal arms of Canada, this is likely on account of the perception at the time that the Royal arms of the U.K. had a more direct "connection" with the sovereign, rather than HM's Royal arms of Canada. Peter Stursberg, *Roland Michener: The Last Viceroy* (Toronto: McGraw-Hill-Ryerson, 1987), see second set of colour plates, p. 6.
27. Governors general of Dominions wore a silver aiguillette, while governors of colonies and high commissioners of British trust territories and protectorates did not.
28. LAC, RG 7, 1590A, Vol. I, Sir E.B. Lytton to Sir Edmund Walker Head.
29. LAC, RG 7, File 1590A, Circular from the British prime minister's office, 1859.
30. LAC RG 7, 1590A, Vol. 1, *Colonial Officer Circular* from Lewis to Sir Edmund Walker Head, 14 July 1860.
31. LAC RG 7, 1590A, Vol. 1, *Colonial Office Circular*, 16 July 1864, Colonial Secretary to Viscount Monck.
32. It was a white drill coat with a high collar, which had dark blue gorgets with gold braid. The amount of braid denoted the rank. Buttons on cuffs, first and second class had three buttons, third and fourth class had two buttons, fifth class had one button. The tropical dress civil uniform was accompanied by a white pith helmet and white feathers. It was a uniform

intended primarily for use in Africa and India and was to be worn when receiving Royal personages, foreign governors, native potentates or chiefs, at military reviews, and at all official ceremonies during the daytime. It was not to be worn during the evening unless others were to be present in uniform. It was stipulated that under most circumstances the regular full dress civil uniform was still to be worn during the opening and closing of the legislature and on the Sovereign's birthday.

33. LAC RG 7, 1509, Vol. 1, 2 March 1905, Lord Lyttelton to Office of the Governor General.
34. LAC RG 7, Colonial Officer to Duke of Connaught, 19 April 1912.
35. LAC RG 7, Secretary of State for Canada to Governor General Secretary, 7 June 1912.
36. LAC RG 7, Under Secretary of State to Secretary to the Governor General, 24 March 1922.
37. The governor general, Lord Minto, received some pressure from senior civil servants to allow them to wear something less austere than the fifth-class uniform, which had almost no gold braid at all. Thus, in 1904 Canadian deputy ministers were permitted to wear the fourth class of uniform. LAC RG 7, Colonial Officer dispatch from Lyttelton to Lord Minto, 2 June 1904.
38. LAC RG 7, Lord Chamberlain to GG, 19 June 1929.
39. LAC RG 7, Lord Clarendon, Lord Chamberlain to Lord Tweedsmuir, 6 December 1938.
40. LAC RG 7, Acting Under Secretary of State to Frederick Pereira, Assistant Secretary to the Governor General, 4 May 1939.
41. LAC RG 7, 800-6, Circular from Colonial Office, Secretary Crewe to Governor General of Canada, 18 August 1908.
42. LAC RG 7, 800-6, G.A. Babbit, Secretary to the Lieutenant Governor of Alberta, 23 October 1906.
43. LAC RG 7, 800-6, Major General Letson to Comptroller of Government House, Ottawa, 28 February 1949.
44. LAC RG 7, 800-6, Memo to File from J.F. Delaute, 23 January 1950.
45. When Vanier was appointed governor general, he held the rank of major general. On 1 January 1964 he was promoted to full general. *Canada Gazette*, Extra Issue, 1 January 1964.
46. Vincent Massey wore the one that once belonged to Lord Tweedsmuir. This uniform was later passed on to Roland Michener. A year into office, Michener realized that the buttons on the uniform still bore the Royal cypher of King George VI, who had died more than fifteen years before.

Michener promptly had the uniform updated with Queen Elizabeth–issue buttons. Michener was rather fond of the governor general's civil dress uniform; indeed, he was the last Canadian governor general to wear it.

47. LAC RG 7, 800-9, Memo to Aides de Campe from Brigadier General Andre Garneau, 26 June 1975.

48. There was a long tradition of "recycling" the governor general's uniforms, which were purchased at the office-holder's expense, and not covered by the Crown. Vincent Massey wore the uniform that belonged to Lord Tweedsmuir, while General Vanier wore Lord Bessborough's uniform (on only a few occasions, including his Karsh photo portrait). Michener initially wore the uniform that belonged to Massey, and then had a new one made. The Bessborough uniform was offered to Léger, but he declined the opportunity to wear it.

49. *Debates of the Legislative Assembly of the Province of British Columbia*, 18 March 1993.

50. In 1974 the newly appointed lieutenant governor of Newfoundland made inquiries with a number of Saville Row London tailors to see about obtaining a new civil uniform. None were to be found, and he was instructed to "enquire if there is any retiring diplomat who would be prepared to sell his uniform." This was not uncommon, and many governors general and lieutenant governors obtained their civil uniforms from predecessors. LAC RG 7, 800-6, Strickland and Sons Ltd. to G.A Winter, 25 September 1974.

51. J. Murray Beck, *The Government of Nova Scotia* (Toronto: University of Toronto Press, 1957), p. 183.

52. *Morning Chronicle*, 24 February 1911.

53. LAC, MG 26-J, Mackenzie King Diary, 9 November 1909.

54. LAC, MG 26-J, Mackenzie King Diary, 8 March 1940. This was an odd comment for Mackenzie King to make, given that he frequently had dreams and visions of himself wearing the full-dress civil uniform, even on horseback. See diary entry for 30 August 1934.

55. LAC RG 2A-5a, Vol. 1893, Cabinet Conclusions, 16 August 1957 and 20 August 1957.

56. Philip Mansel, *Dressed to Rule: Royal and Court Costume from Louis XIV to Elizabeth II* (New Haven: Yale University Press, 2005), p. 148.

57. See William Scully Ltd. Press Release circa 1970s, "Sorry, No Royal Warrants!"

58. Report from Emmanuelle Sajous to C. McCreery by Robert Watt, 15 February 2006.

59. James Risk et al, *Royal Service Volume II.*, p. 89.

60. Given that it is now widely accepted that the lieutenant governors represent the Queen in their particular provinces, it would be more fitting if the badges were presented by the Queen rather than a mid-level civil servant from Rideau Hall.

Chapter Sixteen: Collar of the Sergeant-at-Arms of the House of Commons

1. D'Arcy Boulton, *The Knights of the Crown: The Monarchical Orders of Knighthood in Later Medieval Europe, 1325–1520* (Woodbridge: Boydell Press, 2000).
2. David Williamson, *Debrett's Guide to Heraldry and Regalia* (London: Headline Book Publishing, 1992), p. 37.
3. Elias Ashmole, *The Institution, Laws and Ceremonies of the Most Noble Order of the Garter* (London: Frederick Muller, 1672), p. 224.
4. *Ibid.*
5. Roger Milton, *The English Ceremonial Book: A History of Robes, Insignia and Ceremonies Still in Use in England* (New York: Drake Publishing, 1972).
6. Senate, Usher of the Black Rod Files, W.H. Summers to C.R. Lamoureux, 2 June 1966.
7. Senate, Usher of the Black Rod Files, C.R. Lamoureux to W.H. Summers, 17 June 1966.

Chapter Seventeen: Collars of Office of the Canadian Heraldic Authority

1. It is worthwhile to note that every insignia, collar, chain, and badge of office worn in Canada — or for that matter anywhere in the world — has been created by this "invention of tradition" at some point. All traditions were new at one point.
2. Robert D. Watt, "Two Collars of C's," *Heraldry in Canada*, 2005.
3. In addition to the Chief Herald of Canada, the heralds of the CHA are Saint Laurent Herald, Fraser Herald, Saguenay Herald, Assiniboine Herald, Miramichi Herald, Coppermine Herald, Athabaska Herald (vacant since 2001), Outaouais Herald Emeritus, Rideau Herald Emeritus, Dauphin Herald Extraordinary, Niagara Herald Extraordinary, Cowachin Herald Extraordinary, Albion Herald Extraordinary, Capilano Herald Extraordinary, and Rouge Herald Extraordinary. A collar was also created for the person holding the position of Deputy Chief Herald.

Glossary

Black Rod: The name of the ceremonial rod carried by the Gentleman Usher of the Black Rod; also by tradition the usher is called Black Rod, the same name as his rod of office. Since 1997 in the Canadian Senate the title changed from Gentleman Usher of the Black Rod to Usher of the Black Rod, at the time of the first female appointment to this position, and this form of address has continued with subsequent appointments. (Please refer to Chapters 2 and 3 for the fuller explanation.)

Coat of Arms: This is a heraldic device and pictorial representation to display the armorial bearings of an individual, institution, or country, the main part being the shield, often simply referred to as the "arms." This is usually accompanied by a helmet, wreath, mantling, supporters, a crest, and motto. (*See* Royal Arms)

Enamel: A coloured vitreous substance used to decorate a variety of materials, including silver and gold. This is a decorative technique known since ancient times. A mixture is made up of powdered potash with silica mixed with oil and metallic oxides, and applied to a surface requiring decoration, which is then fired at a low temperature in a kiln, resulting in a glass-like finish. There are a variety of enamelling techniques with differing processes.

Hallmark: This is a form of identification indicating the "Hall" or town assay office where an item was assayed to test the purity of the metal, a British legal requirement that has been in use since around 1300. A hallmark collectively comprises a group of punch marks on a sterling silver, gold, or platinum object, which include a standard mark, a maker's mark, a date letter, and the town mark. Precious metal objects of United Kingdom origin will have a hallmark, though there may be exceptions to this rule, for example in certain circumstances where mixed materials are used. Sometimes the word *hallmark* has been loosely used to indicate general marks applied to a piece.

Mace, components of:

Crowned Head — In the context here, there is usually a dominant crown at the top end or at the head of the mace.

Cap — This is the flat area immediately beneath the crossed arches of the crown, otherwise sometimes called the arms plate. The cap also represents the domed velvet material edged with ermine that is fitted inside arched crowns.

Head — The mace head above which sits the crown is often cup-shaped, and this is the area that usually carries the most decoration and important heraldic devices, such as the Provincial arms and Royal cyphers.

Brackets — These are scroll supports often in a set of four on a mace, but not always, which are usually positioned immediately below the head of the mace and at the top end of the shaft. They can be simple in form or highly decorated.

Shaft — The main stem of the mace usually has knops along its length, which may have a spiral decoration of symbolic elements.

Knop — This is a bulbous decorated ornament, similar to a finial. They can occur down the length of a stem, such as on candlesticks and chalices. On a mace they occur as large globular protrusions down the shaft of the mace.

Foot Knop — A bulbous element similar to a knop, though this is positioned at the lower end of the mace and can be somewhat larger than those down the shaft, and is often more decorative.

Obverse: The obverse (or head) at the front and the reverse (or tail) at the back are the two opposite sides of a coin or medal. These terms can also be used to describe the two sides of a Great Seal.

Reverse: (*See* Obverse)

Royal Arms: Those referred to in this book are the arms of Sovereigns, which are also the arms of sovereignty and thereby represent the arms of Dominion. These Royal arms appear on several maces.

Royal Cypher: This combines a Royal initial with the letter "R" for Regina or Rex; therefore the Royal Cypher of H.M. Queen Elizabeth the Second is "E II R." For each Sovereign, their individual Royal cypher usually has an official typeface style and is easily recognized. Therefore, with subsequent generations, one initial can potentially be distinguishable from another.

Sergeant-at-Arms: The officer of the Crown responsible for carrying the mace of the House of Commons or various provincial and territorial legislatures. This is the familiar spelling most commonly used in Canada. However, other versions may be used in other countries. Depending on the source of references, it can also be written as serjeant at arms, as is customary in the United Kingdom. The Senate employs a mace bearer rather than a sergeant-at-arms, although such a position did exist in the early history of the upper chamber.

Silver-Gilt: This is a term describing silver which has a thin coating of gold applied by a gilding process. An object can also be partially gilded and would be described as "parcel gilt." Ceremonial and presentation objects are often made of silver-gilt, or may be of gilded base metals.

Sterling Silver: This is a fineness of silver, an alloy consisting of 925 parts of silver to 75 parts of copper. In Canada, items made of sterling silver may have the word STERLING stamped on them. Sterling silver and precious metal objects of United Kingdom origin will be hallmarked. (*See* Hallmark)

BIBLIOGRAPHY

Primary Sources

Ashmole, Elias. *The Institution, Laws and Ceremonies of the Most Noble Order of the Garter*. London: Frederick Muller, 1971.

A Definition of the Official Position and Duties of "Black Rod" in England. Ottawa: Hunter Rose Press, 1868.

Gregg, Milton F. *The Mace*, Speech delivered to the Maritime Women's Club of Montreal, 17 November 1934.

House of Commons Archives D 292.

Library and Archives Canada, MG 24-H, Borden Papers.

Library and Archives Canada, RG 85, File 510-15.

Library and Archives Canada, RG 11, Vol 317-318.

Library and Archives Canada, MG 24 B 17, Sir Allan Napier MacNab Papers.

Paquette, Alcide. *The Senate Mace*, Library of Parliament Publication, 1970.

Vancouver City Archives. "Vancouver Golden Jubilee Society Fonds" MSS 177, 513-C-4 File 2

Books and Articles

Abraham, L.A., and S.C. Hawtey. *A Parliamentary Dictionary*. London: Butterworths Press, 1964.

Allen, Gardner W. *A Naval History of the American Revolution*. Boston: Houghton, 1913.

Arch, Nigel, and Joanna Marschner. *Splendour at Court: Dressing for Royal Occasions Since 1700*. London: Unwin Hyman, 1987.

Ashmole, Elias. *The Institution, Laws and Ceremonies of the Most Noble Order of the Garter*, 1672.

"Aspects," *Journal of the Newfoundland Historical Society*, February 1968, Vol. 2., No. 1, p. 14.

Beauchesne's Rules and Forms of the House of Commons of Canada, fifth edition. Toronto: Carswell Company, 1978.

Beck, J. Murray. *The Government of Nova Scotia*. Toronto: University of Toronto Press, 1957.

Begent, Peter, and Hubert Chesshyre. *The Most Noble Order of the Garter; 650 Years*. London: Spink and Son, 1999.

Bennett, H.S. *The Mace*. Winnipeg: Legislative Assembly Library, 1954.

Bliss, J.M. *Canadian History in Documents, 1763–1966*. Toronto: Ryerson Press, 1966.

Bond, Maurice, and David Beamish. *The Gentleman Usher of the Black Rod*. London: HMSO, 1976.

Bourniot, J.E.G. *Parliamentary Procedure and Practice*. Montreal: Lawson Brothers, 1892.

Browning A.R. *The Mace: Its Uses in Australia*. Canberra: Government Printer, 1970.

Bruce, Herbert A. *Our Heritage and Other Addresses*. Toronto: Macmillan, 1934.

Bumstead, J.M. *Land Settlement and Politics on Eighteenth-Century Prince Edward Island*. Montreal: McGill-Queen's University Press, 1987.

Burgess, Fred W. *Silver, Pewter, Sheffield Plate*. New York: Tudor Publishing, 1957.

Callahan, Joseph. *The Mace of the House of Representatives of the United States*, 4th edition. Washington, D.C.: Government Printer, 1950.

The Canadian Parliamentary Guide 1917. Ottawa: Mortimer Company, 1917.

Clarke, Charles C. "The Mace and Its Use," *Rose-Belford's Canadian Monthly and National Review*, August 1881, pp. 109–19.

The Coronation Ceremony and the Crown Jewels. London: Her Majesty's Stationary Office, 1992.

Courage, John, "Parliamentary Priviledge in Newfoundland: The Strange Case of Kielley v Carson," *The Canadian Parliamentary Review*, Vol. 4, No. 3, 1981.

The Crown Jewels: Tower of London. London: Her Majesty's Stationary Office, 1987.

Cunnington, G. Willett, Phillis Cunnington, and Charles Beard. *A Dictionary of English Costume*. London: Adam and Charles Black Press, 1960.

Derriman, James. *The Pagantry of the Law*. London: Eyre and Spottiswoode, 1955.

Dickens, Charles. *American Notes*. Wilson and Company, 1842.

Dominion of Canada. *The New Mace: Presentation at the Guildhall*. London, 28 March 1917.

Dominion of Canada, House of Commons Hansard.

Dominion of Canada, Senate Hansard.

Eggleston, Wilfrid. *The Queen's Choice*. Ottawa: Queen's Printer for Canada, 1961.

The Encyclopedia of Canada, Vol. IV (Toronto: University Associates of Canada, 1948), p. 216.

Ermatinger, C.O. *The Talbot Regime*. St. Thomas: Municipal Press, 1904.

Erskine May's Treaties on the Law and Privileges, Proceedings and Usage of Parliament. London: Butterworth Press, 1971.

Given-Wilson, Chris. *The Royal Household and the King's Affinity: Service, Politics and Finance in England, 1360–1413.* New Haven: Yale University Press, 1986.

Gunn, Gertrude. *The Political History of Newfoundland, 1832–1864.* Toronto: University of Toronto Press, 1966.

Jeffreys, C.W. *The Picture Gallery of Canadian History.* Toronto: Ryerson Press, 1941.

Hackett, Warren. *The Gavel and the Mace.* New York: McClure Phillips, 1902.

Hall, Frank. "Take Away the Fool's Bauble: The Story of the Manitoba Mace," *The Bison,* 1967.

The Heraldry Gazette, "Staffs and Batons of Constables and Marshals," New Series LXXXV, September 2007, p. 7.

History of the House of Commons Security Services, 1920–1995. Ottawa, Stittsville: Love Printing Services, 1995.

Hodgetts, E. *Pioneer Public Service.* Toronto: University of Toronto Press, 1955.

Horrocks, Sir Brian. "Gentleman Usher of the Black Rod," *Journal of the Society of Clerks-at-the-Table in Empire Parliaments,* Vol. xix (1950).

House of Commons Research Paper 99/20 Inflation*: The Value of the Pound, 1750–1998.*

Huot, Charles et la peinture d'histoire au Palais législatif de Quebec (1882–1930), *Bulletin de la Galerie national du Canada,* 1976, p. 27.

Jones, E. Alfred. *The Burlington Magazine for Connoisseurs,* "Some Historical Silver Maces," Vol. 14, No. 69 (December 1908), pp. 170–71.

Jones, E. Alfred. *The Burlington Magazine for Connoisseurs,* Vol. 71, No. 416 (November 1937), pp. 226–28. "Old Plate of the Corporation of Retford."

Journals and Proceedings of the House of Assembly of the Province of Nova Scotia.

Journals of the Legislative Assembly of the Province of Alberta.

Journals of the Legislative Assembly of the Province of British Columbia.

Journals of the Legislative Assembly of the Province of New Brunswick.

Journals of the Legislative Assembly of the Province of Prince Edward Island.

Journals of the Legislative Council of Lower Canada.

Knight, Russell. "The Headers in Life and Legend," *Marblehead Magazine,* 1996.

Laundy, Philip, and Norman Wilding. *An Encyclopedia of Parliament.* London: Cassel Press, 1972.

Le Vine, Victor. *The Journal of Modern African Studies 35, 2 (1997),* pp. 181–206, "The Fall and Rise of Constitutionalism in West Africa."

Legislative Assembly of Nunavut, History of the Mace, 2006.

Levy, Gary, and Graham White (eds). *Provincial and Territorial Legislatures in Canada.* Toronto: University of Toronto Press, 1989.

"The Mace." *Alberta Civil Service Bulletin,* April 1956.

The Mace of the Legislative Assembly of the Northwest Territories. January 1987, Northwest Territories, Culture and Communications Pamphlet.

Mackinnon, Wayne E. *The Life of the Party.* Summerside: Prince Edward Island Liberal Party, 1973.

Mansel, Philip. *Dressed to Rule: Royal and Court Costume from Louis XIV to Elizabeth II.* New Haven: Yale University Press, 2005.

Mansfield, Alan. *Ceremonial Costume: Court, Civil and Civic Costume from 1660 to the Present Day.* Totowana, New Jersey: Barnes and Noble Books, 1980.

Manual of Official Procedure of the Government of Canada. Ottawa: Queen's Printer, 1968.

Matias, Jonathan T. "The Mace: A Symbol of Parliamentary Authority," *Parliamentary Journal,* Vol. XLV, No. 1. January 2004.

McCreery, Christopher. *The Order of Canada: Its Origins, History and Development.* Toronto: University of Toronto Press, 2006.

_____. *The Canadian Honours System.* Toronto: Dundurn Press, 2005.

McDonough, John. "The History of the Maces of the British and Canadian Parliaments," *Canadian Parliamentary Review,* Vol. 2. No. 2., 1979.

Meighen, Arthur. "The Canadian Senate," *Queen's Quarterly,* No. 44, 1937.

Milton, Roger. *The English Ceremonial Book: A History of Robes, Insignia and Ceremonies Still in Use in England.* New York: Drake Publishing, 1972.

Morton, W.L. *The Critical Years: The Union of British North America, 1857–1873.* Toronto: McClelland and Stewart, 1964.

Ontario Public Accounts.

Owusu, Maxwell. *African Studies Review,* Vol. 22, No. 1 (April 1979), "Politics Without Parties: Reflections on the Union Government Proposals in Ghana," pp. 89–108.

Pargellis, S.M. *William and Mary College Quarterly Historical Magazine,* "Procedure of the Virginia House of Burgesses," 2nd Series, Vol. 7, No. 2, April 1927, pp. 73–86.

Proceedings of the House of Assembly of Newfoundland.

Province of Alberta Public Accounts.

Public Accounts of the Province of British Columbia.

Public Papers and Addresses of Franklin D. Roosevelt, Vol. 3, 1934, p. 215. *The Statutes at Large of the United States of America,* Vol. XLVIIII, Part 1, p. 978.

Read, D.B. *The Life and Times of General John Graves Simcoe.* Toronto: George Virtue Publishing, 1890.

Record of the South Carolina General Assembly.

Shapin, Stephen. *Iris*, "The House of Experiment in Seventeenth-Century England." Vol. 79, No. 3 (September 1988), pp. 373–404.

Smith, David E. *The Canadian Senate in Bicameral Perspective.* Toronto: University of Toronto Press, 2003.

Smith, Sir David. *Head of State: The Governor-General, the Monarchy, the Republic and the Dismissal.* Sydney: Maclean Press, 2005.

La Sûreté du Québec de 1870 à 1995, Quebec: Sûreté du Québec, 1995.

Swan, Sir Conrad. *Canada: Symbols of Sovereignty.* Toronto: University of Toronto Press, 1977.

Thorne, Peter. *The Royal Mace.* London: HMSO, 1990.

_____. "Maces: Their Use and Significance," *Journal of the Parliaments of the Commonwealth*, Vol. XLV, No. 1., 1963.

Thorpe, Lewis. *The Bayeux Tapestry and the Norman Invasion.* London: Folio Society, 1973.

Tout, R.F. *Chapters in the Administrative History of Mediaeval England: The Wardrobe, the Chamber and the Small Seals.* London: Longman's Press, 1920.

Young, Carolyn. *The Glory of Ottawa: Canada's First Parliament Building.* Montreal: McGill Queen's Press, 1995.

Uniforms To Be Worn by Her Majesty's Civil Service at Home and in the Colonies. London: HMSO, 1897.

Varkaris, Jane, and Lucile Finsten. *Fire on Parliament Hill!* Erin, Boston Mills Press, 1988.

Warburton, A.B. *A History of Prince Edward Island* (St. John: Barkers Press, 1923).

Wiesinger, Véronique. *Chefs-d'oeuvre du Musée National de la Légion d'honneur et des Ordres de Chevalerie.* Paris : Carte Segrete, 1994.

Woods, A. *Canadian Parliamentary Review*, "The 100th Anniversary of the First Opening of the Saskatchewan Assembly," Summer 2006, p. 33.

Newspapers

The Daily Gleaner
The Halifax Herald
The Nova Scotian
The Regina Leader
The Toronto Globe and Mail
The Toronto Mail and Empire
The Victoria Colonist
The Victoria Standard

PHOTO CREDITS

CHA: Photo courtesy of the Canadian Heraldic Authority
LAC: Photo courtesy of Library and Archives Canada
LP: Photo courtesy of the Library of Parliament
OSGG: Photo courtesy of the Office of the Secretary to the Governor General
SC: Photo courtesy of the Senate of Canada

PHOTO OF	PAGE	CREDIT
Mace Engraving	3	*Illustrated London News*, circa 1840
Queen Elizabeth II	6	Department of Canadian Heritage
David Johnston	18	Department of National Defence
Chapter 3 Senate Black Rod	29	SC
Senate Black Rod, 1867–1916	32	LAC
Senator Identification Pin	33	SC
Borden and the Black Rod	34	LAC
Black Rod Presentation Certificate	35	Photo by C.P. McCreery
Ernest John Chambers	37	LAC
Lieutenant Commander Christopher	38	SC
Senate Black Rod	39	SC
Senate Black Rod	40	SC
Senate Black Rod Upper End	40	SC
Senate Black Rod Middle	40	SC
Senate Black Rod Base	41	SC
Chapter 4 Legislative Council of Newfoundland, 1934	46	Provincial Archives of Newfoundland and Labrador
Quebec Black Rod	48	Assemblée Nationale du Québec
New Brunswick Legislative Council, 1892	49	Legislative Assembly of New Brunswick
New Brunswick Black Rod	50	Legislative Assembly of New Brunswick
Alberta Black Rod	51	Legislative Assembly of Alberta
Alberta Black Rod	52	Legislative Assembly of Alberta
Alberta Black Rod Base	53	Legislative Assembly of Alberta
Alberta Black Rod Head	53	Legislative Assembly of Alberta
Sergeant-at-Arms Knocking	54	Legislative Assembly of Prince Edward Island, photograph by Brian Simpson
Sergeant-at-Arms Adamson	55	Legislative Assembly of Prince Edward Island, photograph by Brian Simpson
P.E.I. Black Rod	56	Legislative Assembly of Prince Edward Island, photograph by Brian Simpson
Chapter 5 Pre-Revolution Baton	58	René Chartrand
Napoleonic Baton	58	Palais de la Légion d'Honneur
British Field Marshal's Baton Top	59	Palais de la Légion d'Honneur
British Field Marshal's Baton	59	Palais de la Légion d'Honneur
British Field Marshal's Baton Top	59	Palais de la Légion d'Honneur

	Fraser Arms	60	CHA
	Fraser Badge	61	CHA
	Milliken Badge	62	CHA
	Milliken with Speaker's Baton	63	LP
	Speaker's Baton	63	LP
	Speaker's Baton Base	64	LP
	Speaker's Baton Head	64	LP
Chapter 6	Herald Chancellor's Shield	65	CHA
	Deputy Herald Chancellor's Shield	65	CHA
	Chief Herald Watt	66	CHA
	Chief Herald's Baton	67	CHA
	Chief Herald's Shield	67	CHA
Chapter 7	Victorian Tipstaff	69	Photo by C.P. McCreery
	Victorian Tipstaff	70	Photo by C.P. McCreery
	Victorian Tipstaff	70	Photo by C.P. McCreery
	Chief Constable's Sword Blade	70	Vancouver Police Department
	Chief Constable's Sword	71	Vancouver Police Department
	Deputy Chief Constable Rolls	71	Vancouver Police Department
	OPP Tipstaff	72	Ontario Provincial Police
	OPP Commissioner Fantino	72	Ontario Provincial Police
	Commissioner Higgitt	73	Royal Canadian Mounted Police
	RCMP Tipstaff	74	Royal Canadian Mounted Police
	RCMP Tipstaff in Case	74	Royal Canadian Mounted Police
	Original RCMP Tipstaff	75	Royal Canadian Mounted Police
	Sûreté du Québec Tipstaff	76	Sûreté du Québec
	Sûreté du Québec Tipstaff Base	76	Sûreté du Québec
	Normand Proulx	77	Sûreté du Québec
Chapter 8	Bishop Odo	83	Photo by C.P. McCreery
	Lesser Retford Mace	87	The Charter of Trustees of East Retford, photo by Ron Beare
	Large Retford Mace	87	The Charter of Trustees of East Retford, photo by Ron Beare
	British HoC Mace	88	Parliamentary Archives, Houses of Parliament, Westminster, London
	British HoC Mace Arms Plate	88	Parliamentary Archives, Houses of Parliament, Westminster, London
	British HoC Mace under Table	89	Parliamentary Archives, Houses of Parliament, Westminster, London
	British HoC Mace on Table	89	Parliamentary Archives, Houses of Parliament, Westminster, London
	South Carolina Mace Head	92	South Carolina House of Representatives
	South Carolina Mace	92	South Carolina House of Representatives
	Norfolk Mace	93	Chrysler Museum of Art
	U.S. Mace	95	Sergeant at Arms of the United States House of Representatives
	1972 Painting	97	Assemblée Nationale du Québec
Chapter 9	Parliament 1880	102	LAC
	Parliament 1916	102	LAC
	Senate Mace	103	SC
	Baillargé's Workbook	104	Musée national des beaux-arts du Québec
	Baillargé's Workbook	105	Musée national des beaux-arts du Québec
	Burning Legislature	106	LAC
	Carving of the Senate Mace	107	SC
	Great Seal of Lower Canada	108	Sir Conrad Swan
	Senate Mace Carried by Jan Potter	110	SC
	Jan Potter	111	SC
	Senate Mace in Chambers	111	SC
	Royal Arms of King George III	112	SC
	Great Seal of Lower Canada	113	SC
	Senate Mace Upper End	114	SC

Chapter 10	Sir Allan Napier MacNab	116	SC
	Original HoC Mace	117	LAC
	Sergeant-at-Arms Smith	117	LAC
	House of Commons, 1905	119	LP
	Parliamentary Fire, 1916	119	LAC
	Mace Remnant Box	121	Canadian Club London, photo by Corinna Pike
	Mace Remnant	122	Canadian Club London, photo by Corinna Pike
	HoC Mace	124	LAC
	HoC Mace with Royal Cypher	125	LAC
	Temporary HoC Mace	125	LP
	Temporary HoC Mace Top	126	LP
	Temporary HoC Mace Top	126	LP
	HoC Mace Crowned Head	127	LP
	HoC Mace Arms Plate	127	LP
	HoC Mace Brackets	128	LP
	HoC Mace Shaft	129	LP
Chapter 11	Ontario Mace in Chamber	134	Legislative Assembly of Ontario
	Ontario Mace in Chamber	135	Legislative Assembly of Ontario
	Upper Canada Mace	136	Legislative Assembly of Ontario
	Ontario Mace	136	Legislative Assembly of Ontario
	Ontario Mace, Top End	137	Legislative Assembly of Ontario
	Ontario Mace Restored	137	Legislative Assembly of Ontario
	Mace of the Legislative Council of Quebec	141	Assemblée Nationale du Québec
	Mace of the National Assembly of Quebec	142	Assemblée Nationale du Québec
	Quebec National Assembly Mace Head	142	Assemblée Nationale du Québec
	Mace of the National Assembly of Quebec	142	Assemblée Nationale du Québec
	Nova Scotia Mace in Chamber	144	Legislative Assembly of Nova Scotia, photo by Shirley Robb
	Sergeant-at-Arms Greenham	145	Legislative Assembly of Nova Scotia, photo by Shirley Robb
	Nova Scotia Mace	146	Legislative Assembly of Nova Scotia, photo by Shirley Robb
	Nova Scotia Mace, Upper End	146	Legislative Assembly of Nova Scotia, photo by Shirley Robb
	Great Seal of Nova Scotia	147	Legislative Assembly of Nova Scotia, photo by Shirley Robb
	New Brunswick Mace in Chamber	149	Legislative Assembly of New Brunswick
	Sergeant-at-Arms Bussières	150	Legislative Assembly of New Brunswick
	New Brunswick Ceremonial Staff	151	Legislative Assembly of New Brunswick
	New Brunswick Mace	152	Legislative Assembly of New Brunswick
	New Brunswick Mace, Upper End	153	Legislative Assembly of New Brunswick
	PEI Chamber	154	Legislative Assembly of Prince Edward Island, photo by Brian Simpson
	Great Seal of PEI	155	Sir Conrad Swan
	Great Seal of PEI	155	Sir Conrad Swan
	Sergeant-at-Arms Adamson	156	Legislative Assembly of Prince Edward Island, photo by Brian Simpson
	PEI Mace	157	Legislative Assembly of Prince Edward Island, photo by Brian Simpson
	PEI Mace Top	158	Legislative Assembly of Prince Edward Island, photo by Brian Simpson
	Sergeant-at-Arms Humphreys	163	Legislative Assembly of British Columbia, photo by Visions West Photography
	Colony of Vancouver Island Mace	164	Legislative Assembly of British Columbia, photo by Visions West Photography

Colony of Vancouver Island Mace, Upper End	164	Legislative Assembly of British Columbia, photo by Visions West Photography
First BC Mace	164	Legislative Assembly of British Columbia, photo by Visions West Photography
First BC Mace, Upper End	165	Legislative Assembly of British Columbia, photo by Visions West Photography
Chicago Mace	165	Legislative Assembly of British Columbia, photo by Visions West Photography
Chicago Mace Top	166	Legislative Assembly of British Columbia, photo by Visions West Photography
Queen Elizabeth II Mace	167	Legislative Assembly of British Columbia, photo by Visions West Photography
Queen Elizabeth II Mace Crown	167	Legislative Assembly of British Columbia, photo by Visions West Photography
Arms of BC	168	Legislative Assembly of British Columbia, photo by Visions West Photography
Queen Elizabeth II Mace End	168	Legislative Assembly of British Columbia, photo by Visions West Photography
Sergeant-at-Arms Clark	170	Legislative Assembly of Manitoba, photo by Tim Pohl
Old Manitoba Mace	171	Legislative Assembly of Manitoba, photo by Tim Pohl
Manitoba Mace	171	Legislative Assembly of Manitoba, photo by Tim Pohl
Mantioba Mace Beavers	172	Legislative Assembly of Manitoba, photo by Tim Pohl
Manitoba Mace Top	172	Legislative Assembly of Manitoba, photo by Tim Pohl
Saskatchewan Mace in Chamber	174	Legislative Assembly of Saskatchewan, photo by Digney Photographics Ltd
Sergeant-at-Arms Shaw	175	Legislative Assembly of Saskatchewan, photo by Digney Photographics Ltd
Saskatchewan Mace	176	Legislative Assembly of Saskatchewan, photo by Digney Photographics Ltd
Saskatchewan Mace Crown	176	Legislative Assembly of Saskatchewan, photo by Digney Photographics Ltd
Saskatchewan Mace Arms Plate	177	Legislative Assembly of Saskatchewan, Photo by Digney Photographics Ltd
Saskatchewan Mace	178	Legislative Assembly of Saskatchewan, Photo by Digney Photographics Ltd
Alberta Legislature, 1906	179	LAC
Sergeant-at-Arms Hodgson	181	Legislative Assembly of Alberta
Alberta Temporary Mace	182	Legislative Assembly of Alberta
Jubilee Mace	182	Legislative Assembly of Alberta
Jubilee Mace Arms	183	Legislative Assembly of Alberta
Jubilee Mace Crown	184	Legislative Assembly of Alberta
Jubilee Mace Bison Heads	185	Legislative Assembly of Alberta
Newfoundland and Labrador Mace in Chamber	189	Legislative Assembly of Newfoundland and Labrador
Sergeant-at-Arms Gallagher	190	Legislative Assembly of Newfoundland and Labrador
Colony of Newfoundland Mace	191	Legislative Assembly of Newfoundland and Labrador
Newfoundland and Labrador Mace	191	Legislative Assembly of Newfoundland and Labrador
Newfoundland and Labrador Mace Crown	192	Legislative Assembly of Newfoundland and Labrador
Newfoundland and Labrador Mace Arms Plate	193	Legislative Assembly of Newfoundland and Labrador
Chapter 12 RCMP Sergeant with NWT Mace	197	LAC

	NWT Chamber	198	Government of the Northwest Territories, photo by Corinna Pike
	NWT 2000 Mace in Chamber	199	Government of the Northwest Territories
	Sergeant-at-Arms Thagard	199	Government of the Northwest Territories
	NWT 1955 Mace	199	Government of the Northwest Territories
	NWT 1955 Mace Crown	200	Government of the Northwest Territories
	NWT 1955 Mace Figures	201	Government of the Northwest Territories
	NWT 1955 Mace Quillwork and Carvings	201	Government of the Northwest Territories
	NWT 1955 Mace Foot Knop	202	Government of the Northwest Territories
	NWT Replica Mace	203	Government of the Northwest Territories
	NWT 2000 Mace	203	Government of the Northwest Territories
	NWT 2000 Mace Crown	204	Government of the Northwest Territories
	NWT 2000 Mace Diamond	205	Government of the Northwest Territories
	Sergeant-at-Arms Couture	207	Government of the Yukon, photo by Robin Armour
	Yukon Territory Mace	208	Government of the Yukon, photo by Robin Armour
	Yukon Territory Mace Crown	209	Government of the Yukon, photo by Robin Armour
	Yukon Territory Mace Topographical Feature	209	Government of the Yukon, photo by Robin Armour
	Nunavut Mace	211	Government of Nunavut
	Nunavut Mace, Upper End	212	Government of Nunavut
	Nunavut Mace Granite Seal	213	Government of Nunavut
	Nunavut Mace Lapis Lazuli Seal	213	Government of Nunavut
	Nunavut Mace End	213	Government of Nunavut
	Nunavut Mace Carved Figurines	214	Government of Nunavut
	Nunavut Mace Carved Elder	214	Government of Nunavut
	Nunavut Mace Carved Woman	215	Government of Nunavut
	Nunavut Mace Carved Child	215	Government of Nunavut
	Nunavut Mace Carved Man	215	Government of Nunavut
	Nunavut Mace in Chamber	216	Government of Nunavut
	Sergeant-at-Arms Kilabuk	217	Government of Nunavut
Chapter 13	Vancouver Mace	221	City of Vancouver
	Vancouver Mace	221	City of Vancouver
Chapter 14	Sovereign's Insignia of the Order of Canada	226	LAC
	Painting of Sovereign's Insignia of the Order of Canada	227	OSGG
	Sovereign's Insignia of the OMM	228	LAC
	Painting of Sovereign's Insignia of the OMM	229	OSGG
	Chancellor's Chain of the Order of Canada	230	LAC
	Reverse of Chancellor's Chain of the Order of Canada	231	OSGG
	Jeanne Sauvé	232	OSGG
	Chancellor's Chain of the OMM	233	LAC
	Chancellor's Chain of the OMPF	235	OSGG
	Principal Commander's Chain of the OMM	236	OSGG
	General Natynczyk	237	Department of National Defence
	Principal Commander's Chain of the OMPF	239	OSGG
	St. John Prior's Chain	240	OSGG
	Michaëlle Jean	241	OSGG
	St. John Chancellor's Chain	243	OSGG
	René Marin	244	Priory of Canada of the Order of St. John
Chapter 15	Sir Edward Peacock	246	Queen's University Archives
	Consular Coat, 1840	246	René Chartrand

	Lord Aylmer, 1830	248	LAC
	Sir Robert Borden	251	LAC
	Henry Bell Irving	251	Office of the Lieutenant Governor of British Columbia
	Full Dress and Levee Dress	252	*Colonial Office Manual*, 1927
	René Kimber	254	LAC
	René Edouard Kimber	255	LAC
	Vincent Massey	257	LAC
	Roland Michener and George R. Pearkes	259	Department of National Defence
	Lord Tweedsmuir	261	LAC
	Lord Tweedsmuir	261	Library of Congress
	Full Dress Governor General's Uniform	262	*Colonial Office Manual*, 1927
	Georges Vanier	263	LAC
	Jeanne Sauvé	264	OSGG
	Ramon Hnatyshyn	264	OSGG
	Michaëlle Jean	265	Department of National Defence
	Roland Michener	266	LAC
	Tropical Uniform	267	*Colonial Office Manual*, 1927
	Mayann E. Francis	269	Office of the Lieutenant Governor of Nova Scotia
	Mayann E. Francis	269	Office of the Lieutenant Governor of Nova Scotia
	Iona Campagnolo	270	Office of the Lieutenant Governor of British Columbia
	William Lyon Mackenzie King	272	LAC
	William Lyon Mackenzie King	272	LAC
	Lord Bessborough	274	Lord Bessborough
	Lord Bessborough in Chamber	274	Lord Bessborough
	Hilary M. Weston	275	Office of the Lieutenant Governor of Ontario
	Lady Jennifer Gretton	275	Office of the Lord Lieutenant of Leicestershire
	Lord Lieutenant's Badge	275	Office of the Lord Lieutenant of Leicestershire
	Viceregal and Commissioner's Recognition Badge	277	OSGG
	Viceregal and Commissioner's Recognition Pin	277	OSGG
	Reverse of Viceregal and Commissioner's Recognition Badge	277	OSGG
	Spouses Viceregal and Commissioner's Recognition Badge	278	OSGG
	Spouses Viceregal and Commissioner's Recognition Pin	278	OSGG
	Civil Uniform Patterns	281–85	Civil Uniform Pattern Book
Chapter 16	Collar of Ss in Case	288	LP
	Collar of Ss Detail	288	LP
	Collar of Ss	289	LP
	Sergeant-at-Arms Cloutier	289	LP
	Central Badge	290	LP
	House of Commons, 1918	290	LAC
	U.K. Black Rod Chain	292	Parliamentary Archives, Houses of Parliament, Westminister, London
	Senate Black Rod Chain	293	Office of the Usher of the Black Rod of the SC
Chapter 17	Governor General's Collar	296	CHA
	Chief Herald's Ceremonial Collar	297	CHA
	Michaëlle Jean	299	CHA
	Dr. Claire Boudreau	299	CHA

Reverse of Canadian Heraldic Authority Collar	299	CHA
Collar of the Deputy Herald Chancellor	300	CHA
Collar of the Deputy Chief Herald of Canada	300	CHA
Collar of the Saint-Laurent Herald	301	CHA
Collar of the Saguenay Herald	301	CHA
Collar of the Assiniboine Herald	301	CHA
Collar of the Mirimichi Herald	301	CHA
Collar of the Fraser Herald	302	CHA
Collar of the Coppermine Herald	302	CHA
Collar of the Outaouais Herald Emeritus	302	CHA
Collar of the Dauphin Herald Extraordinary	302	CHA
Collar of the Niagara Herald Extraordinary	303	CHA
Collar of the Albion Herald Extraordinary	303	CHA
Collar of the Capilano Herald Extraordinary	303	CHA
Collar of the Rouge Herald Extraordinary	303	CHA

INDEX

A

Aarand, Argo, 231–32
Act of Union, 46
Adams, William, 94
Adamson, Curtis, 55, 156
Administrators, 253, 280
Afghanistan, 81
Aitken, W.T., 181
Alberta, 51–53, 55, 96, 179–85, 195, 196, 269–71, 314, 325
Albion Herald Extraordinary, 303
Alexander, Lord, 60, 259–60
American Revolution, 91–92, 132
Anderson, J., 238
Anglican, 107, 152
Anscomb, Herbert, 186
Antigua and Barbuda, 94
Armitage, Blair, 311
Arrest, 26, 69, 87–88, 187
Ashmole, Elias, 32, 287
Askwith, Charles, 31
Assiniboine Herald, 301
Attawapiskat First Nation, 135
Auclair, Gérard, 77
Auditors General, 281
Augustus III, 247
Aupilardjuk, Mariano, 211, 216
Australia, 20, 27, 69, 96, 97, 123, 179, 260
Aylmer, Lord, 248

B

Badge of Office, 69, 229, 245, 274, 276, 307
Bahamas, 93, 94, 96
Bailiff, 69
Baillargé, François, 103–05, 313
Banff, 52
Bannatyne, A.G.B., 169
Barbados, 94
Baril, M., 238
Barnabas, Levi, 211
Bart, Gervase Clifton, 86

Bath, The Most Honourable Order of the, 225, 315
Baton,
    Bâton de commandement, 58, 71, 76–77
    Baton of France, 57
    British Field Marshal's Baton, 58–59
    of the Chief Herald of Canada, 65–67
    French Marshal's Baton, 58
    of the Speaker of the House of Commons, 57–64
Bayeux Tapestry, 82–83
Beatty, Bruce, 228, 231, 234, 238
Beaudoin, Jacques, 77
Beaugrand, Gilles, 77
Beaupré, Victor, 45
Beaverbrook, Lord, 123
Bédard, Marc-André, 77
Bell Irving, Henry, 251
Bennett, W.A.C., 162
Bermuda, 252–53
Bessborough, Lord, 274, 335
Bible, 82
Billy Club, 69
Bird, Alphonse, 174
Birks & Son, Henry, 124, 139, 159, 193, 208, 210, 313, 314
Black, W.D., 162
Black Rod,
    Acting Gentleman Usher of the Black Rod, 31
    Assistant Gentleman Usher of the Black Rod, 30–31
    Black Rod of the Legislative Assembly of the Province of Alberta, 52–54
    Black Rod of the Legislative Council of New Brunswick, 50–52
    Black Rod of the Legislative

    Council of the Province of Quebec, 48–50
    Black Rod of the Prince Edward Island Legislative Assembly, 56
    Black Rod of the Senate of Canada, 29–41, 254, 311
    Deputy Gentleman Usher of the Black Rod, 31, 109
    dormant Black Rods, 44
    Gentleman Usher of the Black Rod, 25–27, 29–32, 36, 43–49, 55, 107, 109, 254, 291–93, 317, 327
    Gentleman Usher of the Blue Rod, 316
    Gentleman Usher of the Purple Rod, 316
    Lady Usher of the Black Rod, 31
    Nova Scotia's Gentleman Usher of the Black Rod, 44
    Usher of the Black Rod, 11, 25, 26, 29, 31, 36, 38, 39, 40, 44, 83, 89, 90, 291, 307–08, 315, 317
    Usher of the Green Rod, 315
    Usher of the Scarlet Rod, 315
    Usher of the White Rod, 315
    Yeoman Usher of the Black Rod, 90, 109
Blain, L.B., 181, 185
Board of Council, (see also Legislative Council), 45
Bond-Boyd Co. Ltd, 73, 75

Bonenfant, Jean-Charles, 140
Booth, Noel, 160
Borden, Sir Robert, 34, 35–36,
        120, 122–23, 251, 256, 272
Boudreau, Claire, 299
Boutillier, William, 47, 317
Bovines, Battle of, 84
Bowie, Henry William, 312
Bowie, Thomas Guy, 311
Boyle, Jean, 238
Brass, 39, 75–76, 96, 109, 113,
        122, 140, 151, 171, 173,
        176, 180, 182, 198, 203,
        313, 314
Breadner Company, 198, 203
Britain, 27, 47, 57, 89, 103, 123,
        132, 247, 253, 273, 295
Britannia, Royal Yacht, 228
British Army, 308
British Columbia, 14, 29, 43, 67,
        93, 98, 131, 159–69, 186,
        192, 193, 195, 234, 239,
        268, 271, 313, 314, 325
British Empire, 20, 123, 133, 143,
        150, 225, 245, 247
British Empire, The Most
        Excellent Order of the, 225
British Guiana, 249
British North America, 43, 44,
        91, 101, 108, 154, 159–60,
        188, 248, 250
British North America Act, 101
British Parliament, 33, 81, 98,
        132, 144
Browne, Peter, 188
Bruce, Herbert, 133
Bruce, Richard, 243
Buckingham Palace, 226
Bunting, C., 161, 165
Burgundy, 84
Bursey-Sabourin, Cathy, 276,
        296
Bussières, Daniel, 150
Butler, Esmond, 19, 260
Butterworth, Rufus, 180, 182
Byzantium, 57

C
Cadieux, Dolphus, 198
Caen, Siege of, 85
Callbeck, Phillips, 155
Campagnolo, Iona, 268, 270–71
Canada, 6, 11, 17–21, 26–27, 30–
        37, 39–41, 50, 52, 54, 66,
        67, 75, 81, 89, 93–94, 118,
        120, 124, 128–29, 131–36,
        150, 152, 154, 158–59, 162,
        167, 173–174, 179, 183,

185, 188, 192, 195–96, 198,
        208, 210, 219, 222, 227,
        28, 230–34, 236, 241–42,
        245–47, 249–51, 253–54,
        256, 258–60, 265, 268–69,
        271, 273–74, 276, 279–80,
        291, 307–09, 311, 313
Canada, Province of, 25, 30, 43,
        45–47, 81, 96–97, 101, 106,
        109, 114–16, 131–34, 139,
        186, 287
Canada Club, 122
Canada East, 43, 115, 133
Canada West, 43, 115, 133–34
Canadian Army, 263
Canadian Association of Chiefs
        of Police, 71, 73
Canadian Expeditionary Force,
        123
Canadian Flag, 157
Canadian Heraldic Authority, 60,
        65, 295–301, 303, 308
Canadian Honours System, 20,
        225–26, 295
Cape Dorset, 197
Capilano Herald Extraordinary,
        303
Capitol Building, 94–95
Caribbean, 91, 94
Carnarvon, Lord, 101
Carson, William, 187–88
Catholic, 107
Ceremony, 19, 29, 39, 47, 52, 62,
        72, 75, 123, 144, 157, 174,
        181, 219, 269, 273
Chains of Office, 17, 19–20,
        223–243
Chambers, Ernest, 32
Chancellery, 225, 276, 278, 300
Chancellor, 18, 34, 41, 65,
        225–26, 228, 230–35, 239,
        241–42, 244, 300, 307–08
Chanteloupe, E., 32
Chapman, William, 287–88
Charles V, King of France, 85
Charlie, Inuk, 216
Charlottetown, 154–56
Chaucer, Geoffrey, 83
Chiasson, H., 298
Chicago Mace, 161–62, 165
Chief Herald, 13, 52, 54, 61, 65–
        67, 276, 295, 297–300, 308
Chief Justice, 144, 148, 249, 287,
        313
Chief of the Defence Staff, 236,
        238, 308
Chisholm, G.K., 115
Chrétien, Jean, 206

Christopher, Terrance, 11, 38
Church of England, 152
Civil Service Association of
        Alberta, 180, 184
Civil Uniform (*see also* Court
        Dress *and* Windsor
        Uniform), 21, 245–53,
        255–60, 262, 265, 268–74,
        279–81, 331
Civil War, American, 94
Clark, Dennis, 114, 135
Clark, Garry, 170
Clarke, Charles, 20, 118, 133,
        144, 149
Clarke, Henry J.H., 169
Clarkson, Adrienne, 232, 234,
        235, 298
Clerk of the Privy Council, 19
Cloutier, Gaston, 289, 312
Coat of Arms, 73, 75–76, 106,
        124, 173, 179, 186, 242, 295
Cocked Hat, 250, 272, 279
Cocobolo wood, 75
Coghill, Henry Judson, 312
Coldwell, Henry, 103
Collar, The Savoyard Order of
        the, 287
Collar of Cs, 296, 298
Collar of Office, 66, 295
Collar of Ss, 287–91, 295, 296, 298
College of Arms, 13
Colonial, 30, 43–45, 48, 50, 55,
        91, 93, 96–97, 101, 132, 144,
        149, 154, 160, 162, 187, 189,
        248–50, 253, 256, 259–60,
        262, 280
Colonial Office, 253, 260
Committee of the Whole, 90, 94
Commonwealth, 11, 21, 27, 31,
        33, 50, 52, 57, 70, 86–87,
        89, 91, 94, 96–98, 121, 135,
        143, 151, 156–57, 159, 179,
        196, 245, 251, 258, 313
Commonwealth of Nations, 11,
        21, 27, 31, 33, 50, 52, 57,
        70, 86–91, 94–98, 121, 135,
        143, 151, 156–59, 179, 196,
        245, 251, 258, 313
Commonwealth Parliamentary
        Association, 33, 52,
        156–57, 159, 313
Confederation, 20, 25, 29, 43, 44,
        47, 49–50, 52, 54, 61, 98,
        101, 106–07, 109, 115, 118,
        124, 131, 134, 138–39, 154,
        156, 159, 161–62, 169, 173,
        185, 196, 246, 249, 256,
        268–69, 287

Connaught, Prince Arthur, Duke of, 60, 123
Constable, 57, 69–71, 76, 220
Constitutional Monarchy, 17, 131, 225
Consular Coat, 246
Cook, Marvin, 231–32
Cookson, Arthur, 73
Coppermine Herald, 302
Corona Jewellers, 136
Cortes Island, 67
Court Dress (see also Civil Uniform and Windsor Uniform), 37, 245–46, 254, 272, 331
Couture, Rudy, 14, 207
Crease, Sir Henry, 160
Crewe, Marquess of, 123
Cromwell, Oliver, 86
Crown, 11, 17, 20–21, 33, 43–44, 46, 47, 56, 70, 73, 81, 87, 90, 91, 94, 98, 132, 135, 139, 144, 208, 225, 245, 247, 253, 256, 269, 273, 274, 276, 278, 295, 308
Crusades, 83–85
Currie, David Vivian, 312

D
Dalton, Robert, 134
Dandurand, Raoul, 273
Dauphin Herald Extraordinary, 302
Davidson, Sir Walter Edward, 189
Dawson, Peter, 181
De Beers, 135
de Chastelain, John, 238
Defacing Ceremony, 19
Democracy, 11, 19–20, 81, 93, 143, 195–96
Deputy Chief Herald, 13, 300
Deputy Herald Chancellor, 65, 300
Deputy Minister, 47, 139, 247, 258, 271, 280–81
D'Estimauville, Robert-Anne, 317
D'Ewes, Sir Simonds, 90
Dextraze, Jacques, 238
Dickens, Charles, 143
Diefenbaker, John, 273
Dinwiddie, Robert, 93
Donegan Hotel, 116
Dorchester, Lord, 108
Doré, Jean, 311
Dorrien Plating and Manufacturing Company, 135
Douglas, Sir James, 160–61
Duppa, Sir Thomas, 27

Duquet, Cyrille, 47, 139, 141
Durham, Lord, 133, 188
Dysart, Allison, 150–51

E
Earl Marshal, 57
Ebony, 32, 50, 52, 53, 94
Edington, John James, 50
Edmonton, 179, 181, 185
Edward III, King, 25, 26, 85
Edward VII, King, 36, 125, 135, 138, 173, 177, 182, 250, 259, 325
Edward VIII, King, 59, 220, 222
Egyptian Kings, 84
Electroplating, 109
Elgin, Earl of, 27
Elizabeth I, Queen, 86
Elizabeth II, Queen, 6, 21, 124–25, 128, 139, 162, 167–68, 227, 325
Elkington & Company, 148, 313
Elliott, William, 239
Empire Parliamentary Association, 33–34, 36, 41
Enamel, 40, 50, 57, 78, 84, 157, 158, 167, 183, 226, 228, 231, 242, 276, 278, 298, 300, 313, 314
England, 20, 25, 27, 30, 57, 60, 69, 73, 84–85, 87, 90–92, 109, 122, 124, 129, 148, 152, 154, 185, 219, 222, 249, 287
English Civil War, 86
Evening Dress Civil Uniform, 253, 259–60

F
Falls, R.H., 238
Fantino, Julian, 72
Fathers of Confederation, 101, 159
Feline, Magdalen, 91–92
Finlay, Lord, 34, 41
Fire, 32–33, 41, 47, 96, 99, 101, 106–07, 109, 115, 118–20, 124, 129, 139, 154, 169–70, 210, 291
Firmin & Sons, 73–75
First World War, 123
Fisher, Charles Wellington, 180
Flag, 21, 94, 157, 169–70, 279, 309
Fleur-de-lys, 78, 113, 165, 172, 182
Forget, Amédée, 173
Fort Langley, 160
Fortier, Alfred, 31

France, 11, 15, 17, 26, 57–58, 81, 84–86, 245
Francis, Mayann, 268–69, 271
Franklin, 155
Franklin, William John, 312
Fraser, Duncan, 269
Fraser, John, 60–61
Fraser Herald, 67, 276, 296, 302
Freeman, Myra, 268
Frock Coat, 250
Full Dress, 279
Fury, HMS, 196–97, 201, 203

G
Gallagher, Elizabeth, 14, 190
Galway, 219
Gargrave, Sir Thomas, 86
Garland, Charles, 46
Garrard, Sebastian, 41
Garrard & Co. Ltd., 33, 41, 226, 228, 231
Garter, The Most Noble Order of the, 25–26, 32, 291
Gelly, Pierre, 317
George III, King, 107, 109, 112–13, 132, 246–47, 250, 323, 325
George IV, King, 58, 247
George V, King, 36, 40, 120–21, 124–28, 173, 259, 260, 325
George VI, King, 124, 150–52, 186, 192, 258, 325
Gervais, James, 276
Gilding, 109, 161, 165, 339
Gilmour, Jeffrey, 243
Given-Wilson, Chris, 20
Gladstone, R.E., 31
Goldsmiths & Silversmiths Co. Ltd., 313
Gomes, Robin, 74
Government House, 250, 259
Governor, 253, 256, 258, 259, 260
Governor General, 17–19, 25–27, 34, 36, 39, 44, 52, 62, 90, 98, 123, 133, 144, 188, 196–97, 208, 225–26, 228, 231–35, 276
Governor General's Uniform, 245–48, 250–53, 258, 260–62, 265–66, 274, 279–81, 195–96, 298, 300, 307–08, 331, 333
Grand Master, 230, 240
Greaves, Kevin, 20
Great Bear Lake, 206
Great Seal, 19, 30, 56, 92, 107–09, 113, 115, 147–48, 152–53, 155, 323

Great Slave Lake, 204
Greek Empire, 82
Green Book, 19
Greenham, Ken, 14, 145
Gregg, Milton Fowler, 312
Grenada, 247
Gretton, Lady Jennifer, 14, 275
Guildhall, 123
Gutknecht, Rene, 311

H
Habeas corpus, 188
Half Dress Uniform, 250, 251,
    272, 279
Hallmark, 41, 50, 64, 121, 129,
    148, 154, 185, 222, 233,
    238, 242, 288
Hancock, 155
Harrison, Robert, 14
Harrison, Roy, 181
Hatt, Samuel Staunton, 317
Head of State, 17, 91
Henault, R.R., 238
Henry IV, King, 287
Henry VII, King, 26
Henry VIII, King, 26, 287
Herald, 52, 54, 61, 65–67, 225,
    276, 295–303, 308
Herald Chancellor, 65, 300, 308
Higgitt, William, 73
High Sheriff, 188
Hillier, Rick, 238
Hnatyshyn, Ray, 232, 234,
    263–64
Hodgson, Brian, 51, 52, 181
Holy Spirit, The Order of the, 26
Home, Ninian, 247
House of Assembly, 44, 91,
    143–44, 148, 186–89, 249
House of Assembly of the
    Bahamas, 93
House of Commons (*see also*
    Parliament *and* Senate), 26,
    39, 41, 57–64, 81, 96, 98,
    106–07, 115–29, 134, 150,
    170, 287, 289–91, 313, 325
    British, 26, 36–37, 84, 85–91,
        118, 121, 189
    members of, 13–14, 34, 36,
        39, 57, 60, 61, 62–64,
        101, 109, 156, 157, 287,
        289– 91, 307–08, 312
House of Lords, 14, 26–27,
    30–31, 33–34, 36, 52, 85,
    87, 101, 292
House of Representatives, 14, 91,
    93, 94–96, 132, 179
Houston, James, 196, 202

Hudson's Bay Company, 173, 195
Humphreys, Anthony, 14, 163
Hungerford, Sir Thomas, 85
Hunley, Helen, 269–270
Huot, Charles, 138

I
Imperial Order of Daughters of
    the Empire, 133
Imperial Service Order, 225
India, 81, 151, 152
Inuit, 196, 211
Ireland, 27, 69, 87, 162, 219

J
Jalbert, René, 31, 311
Jamaica, 27, 94, 95
James Bay, 135
Japan, 258
Jarvis, Frédérick Starr, 317
Jean, Michaëlle, 232, 234, 235,
    241, 242, 265, 299, 300
Johnston, David, 18, 232, 234,
    235, 242
Judicial Committee of the Privy
    Council, 188

K
Kent, John, 187–88
Kerry, Lloyd, 56
Kielly, Edward, 187–88
Kilabuk, Simanuk, 217
Kimber, René, 29, 47, 254, 311, 317
Kimber, René Edouard, 255, 311
Kimmirut, 211, 216
King of Arms, 58
King of France, 84
Kowalsky, Myron, 174

L
Lajoie, Claude, 311
Lam, David See-Chai, 268
Lamoureux, Charles Rock, 291
Lansdowne, Lord, 34
Lapel Pin/Badge, 260, 276, 278
Lapointe, Patricia, 31
Larocque, Gédéon, 139
Larose, Charles, 30
Larose, C. Bonner, 30
Lascelles, Sir Allan, 19
Laurier, Sir Wilfrid, 120, 123,
    271, 272
Leahy, William D., 133
LeBlanc, Phyllis, 31, 316
LeBlanc, Roméo, 232, 234, 276
Léger, Jules, 232, 234, 262
Legislative Assembly, 81, 103,
    131, 134, 139, 160, 273

British Columbia
    Legislative Assembly,
        160–61, 168, 169
Legislative Assembly of
    Alberta, 43, 52, 179,
        180, 185
Legislative Assembly of
    Lower Canada, 47, 91,
        97, 103, 138–39, 140
Legislative Assembly of
    Manitoba, 13, 45,
        169–70, 173
Legislative Assembly of
    New Brunswick, 31,
        43, 48–50, 149–51
Legislative Assembly of
    Newfoundland and
    Labrador, 45, 88,
        186–87, 189
Legislative Assembly
    of the Northwest
    Territories, 198–99
Legislative Assembly
    of Prince Edward
    Island, 13, 43, 54–56,
        154, 156–57, 159
Legislative Assembly of the
    Province of Canada,
        81, 96, 106, 115–16,
        133, 134
Legislative Assembly of
    Quebec, 47, 139
Legislative Assembly of
    the United Canadas,
        32, 139
Ontario Legislative
    Assembly, 47, 134,
        136, 139
Nova Scotia Legislative
    Assembly, 131,
        143–44
Nunavut Legislative
    Assembly, 13,
        210–211, 217
Saskatchewan Legislative
    Assembly, 174
Yukon Legislative
    Assembly, 13
Legislative Council, 25, 43, 46,
    52, 54, 95–96, 106, 131, 253
Legislative Council of
    Canada, 30, 316
Legislative Council of the
    Colony of British
    Columbia, 161
Legislative Council of
    the Dominion of
    Newfoundland, 45–46

Legislative Council of Lower Canada, 29, 34, 43, 45, 46–47, 96, 101, 103–04, 106, 109, 114, 138–39, 313, 317, 325
Legislative Council of Manitoba, 45
Legislative Council of New Brunswick, 27, 48–50, 149
Legislative Council of Nova Scotia, 44
Legislative Council of Prince Edward Island, 54–55, 317
Legislative Council of the Province of Canada, 30, 45, 46–47, 81, 101, 106, 109, 114, 131, 139, 317
Legislative Council of the Province of Quebec, 48, 139, 322
Legislative Council of the Province of the United Canadas, 30
Legislative Council of Quebec, 46–47, 139, 140, 325
Legislative Council of Upper Canada, 45
Legislature, 45, 49, 51–52, 56, 81, 96–98, 101, 118, 120, 124, 133, 135–36, 138, 139, 143, 144, 149, 161, 162, 170, 174, 179–80, 187, 195, 198, 206, 247, 249, 269
LeMoyne, Juchereau de St. Denis, 30, 316
Letters Patent, 25, 30, 308
Levee, 247
Levee Dress, 250–56, 259, 272, 279, 280
Lévis, François Gaston de, 57
Lewton-Brain, Charles, 52, 54
Lictor, 94
Lieutenant Governor, 44, 45, 47, 49, 52, 56, 71–72, 93, 133, 144, 148–49, 151, 157, 173–74, 181, 195, 268–71, 274, 276, 278, 280, 298, 308, 313
Lilly, George, 188
Lindsay, Roger, 242
Lion, 26, 32, 40, 48, 50, 53, 61, 63, 146, 148, 260
Logan, Richard, 31

Lord Chamberlain, 123, 253, 258
Lord Chancellor, 34, 41
Lord High Constable of Scotland, 57
Lord Lieutenant, 248–49, 251, 260, 275, 276, 332
Lord Mayor of London, 120, 123, 129, 219, 287, 313
Lord Protector, 86
Lougheed, Sir James, 36
Louis IX (St. Louis), 84
Louis XIV, King, 57
Louis XV, King, 245
Lower Canada, 25, 29–30, 34, 43, 45–47, 91, 96–98, 101–09, 113–15, 133, 134, 138–40, 143, 206, 313
Lowther, J.W., 34, 41
Loyalists, 91–92, 132

M
MacDonald, Willibald, 157
Macdonald, John Sanfield, 134
Macdonald, W. Ross, 72
Macdonell, Donald William, 312
Mace, 30–31, 44, 45, 47
  Alberta, 185
  Australia, 96, 179
  British Columbia, 163–66
  British House of Commons, 20, 88–89, 96, 121, 189
  components of, 158, 160, 182, 200
  House of Commons, 91, 96, 115, 117–29, 134, 150, 170, 291
  Jamaica, 94–96
  Manitoba, 169–72
  meaning of, 20, 21, 220, 81–88, 101, 140, 173, 181
  municipal, 93
  New Brunswick, 49, 148–51, 153
  New Zealand, 96
  Newfoundland and Labrador, 20, 189–93
  Norfolk, 94
  Northwest Territories, 196, 198–99
  Nova Scotia, 44, 144–47
  Nunavut, 196, 212–14, 216–17, 314
  Ontario, 120, 134–35, 137, 141, 328
  Papua New Guinea, 97
  Parliamentary, 101, 115, 196

positioning of, 20, 30–31, 89–91, 140
  Prince Edward Island, 156–59
  Quebec, 142
  Retford, 87
  Saskatchewan, 173–78
  Senate, 30–31, 32, 50, 90–91, 101, 106–07, 109–15, 120
  South Carolina, 92
  symbolism of, 26, 81–88, 98–99, 131, 133, 144, 192, 206
  Temporary, 96, 120, 160–61, 179, 182
  Upper Canada, 132–33
  U.S., 94
  Vancouver, 15, 219, 221
  Yukon, 206
Mace Bearer, 14, 30–31, 89–91, 109–11
MacKay, Alex, 220
Mackeen, David, 269
Mackenzie King, William Lyon, 19, 271–72
Mackenzie River, 206
MacLaren, Murray, 149–51, 313
MacLaren, Mary, 31
MacLeod, Kevin, 311
MacNab, Sir Allan Napier, 32, 115–16, 118, 122–23, 134, 138, 326
MacNaughton, Alan, 96, 157
Mah, John, 243
Malliki, Paul, 211, 216
Manitoba, 13, 14, 25, 43, 45, 96, 169–73, 195, 196, 314, 325
Manning, Ernest, 181
Manson, Paul, 238
Manual of Official Procedure, 19
Maple Leaf, 36, 63, 153, 177, 210, 220, 226, 228, 231, 233, 237, 242, 277–278, 291
Marin, René, 243–44
Marshal, 57–60, 308
Martin, Paul, 273
Massey, Vincent, 196, 257–58, 260, 274, 335
Massey, W.F., 123
Maudit, Nicholas, 85
Maundy, Thomas, 86, 121
Maxwell, Mr, 37
McCreery, Christopher, 11, 15, 20
McKelvie, B.A., 160, 162
McMaster University, 219
Meighen, Arthur, 101

Metcalfe, Sir Charles, 133
Meyers, Frank, 157
Michener, Roland, 208, 226, 228,
    232, 234, 251, 259, 261–62,
    265–66, 279, 333, 334–35
Middle Ages, 82, 84
Military Merit, The Order of,
    6, 18, 225–29, 232, 234,
    236–39, 307
Milliken, Peter, 62–63
Monarchy, 17, 131, 225
Montcalm, Marquis de, 57
Montgomery, T.R., 157
Montreal, 32, 77, 103, 106, 115,
    124, 139, 170, 173, 208, 273
More, Sir Thomas, 287
Morning Dress/Morning Suit,
    250, 269, 272, 273
Morris, Sir Edward, 189
Moses, Rod of, 82
Motto, 40, 50, 173, 226, 231, 242,
    287–88, 291
Mount Stephen, Lord, 34
Mullock, Sir William, 273
Murray, L.E., 238
Mussallem, Helen, 298

N

Nasogaluak, Bill, 198
National Assembly of Quebec,
    47, 90, 91, 140–42, 325, 327
Natynczyk, Walter, 237, 238
New Brunswick, 25, 27, 29, 31,
    32, 43–44, 48–50, 128, 131,
    148–54, 298, 313, 325
New France, 17, 58, 245
New Westminster, 161
New Zealand, 27, 96, 123
Newfoundland and Labrador,
    185–93, 298, 325
Niagara Herald Extraordinary,
    303
Nicklett, A.F, 133
Norfolk, 14, 93–94
North America, 43, 44, 57, 91,
    101, 108, 131, 143, 154, 159,
    160, 188, 248, 250
North West Mounted Police,
    73, 76
Northern Ireland, 27, 69
Northwest Territories, 52, 195,
    196–206, 314, 325
Nova Scotia, 25, 29, 43, 44, 48,
    81, 128, 131, 143–48, 268,
    271, 313, 325
Nunavut, 13, 14, 195–96, 198,
    210–17, 314, 325
Nuqingaq, Mathew, 211, 216

O

Oath, 44, 98, 103, 106
O'Brien, Audrey, 312
Odes of Horace, 108
Odin, 82–83
Odo, Bishop of Bayeux, 82–83
Olson, Bud, 52
Ontario, 43, 47, 64, 73, 98, 109,
    118, 128, 131–37, 139, 141,
    195, 228, 275, 313, 325
Ontario Provincial Parliament,
    20, 120
Ontario Provincial Police, 14,
    71–72
Outaouais Herald Emeritus, 302

P

Paatz, Walter, 20
Papua New Guinea, 97
Parliament (see also House of
    Commons and Senate),
    17, 20, 25–26, 32–34, 36,
    39, 41, 47, 52, 61–62, 81,
    83–87, 89–91, 93, 95–99,
    101–03, 109, 124, 131–34,
    139, 140, 143. 144, 149,
    154, 156–57, 159, 187–89,
    195–96, 206, 210, 220, 232,
    238–39, 268, 271, 272, 287,
    291, 307–08, 313
Parliamentary Fire, 96, 106–07,
    109, 115–22, 170, 321
Parry, Sir William, 196, 201
Peacock, Sir Edward, 246
Pearkes, George, 259
Pearson, Lester B, 19, 230, 258
Peel, Sir Robert, 69
Pennee, Frank, 317
People's Warden, 152
Perks, John, 49
Perley, Sir George, 123
Perry, Alfred, 115–16
Philip, Prince, 111
Phillip II, King of France, 84
Pitsiulak, Sam, 211
Point, Stephen, 268
Poland, King of, 247
Police, 17, 69–77, 208, 220
Police Forces, The Order of
    Merit of the, 225, 229,
    234–35, 238–39, 307
Potter, Jan, 31, 110–11
Premier, 25, 134, 150–51, 162,
    169, 180–81, 186, 195, 247,
    258, 261
Prescott, Sir Henry, 188
Pressed Metal Products, 234,
    239, 298

Priestley, A.F, 160
Prime Minister, 19, 34, 35, 39,
    101, 122–23, 189, 230, 247,
    258, 260, 271, 273, 280
Prince Edward Island, 13, 14,
    25, 29, 43–44, 54–56, 131,
    154–59, 276, 313, 325
Prince Regent, 58, 247
Principal Commander, 225,
    236–39, 307
Principal Companion, 231
Priory, 242
Priory of Canada, 242
Privy Council, 19, 39, 96, 188,
    251, 252, 257–58, 260,
    271–72, 280
Protocol, 11, 17–21
Proulx, Jean-Claude, 77
Prouse, Harper, 181

Q

Quebec, 20, 25, 43, 46–48, 71,
    76–77, 90–91, 98, 124, 128,
    131, 132, 138–42, 195, 198,
    203, 313
Quebec Act of 1791, 20
Quebec City, 47, 106–07, 118
Queensland, 27

R

Rankin, Robert, 160, 216, 258
Rebellion Losses Bill, 106, 115
Red River, 169–71
Red River Cart, 169–71
Red River Expedition, 169
Regina, 73, 74, 173
Renison University College, 219
Representative Government, 29,
    81, 91, 131, 143, 187
Responsible Government, 98,
    131, 154, 206–07, 253
Restoration (of the monarchy), 87
Retford, 86–87
Retford, Borough of East, 87
Rhodes, Edgar, 291
Richard I, King, 84
Richard II, King, 84
Richard III, King, 57
Rideau Hall, 229, 260, 276, 300
Riel, Louis, 17
Riel Rebellion, 169
Rivett, R.A., 208
Robertson, Gordon, 19
Robitaille, André, 77
Robitaille, Gabriel, 77
Rolls, Bob, 71
Roman, 57, 76, 141
Romans, Robert, 44

Roosevelt, Franklin Delano, 132–33
Roth, Eric, 64
Rouge Herald Extraordinary, 303
Royal Arms, 57, 87, 92, 107, 109, 112, 113, 127, 128, 131, 151, 152, 177, 183, 192, 220, 265, 279, 298
Royal Assent, 29, 36, 39, 49, 52, 62, 149, 270
Royal Canadian Air Force, 263–65
Royal Canadian Legion, 52, 54
Royal Canadian Mint, 231–32
Royal Canadian Mounted Police (RCMP), 71, 73–75, 208, 238, 307
Royal Canadian Navy, 265, 279
Royal Courts of Justice, 69
Royal Cypher, 33, 36, 40, 49–50, 53, 70, 109, 120–21, 124–26, 128, 131, 135, 138, 139, 141, 152, 167, 172–73, 177, 182, 186, 192, 220, 222, 259
Royal Navy, 81, 86
Royal Ontario Museum, 109
Royal Proclamation 1763, 20
Royal Roads Military College, 219
Royal Society of Canada, 219
Royal Tour, 211, 247, 258, 271, 273
Rutherford, C.S., 133
Ryrie Brothers, 173, 177, 314

S
Saint Simplicus, 287
Saint-Esprit, l'Ordre du, 26
Saint-Jacques, Arthur, 317
Saint-Laurent Herald, 301
Sanctus Spiritus, 287
Sandhurst, Lord, 123
Saracens, 83
Sashes of Office, 57
Saskatchewan, 43, 74, 173–79, 195, 308, 314, 325
Sauvé, Jeanne, 232, 234, 260, 263–64
Sceptre, 82, 84
Schreyer, Edward, 232, 234
Schumacher, Stanley, 52
Scotland, Crown of, 148, 325
Second World War, 197, 259, 260
Secret Ballot, 154
Selman, John, 155
Senate (see also House of Commons and Parliament), 11, 13, 14, 19, 25–27, 29–35, 36–37,

39–41, 43, 46, 47, 50, 52, 57, 62, 81, 89–91, 93–98, 101, 103, 105–07, 109–15, 120, 134, 138–40, 156, 157, 253–54, 274, 291, 293, 307, 311, 313, 325
Senate, French, 57
Senate, Speaker of the, 36, 62, 156, 307
Senate Chamber, 30, 32, 36, 39, 90, 97, 109, 274
Senate Protective Services, 31
Sénécal, Roger, 77
Sergeant-at-Arms, 13, 14, 30–31, 36, 39, 44–45, 49, 51–52, 54–56, 81, 83–85, 87, 89–91, 94, 101, 106, 109, 115, 117–18, 120, 131, 133, 135, 139, 143–45, 149–50, 154, 156–57, 163, 170, 175, 180–81, 187–90, 195, 197, 199, 201, 217, 287, 289–93, 296, 308, 316
Sergeant-at-Arms to the Senate, 30
Sewell, John St. Alban, 317
Shamrock, 114, 118, 128, 173, 177, 276, 288
Sharp, F.R., 238
Shaughnessy, Lord, 123
Shaw, Patrick, 175
Shawnigan Lake Boys' School, 160
Sheriff, 69, 120, 129, 188
Sherwood, Alden, 67
Shevet, 82
Silk, Erik, 72
Silver-gilt, 32, 40–41, 50, 53, 86, 96, 277, 288
Simcoe, John Graves, 132
Simmie, Allyson, 198
Skeptron, 82
Smallwood, Joey, 186–87, 190
Smith, Benjamin, 91
Smith, H.R., 291
Sophia, Countess of Albermarle, 122
South Carolina, 91–93
Sovereign, 19, 25, 26, 36, 39, 81, 82, 85–87, 98, 115, 124, 131, 133, 138, 151, 186, 225–26, 245, 247, 253, 268, 295
Sovereign Coin, 41, 52–54
Sovereign Council, 17
Sovereign's Insignia, 6, 226–29, 307
Sovereygne, 287
Spain, 295

Speaker, 20, 30, 34, 36, 39, 41, 45, 52, 56–64, 81, 85–86, 88–91, 93–94, 96, 98, 115–16, 118, 133–35, 138, 140, 143, 156–57, 162, 174, 180–81, 187–88, 199, 206, 208, 211, 216, 217, 249, 291, 307–08
Speech from the Throne, 36, 52, 62, 94, 144, 151, 181, 189, 273
Spink & Son, 233, 238
Sri Lanka, 20, 52, 53
St. Edward's Crown, 21, 74, 76, 226, 228
St. George, 25, 36, 41, 54, 59–60, 225
St. George's Chapel Windsor, 25
St. John, The Order of, 225–26, 240, 242
St. John Molyneux, 311
St. John's, 88, 118, 187–89
St. Lawrence River, 19
St. Michael and St. George, The Most Distinguished Order of, 225, 316
St. Patrick, The Order of, 315
St. Roch, 197
Star of India, The Most Exalted Order of the, 151, 152
State of the Union Address, 94
Stave, 65, 82
Sterling Silver, 40, 50, 75, 96, 121, 127, 146, 152, 155, 157, 167, 173, 183, 185, 186, 192, 220, 242, 287–88, 298, 313–14
Stokes Cap & Regalia, 73
Summers, William, 226, 228
Suqslaq, Joseph, 211, 216
Sûreté du Québec, 14, 71, 76–77
Swan, Sir Conrad, 20
Sword, 43–45, 58, 70–71, 74–75, 82–83, 115, 143, 187, 279, 308
Symbols, 11, 17, 19–21, 82, 84, 86, 93, 94, 98, 115, 174, 177, 185, 187, 195, 196, 210, 219, 225, 245, 271, 287, 307, 309

T
Tabard, 295, 308
Taché, E.E, 47, 139
Talking Stick, 160
Taylor, Fennings, 106
Territorial Commissioner, 195, 276–78

Territorial Commissioner
Recognition Badge, 245, 274
Tessier, Ulric-Joseph, 30
Thagard, Brian, 14, 199
Theriault, G.C., 238
Thistle, 113, 114, 118, 128, 148,
172, 173, 177, 179, 182,
276, 288
Thistle, The Most Ancient Order
of, 315
Thomas, Duke of Lancaster, 85
Thompson, Andrew Ruthvern, 311
Thorne, Sir Peter, 20, 84
Thorpe, Jeremy, 273
Tipstaff, 69–78
Todd, Alfred, 134
Toronto, 72, 73, 106, 118, 120,
132, 133, 135, 173, 177, 300
Tourangeau, Jean-Guy, 77
Tower of London, 85
Tradition, 11, 17, 19, 34, 36, 44,
50, 52, 57, 61, 70, 75, 81,
86, 89, 91–93, 96–97, 120,
124, 131–32, 135, 140, 141,
161, 164, 167, 169, 172–76,
183, 185, 189, 195–96, 199,
200, 204, 210, 217, 219,
225, 226, 230, 234, 250,
260, 268–69, 271, 273,
287, 295
Tramrell, Alan, 298
Travers, Mary, 187, 191
Trinidad and Tobago, 27, 95
Tropical Dress, 251–52, 256,
265, 279
Trudeau, Pierre Elliott, 19
Truncheon, 69–70
Tudor Rose, 276, 291
Turks, 83
Turner, Sir Richard, 123
Tweedsmuir, Lord, 258, 261, 274,
331, 334, 335

U
Uniform, 32, 60, 62, 69–70
civil, 21, 245–74, 279–85
court, 15, 245–47, 272,
277, 278
military, 245, 249–50, 260,
263, 265, 278
United Canadas, Province of the,
30, 139
United Kingdom, 17, 20, 26, 31,
41, 52, 57, 60, 65, 93, 124,
131, 135, 181, 183, 186,
189, 220, 242, 246, 247,
251, 256–57, 260, 265, 269,
273, 275–76, 291, 307, 313

United States of America, 91, 95
United States Congress, 133
United States Naval Academy, 132
Upper Canada, 45, 70, 96, 132,
133, 136, 138

V
Vale Inco, 136
Vallerand, Oliver, 317
Vancouver, 15, 93, 193, 219–22
Vancouver Island, 159–62, 164
Vancouver Police Department,
71, 220
Vandelac, A. Guy, 311
Vanier, Georges, 260, 263, 274,
308, 335
Viceregal Recognition, 275
Vickers, Kevin, 14, 312
Victoria, Queen, 56, 70, 215, 135,
138, 139, 151, 172, 247,
249, 256, 325
Victoria, State of, 179
Victoria Memorial Building,
120, 123
Vincent, Sir Percy, 219, 220, 257,
258, 273–74
Virginia, 14, 91, 93
Vittoria, Battle of, 58

W
Wakefield, Sir Charles, 120, 123,
129, 313
Wales, 69, 118, 219, 247, 256, 265
Wales, Prince of, 118, 247, 265
War of 1812, 94, 132
Washington, George, 155
Washington, D.C., 132, 257, 258
Watson Brother Jewellers, 180
Watt, Robert, 52, 54, 61, 65–66,
276, 295–96
Wellington, Duke of, 58, 60
West Africa, 98
Westminster, 34, 81, 84, 121, 132,
143, 161, 187, 195
Weston, Hilary, 275, 300
Whale Bone, 201
Whitehorse, 209, 257
Whitehorse, William, 25
William, Duke of Normandy, 82
William the Conqueror, 57
William IV, King, 50
William Scully Ltd, 273
Wilmington, USS, 133
Windsor Court Dress, 246
Windsor Uniform (see also Civil
Uniform and Court Dress),
246–47
Winslow Brothers, 161, 167

Withers, R.M., 238
Wolsely, Garnet, 169
Wolsey, Cardinal, 287
World War I, see First World
War
World War II, see Second World
War
World's Fair, 162
Wright, Thomas, 155

Y
York, 9, 45, 132, 133
Yukon, 195, 206–10, 276, 314,
325

Z
Zaccardelli, Guiliano, 75, 239
Zollikoffer, Charles, 47, 134, 138,
139, 142, 313